James Francis Kendal

A history of watches and other timekeepers

James Francis Kendal

A history of watches and other timekeepers

ISBN/EAN: 9783742827296

Manufactured in Europe, USA, Canada, Australia, Japa

Cover: Foto ©ninafisch / pixelio.de

Manufactured and distributed by brebook publishing software (www.brebook.com)

James Francis Kendal

A history of watches and other timekeepers

A HISTORY OF WATCHES

AND OTHER TIMEKEEPERS.

BY

JAMES FRANCIS KENDAL

(KENDAL AND DENT)

MEMBER OF THE BRITISH HOROLOGICAL INSTITUTE,
CHEVALIER OF THE LEGION OF HONOUR; MEMBER OF THE SOCIETY OF ARTS, ETC.

WITH NUMEROUS ILLUSTRATIONS.

LONDON:
CROSBY LOCKWOOD AND SON
7, STATIONERS' HALL COURT, LUDGATE HILL.
1892.
[All Rights Reserved.]

TO

CHARLES J. SAYER, Esq., M.A., LL.D.,

AS AN EARNEST TOKEN

OF GREAT RESPECT AND WARM ESTEEM,

This Volume

IS WITH UNFEIGNED PLEASURE

INSCRIBED

BY HIS SINCERE FRIEND THE AUTHOR.

PREFACE.

IN the following pages I have endeavoured in as concise a manner as possible to trace the origin and history of all methods of reckoning time. The subject is so complex, and the writings upon it so numerous, that many of the materials which I had collected have necessarily been omitted, my aim being to record within the limits of an ordinary volume the gradual development of timekeepers, from the sundial of the ancients to the complicated chronograph of modern times.

To those who have generously assisted me with information, or granted me access to works which but for their kindness it would have been impossible for me to inspect, I here tender my sincere thanks.

In conclusion, I solicit the reader's indulgence, and trust that those omissions he may observe during a perusal of these pages will be rightly attributed to my wish to convey, in a limited space, a general idea of the progress that has been made in the horological art.

JAMES FRANCIS KENDAL.

A HISTORY OF WATCHES
AND OTHER TIMEKEEPERS.

Time.

T is difficult to give a precise definition of time, though the ruins and tombs which mark its course are evidence of its existence, and prove it to be, as Ovid declared, the devourer of all things—
"Tempus edax rerum."

Definition of Time. Johnson says that time is a measure of duration. Another authority explains that time is a succession of phenomena of the universe. Laplace described it as the impression which a series of objects leaves upon the memory, and of which we are certain the existence has been successive.

In the "Talisman" we are told that time is seen not and felt not, and that it is but a shadowy name, the succession of breaths measured forth by night with the clank of a bell, by day with a shadow coursing along a dial stone.

The following is the suggestive thought of the poet Young—

> "From old Eternity's mysterious orb
> Was Time cut off and cast beneath the skies—
> The skies which watch him in his new abode,
> Measuring his motion by revolving spheres
> That horologe machinery divine."

Milton is credited with this apostrophe—

> "Fly, envious Time, till thou run out thy race;
> Call on the lazy leaden-stepping hours,
> Whose speed is but the heavy plummet's pace;
> And glut thyself with what thy womb devours,
> Which is no more than what is false and vain,
> And merely mortal dross;
> So little is our loss,
> So little is thy gain!
> For when as each thing bad thou hast entomb'd,
> And last of all thy greedy self consum'd,
> Then long Eternity shall greet our bliss
> With an individual kiss."

According to Byron—

> "The hollow tongue of Time
> Is a perpetual knell. Each toll
> Peals for a hope the less!"

Time has been called the "conqueror of conquerors," and the "lord of desolation." Shakespeare declared that—

> "—he's a thief too; have you not heard men say
> That time comes stealing on by night and day?"

The well-worn aphorism which declares that "TIME IS MONEY," can hardly be taken seriously as a definition, though many humorous stories are founded on attempts to enforce the synonym, such as that of the impecunious possessor of a valuable watch, who says its truth depends on his ability to obtain an interview with his uncle; and the traveller who, at the end of a week's stay, finds himself unable to pay mine host's bill with current coin, but offers to liquidate it by staying at the house another week.

Times change. Quick travelling of a century ago would now be deemed to be miserably slow; and therefore the old familiar *Tempus*, with a solitary forelock on his venerable brow, and bearing a scythe and an hour glass, seems out of place trudging along on foot. But although the world changes round him the old man still toils on exactly as he did centuries ago.

First Divisions of Time.
We note time but by its flight. Without motion of some kind it could not be measured, and there is but little doubt that in all ages the natural division of time into day and night must have been observed by mankind. It may be assumed that even in the most primitive state of society the motion of the earth with regard to the sun was made available for registering the divisions of days, though the first essays in this direction are beyond the reach of history. The Babylonians, Persians, and Syrians began the day at sunrise, and divided it into twenty-four hours. The Athenians started from sunset, as did also the Jews, who counted twelve hours from sunset to sunrise, and twelve hours from sunrise to sunset. It is said that for nearly five centuries after the building of their city, the Romans only observed sunrise, noon, and sunset. Noon was proclaimed by a herald the moment the sun was perceived between the Forum and a place called the Græcostasis. They afterwards divided the day and night into twenty-four hours, but they counted twelve hours from sunrise to sunset, and twelve from sunset to sunrise. Their hours were, therefore, like the subdivisions adopted by the Jews, of unequal duration, because, except in a few places situated in the torrid zone, the days and nights are equal only twice in the year, when the sun happens to be vertical to the equator.

Divisions of the Day into Hours.

Months, Weeks, and Years.

Months.
JUST as the shepherd of the early ages reckoned by months, or full moons, so does the prairie hunter of the present day. A lunar month is 29 days 12 hours 44 minutes 3 seconds, or rather more than 29½ days. Twelve

lunar months are, therefore, nearly eleven days short of the solar year. Thus the new moons in one year will fall eleven days earlier than they did in the preceding year.

When the ancients began to observe the stars, they fancied certain clusters of them to bear some faint resemblance to figures of men and animals; and afterwards, when they wished to represent the stars in their relative positions they drew these imaginary figures. These figures, called constellations, were formed for the purpose of finding a star with facility by knowing in which part of the imaginary figure to look for it. It was soon noticed that twelve of these constellations, or signs of the zodiac, as they were called, became successively and periodically invisible, owing to the sun seeming to pass between them and the earth, and thus the duration of the year was ascertained.

Constellations of Stars.

The twelve calendar or civil months, by which we compute the year, were so arranged by Julius Cæsar, who ordained that the odd months of January, March, May, etc., should contain thirty-one days, and the even months, April, June, August, etc., thirty, with the exception of February, which had thirty days in leap year only, being in other years composed of twenty-nine.

Naming the Months.

January, fixed by Numa Pompilius as the first month of the year, was named after Janus, a prince who was supposed to have been taught by Saturn the art of dividing the year, as a recompense for his hospitality to this god.

The Romans derived the name of the month February from *Februs*, "to *purify*," because in that month they offered expiatory sacrifices.

March was so named in honour of the god Mars, and by the Romans under Romulus was considered as the first month of the year.

April, from the Latin word *Aprilus*, derived from

aperio, "I open," because in that month the earth opened its bosom for the production of grass and flowers.

May is by some supposed to have received its name from Maia, the mother of Mercury, to whom sacrifices were offered in the commencement of that month. Others derive the word May from Majorum, or, as it is commonly written, Maiorum, because festivals were then held in honour of the senators, who were called majores.

June was so called from Juniorum, because feasts were then appointed in honour of the young men, *juniores*, who had fought for their country.

July was so named by Marc Antony, in honour of Julius Cæsar, who was born in this month. It had previously been called Quintilis, being the fifth month of the year, counting from March.

August, called by the Romans Sextilis, or the sixth, received its present name from Augustus Cæsar, whose vanity has imposed upon us the annoying irregularity in the number of days contained in different months. Unwilling that the month which bore his name should be inferior to the one named after Julius (which contained thirty-one days) he abstracted one day from February, which was already minus, and added it to August.

September was so called from being the seventh month when the year commenced in March; October received its name from being the eighth month; November signified the ninth; and December the tenth.

Romulus, who is supposed to have made the first Roman calendar, divided the year into ten months only, consisting of an unequal number of days, and beginning as we have already stated with March; the total number of days was then only 304, but as it was soon discovered that the civil year, as thus constituted, was much shorter than the solar year, he added two months to every year, but these months were not yet inserted in the calendar, nor were any names assigned them till the following reign.

Representative Gems for each Month. By tradition each month has a particular gem associated with it, and superstition declares that good fortune depends upon the wearing of the stone connected with the birthday month. This conceit has been prettily versified by a transatlantic writer in the following lines.

JANUARY.

By her who in this month is born
No gems save *Garnets* should be worn;
They will insure her constancy,
True friendship and fidelity.

FEBRUARY.

The February born shall find
Sincerity and peace of mind,
Freedom from passion and from care
If they the *Amethyst* will wear.

MARCH.

Who on this world of ours their eyes
In March first open shall be wise,
In days of peril firm and brave,
And wear a *Bloodstone* to their grave.

APRIL.

She who from April dates her years
Diamonds should wear, lest bitter tears
For vain repentance flow; this stone
Emblem of innocence is known.

MAY.

Who first beholds the light of day
In Spring's sweet flowery month of May,
And wears an *Emerald* all her life,
Shall be a loved and happy wife.

JUNE.

Who comes with Summer to this earth,
And owes to June her hour of birth,
With ring of *Agate* on her hand
Can health, wealth, and long life command.

JULY.

The glowing *Ruby* shall adorn
Those who in warm July are born;
Then will they be exempt and free
From love's doubts and anxiety.

AUGUST.

Wear a *Sardonyx*, or for thee
No conjugal felicity;
The August born without this stone,
'Tis said, must live unloved and lone.

SEPTEMBER.

A maiden born when Autumn leaves
Are rustling in September's breeze,
A *Sapphire* on her brow should bind,
'Twill cure diseases of the mind.

OCTOBER.

October's child is born for woe
And life's vicissitudes must know;
But lay an *Opal* on her breast
And hope will lull those woes to rest.

NOVEMBER.

Who first comes to this world below
With drear November's fog and snow,
Should prize the *Topaz's* amber hue,
Emblem of friends and lovers true.

DECEMBER.

If cold December gave you birth—
The month of snow and ice and mirth,
Place on your hand a *Turquoise* blue,
Success will bless whate'er you do.

Hebrew Calendar. The Hebrew calendar computes the time by lunar months. In order to observe their Passover in the spring, and the Feast of Tabernacles in the autumn, as prescribed in the Pentateuch, and likewise that the Day of Atonement should never happen on the day before or following the Sabbath, the Hebrews have occasionally every three or four years an intercalated month before the spring month Adar, called Veh-Adar, or additional Adar, also as a proper distinction generally named First or Second Adar. Up to the third century of the Christian era, the new moon's days were fixed by a special body of legislators, called the Sanhedrin, established in Palestine, guided by astronomical observations and proclaimed by fire-signals on certain mountains to their co-religionists in exile or in Babylon.

Weeks. Probably the four intervals between the change in the phases of the moon suggested the division of the month into weeks.

Many nations of antiquity have given to the seven days of the week titles drawn from the most ancient system of astrology, each day being named after the planet which was supposed to preside over its first hour. These names have been partially retained in modern languages. In Italian, though Sabbato signifies Sabbath, and Domenica, or Lord's day, is derived from Dominus, there still remain Lunedì or Moon's day, Marsedì, or Mars' day, Giovedì, Jove, or Jupiter's day, and Venerdì, Venus' day. The names of the days in French are derived from the same source.

In English, Sunday and Moon or Monday, have been retained, while the corresponding deities of the Scandinavian mythology have been substituted for the others; Tuesday from Tuesco who was identical with Mars; Wednesday, from Woden or Mercury; Thursday from Thor or Jupiter; Friday from Frea or Frigga Venus; and Saturday from Seater or Saturn.

Years. The earth performs its revolution round the sun in 365 days 5 hours 48 minutes 49·7 seconds. No account was taken of the odd hours until, the error in the computation of the year having become very considerable, Julius Cæsar, with the assistance of Sosigenes, an Alexandrian astronomer, undertook, in the year B.C. 45, to reform the calendar, to accomplish which the surplus 5 hours 48 minutes 49·7 seconds were considered as six hours, making one day in four years; this day was, therefore, added to every fourth year by repeating the 24th of February, which, according to the Roman method of computation was the *sixth* day before the calends of March; hence the year in which this double sixth occurred was termed *Bissextilis*. To introduce this new system the year B.C. 46 was made to consist of 455 days, on which account it was called the year of confusion.

There still remained the apparently trifling difference of 11 minutes 11 seconds between the computed year and the real year; this, however, produced an error of about seven days in 900 years.

Gregorian Rectification of the Calendar. In 1582 this error had become so great that the vernal equinox (which at the time of the Council of Nice, A.D. 325, had fallen correctly on the 21st of March) took place on the 11th: this was rectified by Pope Gregory XIII., who took off ten days by calling the 5th of October the 15th. To prevent a recurrence of this error it was decided that three leap years should be omitted in 400 years; thus as 1600 was leap year, the years 1700, 1800, and 1900 are not, but 2000 will be leap year. As our year still exceeds the true year, although by an extremely small fraction, another leap year in addition to these should be omitted once in 4000 years.

Although the learned Roger Bacon had, upwards of three centuries before the time of Gregory, suggested a most effectual means of reforming the calendar, yet the new style was not adopted in England until after the 2nd of September, 1752, when eleven days were struck out, so that the 3rd day of that month was called the 14th; this reform was much opposed by the more ignorant of the people, and mobs assembled to demand the eleven days, which they said had been taken from them.

Hogarth gave expression to the popular feeling in his picture of an excited election crowd, where a banner inscribed, "Give us back our eleven days," is a prominent object.

Of all the countries in Europe the only one which retains the old style in general use is Russia, and there it is usual when corresponding with other countries to put two dates, one in the old and one in the new style, the difference now being twelve days.

Curiously enough, though, the old style is still retained in the accounts of the British Treasury. This is why the Christmas dividends are not considered to be due till twelfth day, and the remaining quarters till the 6th day of the month following quarter day. The Chancellor of the Exchequer still makes the 5th of April, which was formerly Ladyday, the first day of the financial year, and the Queen's taxes are also reckoned for the twelvemonth to April 5th.

Beginning of the Year. There was no particular day universally fixed upon as the beginning of the year. We find that the Athenians commenced the year in June, the Macedonians in September, the Romans first in March and afterwards in January. The Persians began the year on the 11th of August, the Mexicans on the 23rd of February, the Mahometans in July, and astronomers at the vernal equinox. In France, under the first race of kings, the year began in Lent, nearly the same thing as among the Hebrews; and before the change of style in England the year was considered to begin on the 25th of March, but the same Act of Parliament that gave effect to the reformation of the calendar ordained the 1st day of January as the beginning of the year.

Simplification of the Calendar. Many suggestions have been made for simplifying our complex almanac, based on the Gregorian system. One of the best, induced by a prize offered in France a few years ago, pointed out that if the year be divided into four parts or seasons, the quotient will be 91 days and a fraction. The number 91 being divisible by 7, gives for each quarter an equal and whole number of weeks—exactly 13. This permits of having the quarters equal, all commencing by a same day. These four periods giving only 364 days, the 365th day might be placed outside of both month and week, to be considered as a complementary, or extra day, and be made the New Year's day and marked as 0. By this system, the month of 28 days would be suppressed, and calculations relating to the year and quarters thereof rendered easy; but however apparent an improvement may be, its adoption is found to be anything but an easy task in the face of long-continued custom.

The calendar of the Hebrews contains ordinary lunar years of 12 months, consisting of 354 days 8 hours 48 minutes 34 seconds; imperfect lunar years of 12 months, consisting of 353 days; or intercalated lunar years of 13 months, consisting of 383 days. The month Nisan, falling in the spring, is the first of the months in the ecclesiastical year; the month Tishri, falling in the autumn, is the first month in the civil year.

Standards of Time.

Greenwich Mean Time.

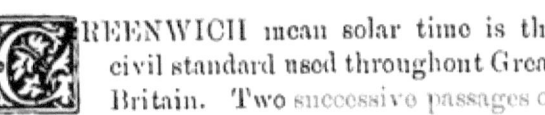

GREENWICH mean solar time is the civil standard used throughout Great Britain. Two successive passages of the sun over a meridian constitute a true solar day, and the instant the sun is seen at its greatest height above the horizon, it is midday at that particular place. In its rotation the earth takes four minutes to pass through one degree of its circumference, and the local time of places east of Greenwich is accordingly fast of Greenwich by that amount, while places to the west of Greenwich are correspondingly slow. For instance, No. 106, Cheapside, is exactly 22 seconds slow of Greenwich; Bodmin, in Cornwall, is 19 minutes slow; and New York 4 hours 56 minutes slow. On the other hand, Dover is 5 minutes 16 seconds fast, and Auckland, New Zealand, as much as 11 hours 39 minutes 4 seconds fast of Greenwich.

Universal Time Chart. Messrs. Kendal and Dent have issued a useful and interesting chart, which shows at a glance the difference between Greenwich and local time at the principal towns throughout the world. There are no less than 306 representations of clock faces, with the hands of each pointing to the time of some particular place when it is noon at Greenwich.

Formerly, each town adhered to its own local time, but the inconvenience of this practice was strongly exemplified when railways were introduced, and it was not an uncommon thing a few years ago to see the public clocks of provincial towns with one minute hand showing local, and another Greenwich, or "railway" time, as it was called.

Equation of Time. The expression *Mean Time* still requires explanation. It might naturally be supposed that the diurnal rotation of the earth would bring each place to the meridian at regular intervals; this would be nearly the case if the earth had no other movement than the rotation on its axis, as a day would then be measured by a revolution of the equator, but the earth at the same time advances in its orbit, and, as the meridians are not perpendicular to the ecliptic, the days are not of equal duration. This may be easily perceived by placing a mark at every 15 degrees of the equator and ecliptic on a terrestrial globe, as by turning the globe to the westward the marks on the ecliptic, from Aries to Cancer, will come to the brazen meridian sooner than the corresponding ones on the equator, those from

Cancer to Libra later, from Libra to Capricorn sooner, and from Capricorn to Aries later; the marks on the ecliptic and equator only coming to the meridian together at Aries, Cancer, Libra, and Capricorn; thus, true and mean time would agree on the days in which the sun enters these signs, which is on the 20th of March, 21st of June, 23rd of September, and 21st of December, were it not that the earth moves with greater rapidity in December, when it is nearest the sun, than it does in July, when it is at its greatest distance from it. The regularity of the earth's motion is also further disturbed by the attraction of the Moon, Venus, and Jupiter. At present true and mean time agree about the 15th of April, the 14th of June, the 31st of August, and the 25th of December; these coincidences vary slightly in different years, because the earth takes about a quarter of a day more than a year to complete a revolution in its orbit, and this error accumulates from leap year till the fourth year after, when the extra day is taken in. The greatest differences between true and mean time occur about the 23rd of October, when the clock is said to be sixteen minutes slow of the sun, and about the 30th of January, when it is said to be fourteen minutes fast of the sun. The Greenwich *mean* solar day, then, is really the mean of all the solar days in the year, and the equation of time is the amount to be added to or subtracted from true time in order to convert it into mean time. The variation between the two at different periods of the year is shown in the table on p. 14.

Many old English clocks were furnished with equation mechanism to enable them to show true as well as mean time.

In France it was the custom, till 1826, for clocks to show true solar instead of mean solar time; and a cam, known here, on account of its shape, as a kidney piece, was introduced to advance or retard the hands of the clock as required.

Sun-dials, of course, show true solar time.

Equation Table computed to Minutes of Time.

Clock faster than the Sun.			Clock slower than the Sun.			Clock faster than the Sun.			Clock slower than the Sun.		
		Min			Min.			Min.			Min.
December	26	1	April	17	1	June	17	1	September	2	1
,,	28	2	,,	22	2	,,	22	2	,,	6	2
,,	30	3	,,	28	3	,,	26	3	,,	8	3
January	1	4	May	6	4	July	1	4	,,	11	4
,,	3	5	,,	23	3	,,	7	5	,,	14	5
,,	5	6	June	1	2	,,	14	6	,,	17	6
,,	7	7	,,	7	1	August	8	5	,,	20	7
,,	9	8	,,	14	0	,,	14	4	,,	23	8
,,	12	9				,,	19	3	,,	26	9
,,	15	10				,,	23	2	,,	29	10
,,	18	11				,,	27	1	October	2	11
,,	21	12				,,	31	0	,,	5	12
,,	25	13							,,	9	13
,,	30	14							,,	12	14
February	24	13							,,	17	15
March	1	12							,,	23	16
,,	6	11							November	14	15
,,	10	10							,,	19	14
,,	14	9							,,	23	13
,,	17	8							,,	26	12
,,	21	7							,,	29	11
,,	24	6							December	2	10
,,	27	5							,,	4	9
,,	30	4							,,	7	8
April	3	3							,,	9	7
,,	6	2							,,	11	6
,,	10	1							,,	13	5
,,	15	0							,,	15	4
									,,	18	3
									,,	20	2
									,,	22	1
									,,	25	0

NOTE.—In an equation table for use in any year of the **four** from leap year to leap year, absolute exactness is impossible, on account of the error in the computation of the year, which is referred to on p. 9. Seconds and intermediate days are therefore omitted.

AND OTHER TIMEKEEPERS.

Unification of Time Needed. From what has already been said it will be seen that our present system of timekeeping is a curious compromise between ancient custom and modern requirement. We have abandoned the unequal hours inseparable from dividing the whole day into twelve hours of light and twelve hours of darkness, but we still split the twenty-four hours into two periods of twelve hours each. We admit the impracticability of keeping local time by adopting one standard for the whole of Great Britain, yet we hesitate to extend the benefit of universal time by adopting one standard for the whole world. Now that such intimate commercial relations are established between nations scattered over various parts of the earth under different meridians of longitude, the selection of an universal datum, or initial meridian, is most desirable, in order to avoid the perplexities of varying times in intercommunication by telegraph, and in the recording of incidents.

Throughout Ireland, Dublin time, which is 25 minutes 22 seconds slow of Greenwich, is kept.

American Standards of Time. In America, the authorities, weary of the annoyance and perplexity arising from local time, have recently established five different standards. A central meridian, 90 degrees west, and six hours slow of Greenwich, serves for the Mississippi Valley, Missouri Valley, Upper Lakes, and Texas, and is called "Valley Time." A meridian 75 degrees west, and five hours slow of Greenwich, called "Atlantic Time," serves for the district from Maine to Florida, from Ohio to Alabama and the Lower Lakes, as well as for Canada. A meridian 60 degrees west, and four hours slow of Greenwich, known as "Eastern Time," serves for Newfoundland, New Brunswick, and Nova Scotia. A meridian 105 degrees west, and seven hours slow of Greenwich, known as "Mountain Time," serves for the Rocky Mountain region. A meridian 120 degrees west, and eight hours slow of Greenwich, known as "Pacific Time," serves for the Pacific States and British Columbia. But this alteration really accentuates the necessity for one universal meridian, as it makes confusion worse confounded on the border lines of the standards.

Two standards of time have lately been adopted for the whole of Austria-Hungary, but a dweller at Lake Constance will still find he has to consider which of three or four times is meant before he decides on fulfilling an appointment.

Military strategists find the varying times most annoying. The late veteran Count von Moltke earnestly entreated the Reichstag to introduce one time for the German empire. He suggested the time of the fifteenth degree east of Greenwich as the most suitable, because it passes through Sweden, Germany, Austria, and Italy, and might, he thought, become the basis for a normal time for the whole of Central Europe. I trust that a broader view will be taken, and that Germany will use its influence to further what all must admit is the real solution of the problem, and that is the adoption of universal time.

In using the telephone recently completed between London and Paris, the want of universal time is already making itself felt. As the rates for using the instrument are necessarily high, possession of the terminals is held, as a rule, for very short periods, and much of the conversation is carried on by appointment, so that the difference of 9 minutes 21 seconds between the time of the two cities is often productive of perplexity and disappointment.

Beyond the adoption of an universal meridian, a reckoning of the hours continuously from midnight to midnight is much needed, and the general acceptance of these two reforms is only a question of the ripening of public opinion against the prejudice of long custom. People can be found to defend the present system on the ground that it would be difficult to count up to twenty-four. And so it would at first, no doubt, but that is no reason for depriving ourselves and our children of the undoubted benefit of a simpler and better notation than we received from our forefathers. Such an argument, indeed, would prevent the introduction of any reform if it were allowed to weigh. There is no more difficulty in reckoning twenty-four hours, than in computing twenty-four pounds or twenty-four tons.

Continuous Counting of the Hours versus Bisection. If we were dealing with, say, eighteen cwt. of sugar, we should not speak of it as half a ton and eight cwt.; nor do we divide the hour into two periods of thirty minutes each. Why, then, should we needlessly complicate the twenty-four hours of the day by splitting them into halves of twelve hours, so that, in expressing any one hour, we have to make some addition to distinguish whether we mean the morning or the afternoon—a cumbersome process, leading to many mistakes and confusion with A.M. and P.M., especially in the timing of railway trains?

It would evidently be as easy for the community in general to count the hours continuously as it is for astronomers to do so. But it may even be conceded that the objection to counting up to twenty-four would be insuperable; the bisection of the day could then be avoided by making twelve hours cover the whole day from midnight to midnight, the duration of each hour and each minute would in that case, of course, be twice as long as it is at present.

I must ask to be forgiven if I appear to dwell unduly on the reforms of universal day and continuous notation of the hours. It is a subject on which I feel strongly, and, both personally and through the firm of Kendal and Dent, I have, by offering substantial prizes, and by the introduction of simple mechanism for timekeepers under the proposed new system, striven to roll away from the path of progress the huge mountain of supineness and ignorant obstruction which still blocks the way. But the necessity is pressing, and I do not intend to relax my efforts, remembering that all reforms of any moment have only been obtained after long and continuous stuggle.

Sidereal Time. Sidereal time is the standard used by astronomers, and is measured by the diurnal rotation of the earth, which turns on its axis in 23 hours, 56 minutes, 4·1 seconds. The fixed stars are at such immense distances from the earth, and the orbit of the latter is so small in comparison, that the earth in regard to the stars appears to have no other motion than its diurnal rotation. Consequently, a complete revolution of the terrestrial equator brings the same stars to the meridian at perfectly regular intervals, and this uniformity of the sidereal as compared with the solar day renders the former more suited as a standard for astronomical purposes.

The sidereal day being shorter than the mean solar day by 3 minutes 56 seconds, a clock to show sidereal time would have its pendulum a trifle shorter than a mean time clock of the same construction. About the 15th of April the sidereal and the mean time clock would agree, but from that time the divergence between the two would be increased each day by 3 minutes 56 seconds.

Division of Dial Astronomical Clock. The astronomical day begins at noon, and the hour circles of astronomical clocks are invariably divided into twenty-four, whether solar or sidereal time is indicated.

Transit Instrument. Sidereal and solar time are obtained by means of a transit instrument, as shown in Fig. 1. It consists of a telescope placed in the meridian, and mounted in bearings so that it may be turned from north to south. One horizontal and three or more vertical wires, or "spider lines," are stretched across the focus, and by looking through the telescope the time of the passage of the sun or a star across the wires may be accurately noted. The time at which

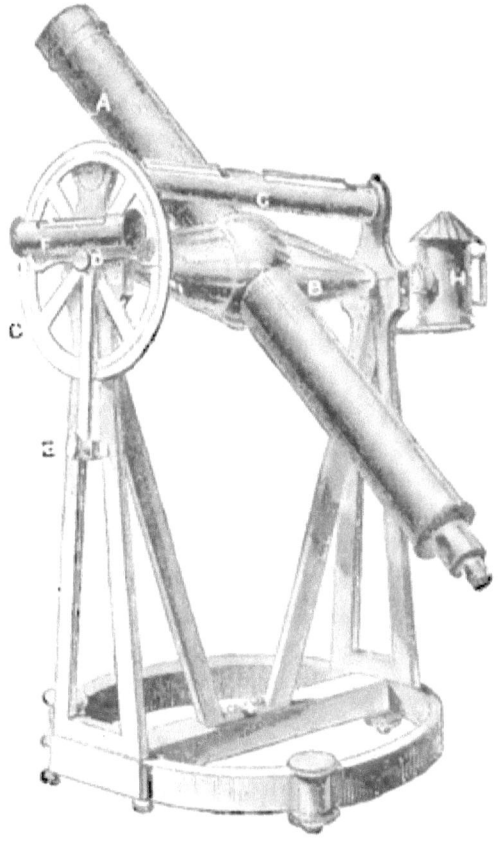

Fig. 1.—Transit Instrument.
A, telescope; B, hollow axis; C, striding level; D, vernier; E, binding screw; F, cross level; H, lamp.

certain stars pass the meridian of Greenwich is given in the "Nautical Almanac," and other publications. A suitable star having been selected, the instrument is pointed to the known altitude of the star, and clamped there. The altitudes given are those for places in the latitude of

Greenwich, and would require correction for other latitudes. Mr. Latimer Clark suggests a very simple method. Set the instrument, so that it points exactly right to a star, the altitude of which for Greenwich is given; then turn round the graduated circle at the side of the instrument till the given altitude is indicated, and fix the circle there. No further correction for latitude need then be made as long as the instrument remains in the same place. The instant the star passes the centre wire will be the time given in the "Nautical Almanac" as the right ascension of the star, plus or minus the correction for longitude of the particular place where the instrument is fixed. This, of course, is sidereal time. The passage of the sun across the vertical wire of the telescope gives solar noon. As the sun is a large body, the usual course is to observe the instant when the edge of the sun enters and leaves the centre wire, and take the mean of the two. This may be converted into mean solar noon by correcting for longitude and adding or subtracting the amount given in the equation table.

Easy permanent Correction for Latitude.

Solar Observations.

Mean time clocks can be regulated by the stars just as easily as by the sun, for the motion of the earth with regard to the fixed stars is uniform, and a star will always appear at the meridian 3 minutes 56 seconds sooner than it did on the preceding day. In the absence of a transit instrument and a table giving the right ascension of particular stars, choose a window having a southern aspect, from which the steeple of a church, a chimney, or any other fixed point may be seen. To the side of the window attach a thin plate of brass having a small hole in it, in such a manner that by looking through the hole towards the edge of the elevated object, some of the fixed stars may be seen; the progress of one of these being watched, the instant it vanishes behind the fixed point a signal is

How to Regulate a Mean Time Clock by the Stars.

made to a person observing the clock, who then notes the exact time at which the star disappeared, and on the following night the same star will vanish behind the same object 3 minutes 56 seconds sooner. If a clock mark 10 hours when the observation is made, when the star vanishes the following night it should indicate 3 minutes 56 seconds less than 10 hours. If several cloudy nights have rendered it impossible to compare the clock with the star, it will then be necessary to multiply 3 minutes 56 seconds by the number of days that have elapsed since the observation, and the product deducted from the hour the clock then indicates gives the time the clock ought to show. The same star can only be observed during a few weeks, for as it gains nearly one hour in a fortnight it will, in a short time, come to the meridian in broad daylight, and become invisible; to continue the observation, another star must be selected. Care must be taken that a planet is not observed instead of a star; Mars, Jupiter, and Saturn are those most likely to occasion this error, especially Saturn, which, from being the most distant of the three, resembles a star of the first magnitude. The planets may, however, be easily distinguished, for being comparatively near the earth, they appear larger than the stars; their light is also steady, because reflected, while the fixed stars scintillate, and have a twinkling light. A sure means of distinguishing between them is to watch a star attentively for a few nights; if it change its place with regard to the other stars it is a planet.

Nautical Day. The nautical day commences when the sun is on the meridian; eight blows are then struck on the ship's bell, and the afternoon watch is begun. At 12.30 one blow is struck, and the time is spoken of as "one bell;" at 1 o'clock, two bells; at 1.30, three bells; at 2, four bells; at 2.30, five bells; 3, six bells; 3.30, seven bells; at 4 o'clock, eight bells again. At 4 o'clock begins the first dog watch, which lasts two hours, the periods being struck as before, ending at 6 o'clock, with four bells. Then begins the second dog watch, also of two hours' duration, ending at eight o'clock, half-hour intervals being struck, 1, 2, 3, 8; eight bells marking the completion of the second dog watch. Next comes the middle watch, lasting four hours, and struck like the afternoon watch. The night watch, the morning watch, the forenoon watch, each of four hours similarly marked, follow in succession ; the forenoon watch ending at noon with eight bells, completes the day.

Cycles of Time.

Cycle of the Sun.  A CYCLE of the sun is a period of twenty-eight years, after which the days of the week again fall on the same days of the month as during the first year of the former cycle. The cycle of the sun has no relation to the sun's course, but was invented for the purpose of finding the Dominical letter which points out the days of the month on which the Sundays fall during each year of the cycle. Cycles of the sun date nine years before the Christian era. If it be required to know the year of the cycle in 1892, nine added will make 1901, which, divided by 28, gives the quotient 67, the number of cycles which have passed, and the remainder, 25, will be the year of the cycle answering to 1892.

The Golden Number. Meton, an Athenian astronomer, B.C. 432, discovered that after a period of nineteen years, the new and full moons returned on the same days of the month as they had done before. This period is called the cycle of the moon.

The Greeks thought so highly of this calculation that they had it written in letters of gold, hence the name Golden Number; and at the Council of Nice, A.D. 325, it was determined that Meton's cycle should be used to regulate the movable feasts of the church.

Our Saviour was born in the second year of the lunar cycle. To find the year of the cycle, add one to the present year, divide this by 19, and the remainder will give the year of the cycle. 1892 + 1 divided by 19 leaves a remainder of 12, which is therefore the Golden Number for 1892.

The Epact. The Epact serves to find the moon's age by showing the number of days which must be added to each lunar year, in order to complete a solar year.

A lunar month is composed of 29 days 12 hours 44 minutes 3 seconds, or rather more than 29½ days; twelve lunar months are, therefore, nearly eleven days short of the solar year—thus, the new moons in one year will fall eleven days earlier than they did on the preceding year, so that were it new moon on the 1st of January, it would be nearly eleven days old on the 1st of January of the ensuing year, and twenty-two days on the third year; on the fourth year it would be thirty-three; but thirty days are taken off as an intercalary month (the moon having made a revolution in that time), and the three remaining would be the Epact; the Epact thus continues to vary, until, at the expiration of nineteen years, the new moons again return in the same order as before.

If the solar year were exactly eleven days longer than twelve lunar months, it would only be necessary to multiply the golden number by 11, divide the product by 30, and the remainder would be the Epact; but as the difference is not quite 11 days, 1 must be taken from the Golden Number, the remainder multiplied by 11, and the product, if less than 30, shows the Epact; but if more it must be divided by 30, and the remainder is the Epact for that year. The golden number for 1892 being 12, 11 multiplied by 11 = 121, and 121 divided by 30 leaves a remainder of 1, which is the Epact for 1892.

To find the moon's age upon any particular day, add the number placed against the month in the following table to the Epact and day of the month, the product, if under 30, will be the moon's age; should it exceed this number, divide by 30, and the remainder will show it:—

January ... 2	April ... 2	July ... 5	October ... 8
February ... 3	May ... 3	August ... 7	November ... 10
March ... 1	June ... 4	September ... 7	December ... 10

From the irregularity of the number of days in the calendar months, and other causes, it is difficult to make an exact calculation, but the error resulting from this rule does not exceed one day.

The Number of Direction. The Council of Nice decided, A.D. 325, that Easter Day is always the first Sunday after the full moon which happens upon or next after the 21st of March. Easter Day, therefore, cannot take place earlier than the 22nd of March, or later than the 25th of April. The Number of Direction is that day of the thirty-five on which Easter Sunday falls.

The Roman Indiction. The Roman Indiction was a period of fifteen years appointed A.D. 312, by the Emperor Constantine, for the payment of certain taxes.

The Julian Period. The Julian period of 7980 years is the product obtained by multiplying together 28, 19, and 15, which numbers represent the cycles of the sun, the moon, and the Roman Indiction. The beginning of the Julian Period is reckoned from 709 before the creation of the world, so that its completion will occur A.D. 3267, until which time there cannot be two years having the same numbers for the three cycles.

Time Recorders.

OF these, shadows from the sun undoubtedly formed the first in attempts to measure subdivisions of a day. The sun-dial of Ahaz, mentioned in the Second Book of Kings, is the earliest on record. There is no word to express a dial in Hebrew, and the reference to the dial of Ahaz mentions steps or degrees. This has led commentators to conclude that this famous dial was merely a stair, formed so that the shadows of the steps expressed the hours and course of the sun. Evidence exists that the famous obelisks of the Egyptians were intended as gnomons; but the earliest sun-dial of which we have any definite description is the hemicycle, or hemisphere, of the Chaldean astronomer, Berosus, who probably lived about 540 years B.C. There was found in 1726, at Mount Tusculum, near Rome, a marble dial in the form of a portion of a hollow sphere, of which a representation is given in Fig. 2. This is supposed to be the principle on which the dial of Berosus was planned. At the centre of the sphere, of which the dial is a portion, was fixed a ball. The dial being placed with the concavity towards the zenith, the shadow of the ball would enter the sphere as the sun rises and trace its path on the inside as the day advanced.

Hemicycle of Berosus.

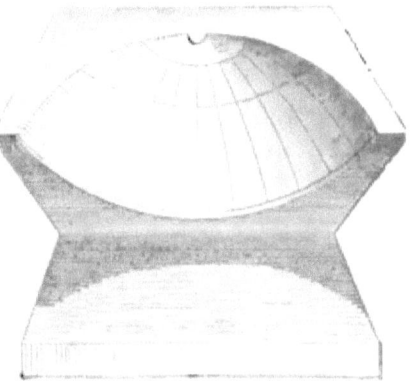

Fig. 2.—Hemicycle of Berosus.

Among the Elgin collection in the British Museum there is a dial with four faces which, it is conjectured, was intended to show the hours at one of the crossways of Athens, in which city it was discovered.

Pompeian Sun-dial. Martini, speaking of a dial found in 1762, at Pompeii, says that it was made for the latitude of Memphis, and may therefore be the work of Egyptians, if not constructed in the schools of Alexandria. It may, indeed, be supposed that every nation that cultivated astronomy found it necessary to use some means of dividing and measuring time. It appears that the Egyptians had found in the heavens some means of attaining this object, but no sun-dial has been found among the antiquities of that country, and their sculptures give us no indication of any having existed.

Plautus's Declamation against Sun-dials. It appears that sun-dials had been common in the days of Plautus, in a fragment of one of whose comedies, as preserved by Aulus Gellius, he makes a parasite declaim against sun-dials something in the following style:—

> "The gods confound the man who first found out
> How to distinguish hours! Confound them too,
> Who in this place set up a sun-dial,
> To cut and hack my days so wretchedly
> Into small portions! When I was a boy
> My belly was my sun-dial; one more sure,
> Truer and more exact than any of them.
> This dial told me when 'twas proper time
> To go to dinner (when I had aught to eat),
> But nowadays, when—(even I have)—
> I can't fall to unless the sun give leave.
> The town's so full of these confounded dials
> The greatest part of its inhabitants,
> Shrunk up with hunger, creep along the streets."

In Arabia and China traces of ancient sun-dials abound.

Sun-dials to record Religious Rites among Mahomedans. Mahomedan countries still favour sun-dials. There are dials in all the mosques of Constantinople. Prayer is a rite which is to be performed five times in twenty-four hours; and the dials indicate to the people the times for worship. On some of the dials, in addition to the marks which indicate the course of the sun, is a line pointing to the sacred town of Mecca, towards which the faces of the faithful must be turned during the performance of their religious offices. It is said that the Turks never fail to erect a sun-dial when building a mosque.

Early Dials in England. Among the ancient Britons pillars to form gnomons were erected. The shadow from the pillar was cast on flat stones placed at intervals in a ring. Sometimes natural projections of rocks were utilized as gnomons.

Anglo-Saxon dials, cut on the walls of churches, still exist in different parts of England. But from the time of the Norman Conquest, but little interest appears to have been taken in gnomonics till the sixteenth century. Then, and during the seventeenth and eighteenth centuries, many books were written on dialling; and the attention thus drawn to the subject resulted in the erection of dials of various kinds in large numbers, the majority of them being either horizontal or vertical. Mottoes, quaint sayings, and verses, more or less appropriate, were occasionally carved or painted on the face. The late Mrs. Gatty devoted herself to the examination of sun-dial literature, and published a large collection of these maxims.

Of the more pertinent inscriptions, "Non sine Lumine" ("Not without light"), is well known. It may be seen on a dial built into the front of the church of St. Mary Cree, in Leadenhall Street.

There is a large vertical dial of stone on the Dutch church in Austin Friars, bearing the words, "Docet Umbra" ("The shadow teaches").

"It flies whilst thou lookest,"
may be interpreted either as a rendering of *Tempus Fugit*, or as a reference to the sudden clouding of the sun.

"Ough isabe by a ray from heaven."
This is strictly true as applied to information from a sundial, and is also capable of a much wider interpretation.

"It is the hour for well doing,"

appears on a dial at Nice.

"I wait for no one,"

is unassailable, as are also

"You ask the hour; meanwhile you see it fly,
Nor can the hour return that passes by,"

and,

"The iron bell may wrongly tell,
I err not, if the sun shine well,"

which is paraphrased in another couplet:

"The clock may mistake the hours of the day,
But the orb of the sun never goeth astray."

"Time and tide tarry for no man"

is on a dial in Brick Court, Temple, and, among other places, used to be seen at the hall of New Inn, Wych Street.

The well-known classical lament,

"So passes the glory of the world,"

and the equally familiar scriptural injunction,

"Let your light so shine before men,"

are especially favoured by diallists.

"Tells the hour all round
Without making a sound,"

appears to be of Italian origin, and is found in the vernacular on many dials in Italy.

"So glide the hours, so wears the day,
These moments measure life away,"

often recurs.

What can be better than St. Paul's monition,

"Let not the sun go down upon your wrath,"

which is said to have been adopted for a sun-dial by Bishop Coplestone?

"**I speak, but not to the blind,**"

was on a dial at Bath some years ago; and at Combe Down, near the same city, is,

"**The hour past cannot be recalled.**"

"**Lumen me regit, vos umbra,**"
("The light guides me—the shadow you"),

is on a very old dial at Barlow Hall, Lancashire.

"**Memento Mori**" furnishes the text for a number of inscriptions which insist on reminding the reader of the uncertainty and fleeting nature of human life. Some of these are addressed with startling directness to the person who ventures to consult the dial. Here is one from the National Museum at Munich—

"**Any hour is the signal for thy death.**"

"**Look upon the hour and remember death,**"

is the classical "**Aspice in Horam et memento mori.**" which, in another instance, is rhymed into,

"**As the hour here you see,
Think on death and ready be.**"

"**I come and go, and go and come each day;
But thou without return shall pass away,**"

comes from Cornwall.

"**Life's but a shadow,
Man's but dust,
This dyall sayes
Dy all we must,**"

from the Church of All Saints, Winkleigh, Devon, is noticeable for the determination to perpetrate a pun.

"**Time passes away, eternity draws near.**"

is also from Devon.

"**Meam non tuam noscis**"
("Thou knowest my hour, not thine own").

is from Porrimo, Piedmont.

"Remember, ye that mark my face,
That death's behind you pace by pace,
Whence ye are come ye do not know,
Nor whither afterwards you'll go,"

is copied from a dial in Somerset; but a rendering of it in French is taken from a village high up in the Alps.

"Every hour shortens life"

was on an old dial at Barnard Castle church.

"Do to-day's work to-day,"

which is said to have been a fixed rule with the great Duke of Wellington, is engraved on a dial in the grounds of Sir Spencer Wells, at Hampstead.

"To friends any hour they please,"

breathes a hospitable sentiment, welcome to the tired traveller.

"The hour for drinking,"

which the landlord of a public-house at Grenoble has adopted, was, no doubt, inspired by a hope of profit. But what could have been the motive for the following:

"It is later than you believe"?

Possibly it was the assertion of a victim to unpunctuality.

"He that will thrive
Muste rise at five,
He that hath thriven
May lie till seven,
He that will never thrive
May lie till eleven,"

on the front of Stanwardine Hall, Salop, was doubtless the diction of one who had thriven.

The peremptory mandate,

"Begone about your business"

appears on several dials; and a story is related that it originated with a bencher of the Inner Temple, who, annoyed at the interruption of a messenger from the dial maker, who desired instructions as to the motto, gave utterance to the words, which were considered to be sufficiently apposite for the purpose. At Bangor a slightly different rendering is cut up to form a cryptogram, thus,

"𝕲𝖔𝖆 𝖇𝖔𝖚 𝖙𝖕𝖔 𝖚𝖗𝖇 𝖚𝖘 𝖎𝖓 𝖗𝖘𝖘."

"𝕬𝖚𝖙 𝖉𝖎𝖘𝖈𝖊, 𝖆𝖚𝖙 𝖉𝖎𝖘𝖈𝖊𝖉𝖊"
("Either learn or go"),

says the solar timekeeper at the Royal Academy, Woolwich.

"𝕮𝖚𝖒 𝖚𝖒𝖇𝖗𝖆 𝖓𝖎𝖍𝖎𝖑; 𝖘𝖎𝖓𝖊 𝖚𝖒𝖇𝖗𝖆 𝖓𝖎𝖍𝖎𝖑"
("With shadow nothing; without shadow nothing"),

is the paradoxical truth propounded by the dial in an Italian Custom House.

"𝖂𝖆𝖘𝖙𝖊, 𝖙𝖗𝖆𝖛𝖊𝖑𝖑𝖊𝖗, 𝖙𝖍𝖊 𝖘𝖚𝖓 𝖎𝖘 𝖘𝖎𝖓𝖐𝖎𝖓𝖌 𝖑𝖔𝖜;
𝖂𝖊 𝖘𝖍𝖆𝖑𝖑 𝖗𝖊𝖙𝖚𝖗𝖓 𝖆𝖌𝖆𝖎𝖓, 𝖇𝖚𝖙 𝖓𝖊𝖛𝖊𝖗 𝖙𝖍𝖔𝖚,"

which is inscribed on a dial at Tytherton Kellaways, Wilts, is rather an alarming greeting to the wayfarer who meditates but a short sojourn.

"𝕿𝖍𝖊 𝖍𝖊𝖆𝖛𝖊𝖓𝖘 𝖔𝖓 𝖍𝖎𝖌𝖍 𝖕𝖊𝖗𝖕𝖊𝖙𝖚𝖆𝖑𝖑𝖞 𝖉𝖔 𝖒𝖔𝖛𝖊,
𝕭𝖞 𝖒𝖎𝖓𝖚𝖙𝖊𝖘 𝖘𝖒𝖆𝖑𝖑 𝖙𝖍𝖊 𝖍𝖔𝖚𝖗 𝖉𝖔𝖙𝖍 𝖘𝖙𝖊𝖆𝖑 𝖆𝖜𝖆𝖞,
𝕭𝖞 𝖍𝖔𝖚𝖗𝖘 𝖙𝖍𝖊 𝖉𝖆𝖞𝖘, 𝖇𝖞 𝖉𝖆𝖞𝖘 𝖙𝖍𝖊 𝖒𝖔𝖓𝖙𝖍𝖘 𝖗𝖊𝖒𝖔𝖛𝖊,
𝕬𝖓𝖉 𝖙𝖍𝖊𝖓 𝖇𝖞 𝖒𝖔𝖓𝖙𝖍𝖘 𝖙𝖍𝖊 𝖞𝖊𝖆𝖗𝖘 𝖆𝖘 𝖋𝖆𝖘𝖙 𝖉𝖊𝖈𝖆𝖞."

These lines were written by Dr. Watts as the motto on a handsome pillar-dial, which formerly stood in the garden of Lady Abney, at Stoke Newington. Sir Thomas Abney was Lord Mayor of London in 1700, and died in 1722.

Miss Martineau's Sun-dial. A friend, knowing that Harriet Martineau desired a sun-dial on the terrace of her house at Ambleside, presented her with one of grey granite, in the form of an ancient font, to which she attached the words of Wordsworth,

"𝕮𝖔𝖒𝖊 𝖑𝖎𝖌𝖍𝖙! 𝖁𝖎𝖘𝖎𝖙 𝖒𝖊!"

Cowper's Sun-dial. Cowper also coveted a sun-dial for his garden at Weston Underwood, and it is recorded that Dr. Johnson had one set up unknown to the poet, who beheld it, on taking a morning ramble, with surprise and gratification.

Dial at Kew in commemoration of Bradley. In the grounds of Kew Palace is a horizontal dial to commemorate the discovery, by Bradley, of the aberration of light. The stone on which his telescope was fixed is now the base of the pedestal supporting the dial.

Great Dial in India. In Murray's "Handbook to Bengal" is mentioned a great dial at Delhi, constructed in 1724, by Jey Singh, Rajah of Jeypore, of which the dimensions of the gnomon are as follows:—

	ft.	in.
Length of hypothenuse	118	5
,, ,, base	104	0
,, ,, perpendicular	56	7

The gnomon is of solid masonry, coped with marble; and the shadow is thrown upon a graduated circle, also of marble.

Dial in Temple Gardens. In the gardens of the Inner Temple, facing the Thames Embankment, is the life-size figure of a Moor, kneeling and supporting a sun-dial on his head. Until 1884 it stood in the garden of Clement's Inn, in the Strand; and Peter Cunningham, in his "Handbook of London," says it was brought from Italy, and presented to Clement's Inn by Holles, Earl of Clare. The date inscribed on the dial-plate is 1731.

Exact Dial at Monaco. On the guard-house at the palace of the Prince of Monaco is a very fine dial, of which the head of the gnomon is flattened and has a hole with knife edges, so that a bright round spot of light falls upon the hour lines. In this way more exact observations may be secured.

Humorous Mock Dial. At an old inn in Somerset is a dial something like the sketch (Fig. 3), with the following:—

"The hour is shown on other dials but when the sun doth shine,
They have a style projecting whose shadow casts a line,
But always whether sun do shine or whether clouds do lower
One of my hands will never fail to point to the true hour."

Of course it is not a timekeeper at all, but merely the joke of some humourist. Yet a good many wayfarers,

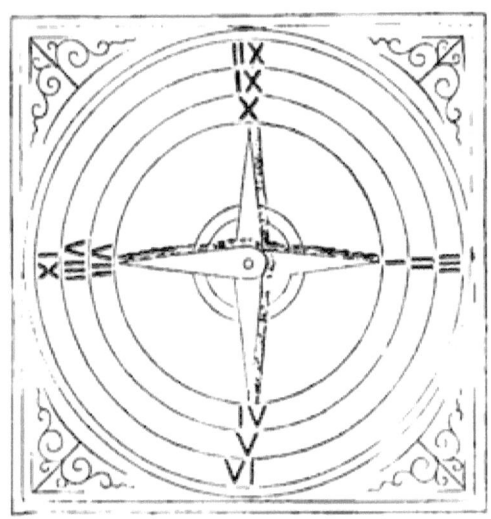

Fig. 3.—Humorous mock dial.

after examination of the dial, read the inscription over and over with a puzzled air, much to the delight of the natives.

Portable Dials. Portable dials, such as were much used in the seventeenth century, may be divided into

Fig. 4.—Pocket sun-dial with hinged gnomen.

two classes. The first kind consisted of a horizontal dial, the gnomon of which was often hinged to lie flat when not in use, as in Fig. 4. Beside the dial was a compass to set the gnomon true north and south.

The second class of pocket dials were presented to the sun wherever he happened to be, and therefore required some adjustment to suit the varying altitude of the sun at different periods of the year.

Pocket Ring-dial. Ring-dials, like the one shown in Fig. 5, were a common form. On the inside of the ring were lines corresponding to the hours of the morning and afternoon. Outside the ring in four

Fig. 5.—Pocket Ring-dial.

groups of three each, were either the initials of the maker or the signs of the Zodiac. Slipped into a circular groove formed in the middle of the outer surface of the ring was a slide to be moved round so as to bring a mark on it opposite the date when the dial was being used. Then the light from the sun passed through a very small hole in the slide and infringed on the hour-line in the interior of the ring. It is generally supposed that Shakespeare referred to a dial of this kind, when Jacques, in "As You Like It," recounting his meeting with the fool, says he

> "... drew a dial from his poke;
> And looking on it with lack-lustre eye,
> Says, very wisely, 'It is ten o'clock :
> Thus we may see,' quoth he ' how the world wags;
> 'Tis but an hour ago since it was nine,
> And after one hour more 'twill be eleven.'"

It is doubtful if the record of the time obtained by these ring-dials was any nearer than could be judged by persons accustomed to noting the position of the sun at different periods of the day.

Pyrenean Pocket-dial. I have in my possession a very superior pocket-dial, of French make (Fig. 6), such as is still used by the peasants of the Pyrenees. It is of wood, and when closed is a cylinder less than an inch in diameter, and about three inches long, with an oval handle. To use it the handle is pulled out, and a blade, similar to a knife-blade, unfolded; the handle is then pushed in again as far as it will go, leaving the blade projecting at right angles to the axis of the cylinder. The surface of the cylinder is covered with longitudinal lines, crossed by curves to represent the altitude of the sun throughout the year. When taking an observation the blade which forms the gnomon is adjusted to the date, and the length of its shadow on the cylinder indicates the hour.

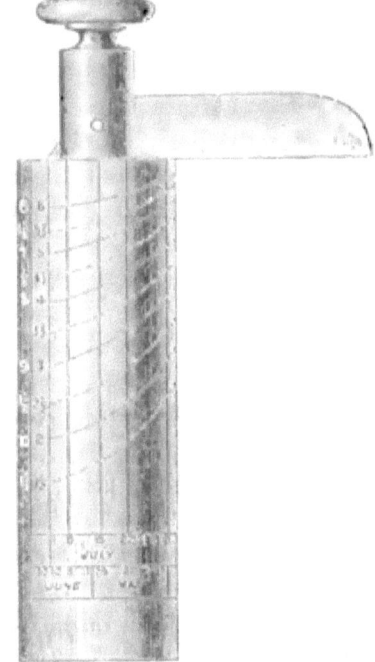

Fig. 6.—Pyrenean Pocket-dial.

The mechanical timekeepers of later days have not entirely banished sun-dials, which still linger in the affections of many, and are often set up either to indulge a fancy, or in the form of a meridian dial for the regulation of other timekeepers.

Meridian Dial. A meridian dial, useful for ascertaining solar noon at any particular spot, may be easily constructed by following Ferguson's concise instructions: "Make four or five concentric circles, a quarter of an inch from one another, on a flat stone, and let the outmost circle be but little less than the stone will contain. Fix a pin perpendicularly in the centre, and of such a length that its whole shadow may fall within the innermost circle for at least four hours in the middle of the day. The pin ought to be about an eighth of an inch thick, with a round blunt point. The stone being set exactly level in a place where the sun shines, suppose from eight in the morning till four in the afternoon, before and after which hours the shadow should fall without all the circles; watch the times in the forenoon when the extremity of the shortening shadow just touches the several circles, and there make marks. Then in the afternoon of the same day watch the lengthening shadow, and where its end touches the several circles in going over them make marks also. With a pair of compasses find exactly the middle points between the two marks on any circle, and draw a straight line from the centre to that point, which line will be covered at noon by the shadow of a small upright wire which should be put in place of the pin."

Of course with an accurate timekeeper, and an "Equation of Time" table, a meridian line may be at once drawn, without recourse to the preceding plan of Ferguson's.

Lord Grimthorpe recommends, for obtaining a more accurate meridian dial, a slot in the gnomon terminating in a round hole, as in the Monaco sun-dial.

AND OTHER TIMEKEEPERS.

Construction of Sun-dials. By observation, the hours of the morning and afternoon may also be marked on the meridian dial, and it will be noticed that although the position of the hour immediately preceding noon corresponds with the one immediately after noon, the space representing one of these will not answer for any of the remaining hours. In fact, the art of dialling is more complex than may be at first supposed. A sundial may be regarded as a circle round the earth, or as the edge of a disc which passes through the centre of the earth from the spot where the dial is fixed, the edge of the gnomon or style whose shadow marks the time being parallel to the axis of the earth. A glance at the diagram, Fig. 7, will show at once why, except for

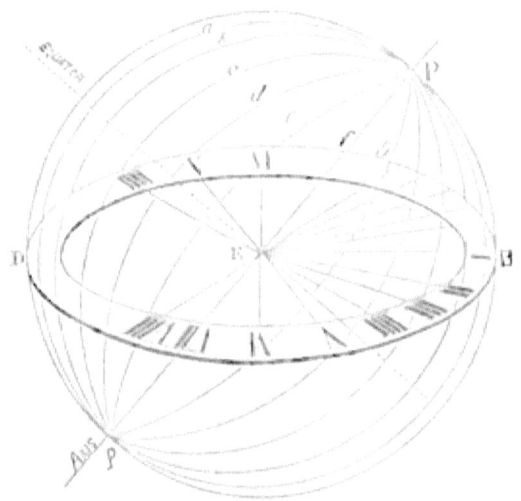

Fig. 7.

places on the equator, the hour spaces are not equal; a, b, c, d, e, f, g, etc., are longitudinal circles representing the hours, B the spot where the dial is situated, D the corresponding latitude, P p the poles, and E the centre of the earth. The only way the hour spaces can be obtained equal is by making the dial cylindrical, the gnomon being the diameter of the cylinder. It will be evident that a dial prepared for any particular place is useless for another place in a different latitude. With this exception, a horizontal dial for a certain spot is a vertical dial for the complementary latitude, or its difference from 90°; for instance, a horizontal dial for 30° would be a vertical dial for 60°. In dials which do not face the south, *i.e.* incline to the east or the west, corresponding hour spaces before and after noon will obviously not be equal.

With a sun-dial of adequate size, and carefully constructed so as to be useful for regulating timekeepers, it may be worth while to mark the hours to show Greenwich instead of local time; mean time for any particular day can then be readily obtained by reference to the "Equation of Time" table on page 14.

Clepsydræ.

Chaldean Clepsydræ.

THE Clepsydra, or water-clock, which was the first contrivance for measuring spaces of time independently of the motion of the earth, is of great antiquity among Eastern nations, and the varied forms in which water clocks have been found, testify to the great amount of ingenuity expended in their production through many ages. The Chaldeans, it is said, divided the day into twelve equal parts, as they supposed, by allowing water to run out of a small orifice during the whole revolution of a star, and dividing the fluid into twelve equal portions. Sextus Empiricus remarked that the unequal flowing of the water, and the variations of temperature, would affect the accuracy of the result in this arrangement.

Egyptian Clepsydræ.

One of the earliest forms of the clepsydra which was in use in Egypt about 300 B.C., is shown in Fig. 8. A supply of water ran through the pipe H into the cone A, and from there dropped into the cylinder E. A conical stopper, B, regulated the flow, and the superfluous water escaped by the waste pipe I. As the Egyptians divided the period between sunrise and sunset into twelve equal hours, the conical stopper had to be adjusted for each day, and marks for every day in the year, and for the particular latitude of the place, were cut on the stalk, D, as a guide to the position of the stopper. A loose, floating piston, terminating in a rack, served to actuate a pinion, to the arbor of which an hour hand was fixed.

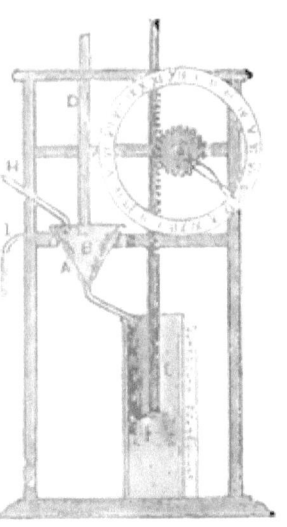

Fig. 8.—Egyptian Clepsydra.

The next attempt to improve the clepsydra, which we also get from Vitruvius, was by adding an index to the sun's place in the ecliptic circle, so that the water aperture might be by it adjusted as the year advanced. Fig. 9 represents a clepsydra on this plan. From a reservoir with an overflow pipe the water was conducted by the pipe B to a drum M N, on the face of which were engraved the signs of the ecliptic. Within the large one a smaller drum passes, having cut through it a groove or slot, $a\ b$, which is tapering in breadth. The inner drum turns on a pipe F, which has a funnel, and when the inner drum is in its place, the tapering groove comes just under the orifice of the supply pipe B. The index L O served to adjust the flow of water according to the sign of the ecliptic. The water, regulated by the index, dropped into the cylinder H, within which was a float, connected, by means of a chain passing over the pulley P, with the

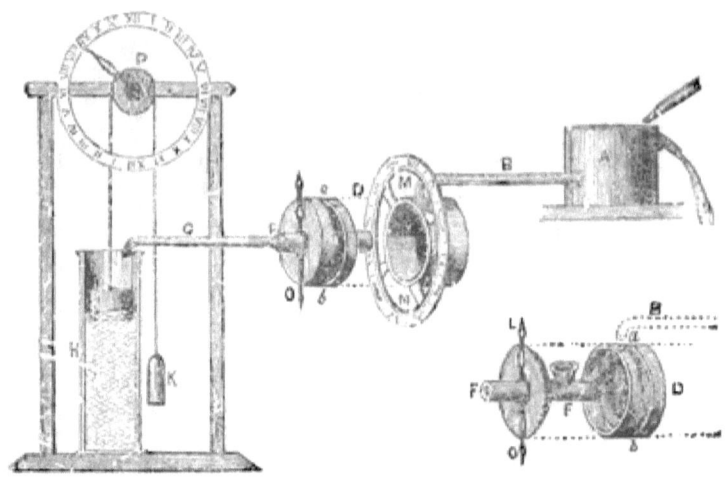

Fig. 9.—Clepsydra of Vitruvius.

counterweight K. The pulley P carries a hand pointing to the hours on a circle.

Clepsydræ of Ctesibus. Ctesibus, the son of a barber of Alexandria, seems, about 240 B.C., to have devised many clepsydræ, and possibly the preceding one was of his invention. His name is, however, more definitely connected with the automatic arrangement for meeting the difficulty arising from the inequality of the Egyptian hours, shown in Fig. 10, of which he is acknowledged to be the originator. The water dropped from the eyes of a figure, fed from a full reservoir to ensure a constant pressure into the funnel A, from whence, through the pipe M, it was conveyed to an open cylinder. From a float on the water in the cylinder rises the stalk C, terminating in a human figure carrying a wand, with which it pointed to the hour on a column. As the water rises in the cylinder it also rises in the short leg of a syphon B E F, till it reaches the top, when it flows over the bent part and quickly empties the cylinder, bringing down the float, and with it the index, to the starting point. The water as it flowed from the syphon fell into a chambered drum K, which turned with the weight as each compartment became filled. On the axis of the drum is a pinion gearing with a contrate-wheel I, on whose axis is another pinion II, which turns the wheel G on the axis L of the column. The hours being engraved in slanting lines on the column to correspond with the varying length of the days throughout the year, the column was by this means adjusted to the position required for the correct record of each succeeding day.

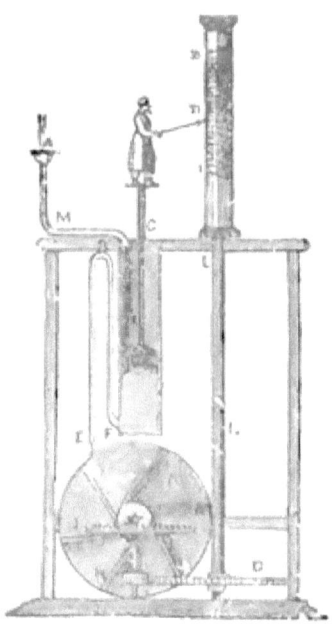

Fig. 10.—Clepsydra of Ctesibus.

Grecian Clepsydræ.
The clepsydra was introduced into Greece by Plato. Athenæus relates that the so-called "divine philosopher" invented a night clock, which was a clepsydra, or water-clock, that played upon flutes certain sounds which indicated the hours of the night at a time when they could not be seen on the index. Athenæus says of it that it resembled in appearance a round altar; that it was not to be ranked with stringed instruments, but was a wind instrument composed of pipes, the orifices of which being toward the water as it fell produced a soft and pleasing sound. The introduction of the clepsydra into Rome took place about 157 B.C. by

Scipio Nasica. Pliny tells us that Pompey brought a valuable one among the spoils from the eastern nations, which he made use of for limiting the speeches of the Roman orators. It is much to be regretted that horological machines are not more used for the purpose in these days. Julius Cæsar is said to have met with an instrument of the kind in England, by the help of which he observed that the summer nights of this climate are shorter than they are in Italy, which fact is mentioned in his Commentaries. It is most probable that they had been long known to our ancestors in consequence of the very early intercourse they had with the Phœnicians.

Fig. 11.—Striking Clepsydra, presented to Charlemagne, 807 A.D.

Extraordinary Striking Among the presents sent in 807 A.D. to Charlemagne by the King of Persia was a water-clock

Clepsydra presented to Charlemagne. which struck the hours, and is thus described by Gifford in his "History of France." "The dial was composed of twelve small doors, which represented the division of the hours; each door opened at the hour it was intended to represent, and out of it came the same number of little balls, which fell one by one, at equal distances of time, on a brass drum. It might be told by the eye what hour it was by the number of doors that were open, and by the ear by the number of balls that fell. When it was twelve o'clock twelve horsemen in miniature issued forth at the same time and shut all the doors. A view of the exterior of this remarkable clock, taken from a piece of old Sèvres china, is given in Fig. 11.

Sounding Clepsydræ of the Romans. By this time the Romans had learned to make sounding clepsydræ; and later still, Lucian describes, among the numerous conveniences of certain newly built baths, a horologium that proclaimed the hour by means of a roaring sound. This sound, it is conjectured, was produced by the release of air compressed by water.

Indian Clepsydræ. That water-clocks were early used in India there is good presumption afforded by the arithmetical treatise of one Bhascara Acharya, written in the twelfth century, and called "Liliwati." This was the name of the author's daughter, at whose birth it was predicted that she should die unmarried. The father determined to have at least one struggle against the prophecy, and accordingly procured a bridegroom and an astrological determination of a lucky hour. The damsel, adorned as a bride, watched at the clepsydra for the auspicious hour. But in vain, for it passed unobserved; and on looking to the clock which should have prevented such a mischance, the maiden found that a pearl which had become detached from her dress had fallen into the water, and closed the opening through which it should have flowed. The father, thus grievously baffled, sought to console his child, and said to her, "I will write a book of your name which shall remain till the latest times. The "Liliwati" was accordingly written. It is a work well known to Hindu scholars, and so bids fair to realize the prediction.

Primitive Clepsydra still in use in India. The Brahmins of India still divide the natural day into sixty hours of twenty-four minutes each, called ghurees; they measure the ghurees occasionally with a 24-minute sand-glass, but more commonly by means of a copper bowl with a very small hole in the bottom of it. This bowl is placed on the surface of the water contained in a larger vessel, and as the water enters by the small hole in the bottom it gradually fills. If the hole is correctly sized, the bowl sinks when twenty-four minutes have elapsed, and this registers the duration of a ghuree. The attendant then empties it, and strikes the hour of the day or night on a gong.

Clepsydræ of the Seventeenth Century. Though the introduction of weight-clocks caused a decline in the popularity of clepsydræ, the performance of the early instruments controlled by a balance fell short of what was expected by many, and other forms of timekeepers actuated by water were originated. Beckmann, in his "History of Inventions," dates the revival of clepsydræ to some time between 1643 and 1646; and Dr. Hutton mentions a water-clock brought to Paris from Burgundy. He says that Father Timothy, a Barnabite monk, had given the machine all the excellence it was capable of, by constructing it so as to make it go a month without replenishing, and to exhibit not only the hours on a dial plate, but also the sun's place, day of the month, and festivals throughout the year.

A favourite form of clepsydra in the seventeenth century

is shown in Fig. 12. It consists of an oblong frame of wood, A B C D, to the upper part of which two cords are fixed at their superior extremities, and at their inferior extremities are wound round the axis of the drum, E. As seen in section in Fig. 13, this drum has seven water-

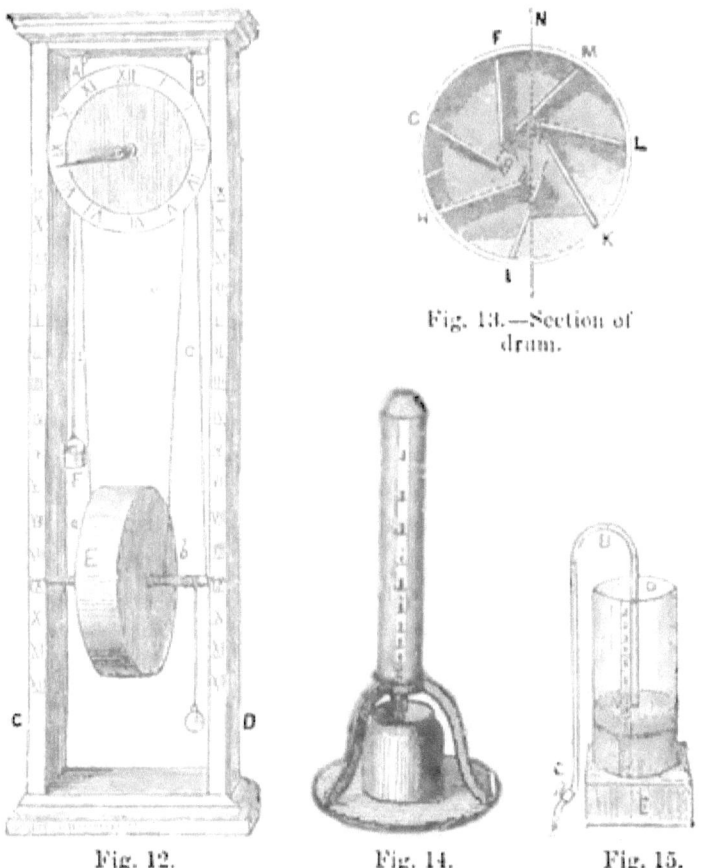

Fig. 13.—Section of drum.

Fig. 12.   Fig. 14.   Fig. 15.
Clepsydræ of the Seventeenth Century.

tight metallic partitions. If the cords be wound round the axis till the drum rises to the top of the frame, and the drum be left to obey the force of gravity, it will of course tend to fall, and the cords resisting this tendency would cause it to rotate as it descended. But if water is introduced into the drum it will be retained in certain parts of the circumference by the partitions, and one side being thus heavier than the other, the tendency to rotate would be counteracted, and the drum remain stationary. But a small hole is pierced near the bottom of each cell, to allow the water to slowly ooze from it to the next one, and so the drum is allowed to slowly rotate, the rate of motion being regulated by adjusting the size of the holes. If this is properly done the axis will point out the hours on the side of the frame. Or a cord, $c\ d$, with a weight F, may be made to pass over a pulley attached to an arbor bearing an index or hand to point out the hours on a circle properly engraved or painted. Either method was employed at pleasure.

Fig. 14 represents another, and a very simple, form of clepsydra used in the seventeenth century. It is merely a glass vessel having an orifice at the bottom, and filled with as much water as would flow out in exactly twelve hours, figures being placed at the proper distances to denote the successive hours.

In Fig. 15 an open vessel is used. The shorter limb of a syphon is attached to a float, and the syphon being filled with water it empties the vessel of the whole of the contained fluid. As the float falls with the water the proportion between the length of the legs of the syphon is maintained, and the rate at which the water issues constant, so that the hour-marks on the side of the vessel are equidistant.

The construction of clepsydræ and weight-clocks went on contemporaneously for a long period, but with the introduction of the pendulum the superior performance and convenience of the latter were too apparent to be resisted.

Clepsydra for Equatorial at Greenwich. At the Royal Observatory, Greenwich, a water-clock is still employed to drive the equatorial telescope. Water at a constant pressure from a pipe of a certain height is allowed to issue from holes on opposite sides of two horizontal hollow arms, projecting from and in communication with the vertical supply pipe, which runs on a pivot; and the arms, being relieved of the pressure where the holes are pierced, recoil. As the pipes are free to revolve, a constant circular movement is maintained, the steadiness of motion being assisted by a revolving pendulum. This arrangement is a very suitable one for continuous progression, as is necessary where a telescope has to follow the motion of a star, and where, therefore, the intermittent motion incidental to ordinary escapement clocks would be out of the question. The rotation obtained by the issue of fluids at a pressure from horizontal tubes is the principle of a device known as Barker's Mill, and in breweries as a sparger, where it is used for sprinkling the malt. Latterly it has been applied for watering lawns and gardens.

Candle-clocks. Candle-clocks may be mentioned as one of the early devices adopted for the apportionment of time. According to Asser, Alfred the Great, in fulfilment of a vow, devoted eight hours of the day to acts of religion, eight to public business, and as many to sleep, study, and refreshment. To this end he caused wax candles twelve inches long to be made, one inch of which burnt away in twenty minutes. The tending of the candle-clock was entrusted to the king's domestic chaplains, who lighted a fresh candle every four hours throughout the day and night. Horn scraped so thin as to be transparent, and let into frames of wood, was used as screens to keep the draughts from the light and permit of a uniform consumption of the candle.

Sand-glasses. Sand-glasses, introduced about A.D. 330, consisted of a double bulb of glass with an intervening neck; the upper bulb was charged with sufficient dry sand to run through the neck into the lower bulb in exactly one hour, hence the title hour-glasses.

Though the constant attention which sand-glasses required precluded their general use for marking the division of a day, special uses have been found for them. To this day they are used in Parliament for noting prescribed periods, and a few years ago it was not at all uncommon to see the preacher turn his sand-glass as he began his sermon. Until his death in 1890, the Rev. Henry White, the popular minister of the Savoy, used a twenty-minute sand-glass to measure the duration of his discourse.

Fig. 16 is a very elegant sand-glass of the sixteenth century.

The Brahmins of India occasionally use a twenty-four-minute sand-glass to record their ghurees, or hours, though the copper bowl mentioned in connection with clepsydræ is more common.

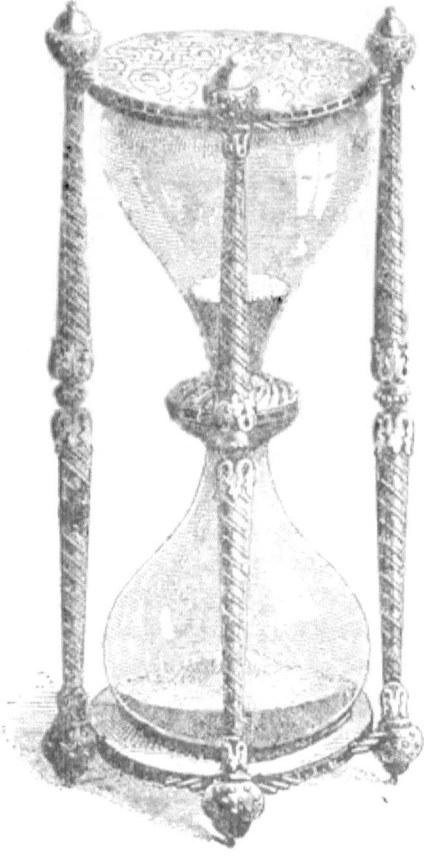

Fig. 16.—Sand-glass, Sixteenth Century.

Sand-glasses are almost universally used to time the period necessary for boiling an egg, and the story of the individual who used a watch for the purpose, and in a fit of absent-mindedness placed the watch in the saucepan and held the egg in his hand, may be taken to be only the exception that proves the rule.

Weight Clocks.

SOME of the varieties of the clepsydra would naturally suggest to a mechanical mind the idea of obtaining the necessary motive force for a machine to mark time, by allowing gravity to act upon a body other than water, so that it is not surprising to find men of known inventive power, from Archimedes, before the Christian era, and Gerbert, a monk who lived at the end of the tenth century, named with confidence as the inventors of clocks composed of wheels actuated by a weight.

But to whomsoever we may be indebted for the first idea, it appears certain that "horologes" of some kind, with other motive power than water, were known about 1120, and that they were set up in churches as early as 1174. Towards the middle of the thirteenth century, a Saracen is stated to have received a sum equal to £2000 for having made a clock moved by weights. This machine was afterwards presented to Frederick II., Emperor of Germany. In the reign of Henry VI. a pension was granted to the dean and chapter of St. Stephen's, for taking charge of a clock placed in a turret in Palace Yard, opposite Westminster Hall. It was erected in the time of Edward I., about 1298, from a fine imposed on the Chief Justice of the King's Bench; and near the same time a clock is said to have been placed in Canterbury Cathedral, but there is nothing tangibly descriptive of a clock till 1326, when Richard Wallingford, Abbot of Saint Albans, placed one in his monastery. It showed the hours, the apparent motion of the sun, the changes of the moon, the ebb and flow of the tides, etc., and it continued to go until the time of Henry VIII., when, Leland says, "all Europe could not produce such another." The account which Wallingford gave of his "horologe" is still preserved in the Bodleian Library at

Early Clocks merely Planataria. Oxford, and it seems that even this was really more of a planatarium, that when wound showed the course of the heavenly bodies, rather than an instrument for recording the time with any pretence to accuracy, for there is no mention of an escapement.

Fig. 17.—Dial of Glastonbury clock, now at Wells Cathedral.

First real Clocks, Lightfoot and De Vick. In 1340, Peter Lightfoot, a monk, made for Glastonbury Abbey a clock, which was at the Reformation removed to Wells Cathedral, where some part of it still remains. This was certainly a "timekeeper" with an escapement and a regulator for securing equable motion, and very different from all previous astrological and horological machines. In 1835, the mechanism being entirely worn out, the clock was supplied with new works and the dial somewhat remodelled. Fig. 17, is a view of it as it appears now. The outer circle is 6 feet 6 inches in diameter and the band within is of a blue colour, with gilt stars scattered over it; the hour numerals are painted in old English characters on circular tablets, and are in two series of twelve each. The centre portion of the dial rotates once in a lunar month, showing the phases of the moon through a circular aperture. An index mark on the edge of the rotating centre points to the age of the moon. Emerging from behind the age of the moon circle, is a gilt star with a long ray pointing to the minute, and mounted on a stalk is another star to indicate the hour. The minute circle and index were added when the clock was reconstructed in 1835. However useful the addition, one cannot repress a feeling of regret that the integrity of so rare an example of early English horology should have been destroyed. At the base of the arched pediment which surmounts the square of the dial, is an octagonal projection from which rises a panelled turret. Around this, fixed to two rings of wood, are sets of horsemen which formerly revolved in opposite directions as the hour was struck. The original movement is, or was a short time ago, to be seen in the Patent Museum at South Kensington. It had iron frames and wheels and, except that it was controlled by a balance instead of a pendulum, it bore a remarkable resemblance to the turret clocks of a few years ago.

<small>Lightfoot's Glastonbury Clock.</small>

The action of these fourteenth century clocks will be understood by an examination of the drawings on page 53, which represent a clock very similar to Lightfoot's, which was made about 1364, by Henry de Vick for Charles V. of France. It was on the bell of De Vick's clock that the signal for the massacre of St. Bartholomew was given.

Clockmakers in England. It may be taken for granted that for a long period clocks were produced at rare intervals, and were chiefly the handiwork of monks and others connected with monasteries and similar religious retreats. Chaucer, who died in 1400, wrote of the cock crowing as regularly as clock or abbey horologe. In his "History of Taxation and Duties in England," Mr. Dowell asserts that the manufacture of clocks in England was commenced by the three horologists from Delft, in Holland, to whom Edward III. granted licence in 1368 to come and practise their occupation here.

Mechanism of Fourteenth Century Clocks. Rude as the mechanism undoubtedly was, the clocks of Lightfoot and De Vick form the basis from which our timekeepers of to-day have been evolved by successive improvements, and their construction is therefore worthy of a brief description. A heavy weight being tied to a rope which was wound round a cylinder or barrel served as the power to cause the hand to revolve; but the hand, instead of being fixed to the axis of the barrel, had its motion communicated through toothed wheels, called a train, arranged in such a manner that the hand made several revolutions for one rotation of the barrel, so that the weight did not need to be wound up so frequently. If the weight were allowed to act freely on the hand, its motion would have been accelerated, therefore what is now known as an escapement had to be devised, to ensure uniformity in the rate of progress of the hand.

Attached to a vertical axis were two arms, each carrying a weight; upon the same axis were two vanes or pallets, at right angles, and apart from each other a distance equal to the diameter of the last wheel in the train. This wheel had an odd number of teeth, which were formed on its side instead of on its periphery, and one of the pallets projecting in the path of the wheel teeth had to be pushed aside before the wheel could

AND OTHER TIMEKEEPERS. 53

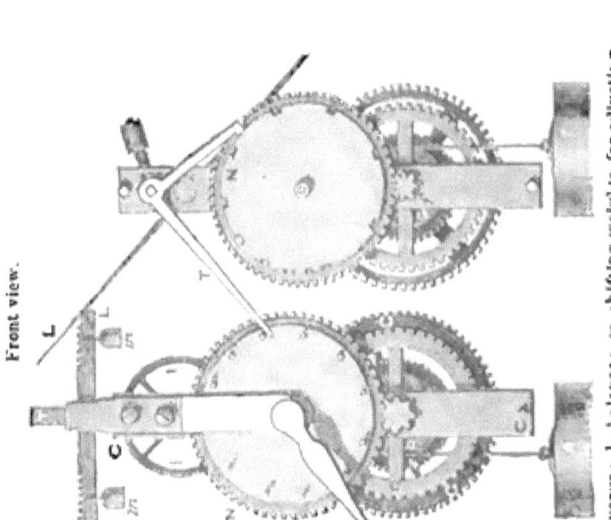

Fourteenth Century Clock.

Side view of Striking part.

Front view.

Side view of Going part.

F, weight; A H, plates; C, barrel; c, pins for raising the hammer tail; E, fly; f, pinion for driving count wheel; N, count wheel or locking plate; T, lever for letting off striking work.

K, verge; l, balance; m, shifting weights for adjusting the clock to time; o, pinion for driving hour wheel; N, hour wheel the arbor of which carries the hand.

D, barrel; C D E, plates; F, ratchet and click; G, great wheel; P O, winding pinion and wheel; H, second wheel; g, escape pinion.

rotate. The tooth in turning the pallet round its axis had to overcome the inertia of the weights hung upon the arms; and the arms having notches in them to allow the weights to be moved farther from or nearer to the centre of motion, the operation of pushing the pallet on one side could be arranged to occupy approximately the required time. But having succeeded in getting clear of one pallet, the progress of the wheel was barred by the second pallet, which would in its turn be presented to the tooth on the other side of the centre, and in being thrust aside would carry the arms and weights in an opposite direction. The whole operation being continually

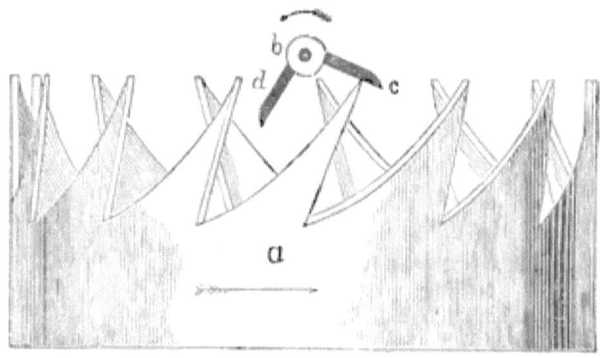

Verge Escapement.
a wheel; *b* verge; *c* and *d* pallets.

repeated resulted in a constantly alternating motion of the arms and weights, whereby the progression of the hand was kept tolerably uniform.

The form of escapement here described is known as the verge, and it held its own for three centuries, while the reciprocating motion of matter as a means of regulating the motive force of timekeepers has never been superseded.

The barrel was tight on its arbor, but the driving-wheel on the same arbor was loosely fitted, the connection between the two being established by means of a ratchet wheel and click; so that when the weight had run down it could be again raised by placing a cranked handle on

the square extremity of the arbor, and turning the barrel
the reverse way.

Striking Work of Fourteenth Century Clocks.
On reference to the engravings on page 53, it will be observed that there are twelve pins projecting from the wheel to which the hand is attached. At each hour one of these pins pushed aside an arm of a bell-cranked lever, thereby releasing the striking-train, which had been held by a catch on the other arm of the lever entering one of a series of notches in the edge of a disc or locking plate. As the wheels of the striking-train solicited by the weight begin to rotate as the train is released, the pins at *c* lift the hammer, which on its return strikes a blow on the bell. The notches round the edge of the locking plate are placed at such distances that at one o'clock the catch enters a notch directly one blow has been struck on the bell. At the next hour there is a longer space before a notch is reached, and so two blows are struck before the train is again locked; at the succeeding hour the space permits of three blows, and so on till at twelve o'clock the plate has made a complete rotation, and the action of the preceding twelve hours recurs. The striking-train would run down with increasing velocity but for the fan L, which keeps the periods between the strokes of the bell perfectly uniform. This is the principle in the striking work still used in most turret clocks, and till recently in nearly all small clocks of French make. The chief objection to it is that the hours are struck in regular progression without reference to the position of the hands; so that if the clock happens to run down, the striking will be all wrong when the clock is started again, unless the precaution is taken to set it going at the same hour as that at which it stopped.

For nearly two centuries Barlow's rack and snail-repeating mechanism has been used as striking work in English house clocks.

The vibrating arms or balance, though an almost perfect regulator when controlled by a spring, as it now is in watches and other portable timekeepers, was nevertheless sadly deficient without this adjunct.

Fig. 18.—Exterior of Fourteenth Century clock at Wimborne.

At Wimborne, in Dorsetshire, is a very old clock, somewhat on the lines of the one at Wells, and it is believed that this one also was devised by Peter Lightfoot. A view of the exterior is given above.

During the sixteenth century most public clocks were under the care of "setters," a title suggestive of erratic going. Shakespeare, who allowed very little to escape his notice, makes Falconbridge tell King John that Old Time is a clock setter.

Cardinal Wolsey's Clock. In the "Calendar of State Papers," *temp.* Henry VIII., there is a letter, dated 13th of August, 1516, from Tunstal to Cardinal Wolsey, in which the writer says that he has prepared for the prelate "a clock such as Richmond (described to) your grace. It is all ready, save the case, and that it (may stay) a season by the maker to see as it goeth, that if any (lack) be it may be amended. As soon as it is trimmed I shall have it conveyed to your grace." On the 1st of September following, Tunstal, dating from Brussels, again wrote to Wolsey, stating that he sent by Richmond a clock as a present, which Richmond would inform him how to set, and he enclosed the key of the case and the vice, which latter was probably the winder.

Wolsey said to have predicted his Death. Wolsey died as a clock struck eight on the 28th of November, 1530, and there is a remarkable legend to the effect that he had during his preceding illness predicted that he should die at that hour.

Anne Boleyn's Clock. There is in the possession of Her Majesty at Windsor Castle the case of a clock which was given by Henry VIII. to Anne Boleyn on their marriage, in 1532; but the original movement has been unfortunately replaced by a modern one. The case is about four inches square, of brass, gilt, richly chased with fleur de lys, little heads, etc. On the top sits a lion holding the arms of England. The height from the base to the cornice is five and a half inches, thence to the top of the lion's head five inches more. The weights are chased with the initials of Henry and Anne within true lovers' knots. One bears the inscription, "The most happye;" the other the royal motto.

The clock seems to have been given by Lady Elizabeth Germaine to Horace Walpole; and when his effects were sold at Strawberry Hill, it was bought by the Queen for £110 5s. The Rev. H. L. Nelthropp and other writers speak of it as a portable clock. I have not been able to see it; but whatever it may be now, the mention of the weights seems to negative the idea that it was originally driven by springs.

Old Clock at Hampton Court. William Derham, the earliest English horological writer, describes an astronomical clock which was placed in one of the towers of Hampton Court Palace in 1541. When in action, it showed the rising and setting of the sun, motions of several of the planets, phases of the moon, etc. From some marks resembling the letters N.C., it is conjectured that the maker was Nicholas Cratzen, a Bavarian, who was "deviser of the King's horologeries" in the time of Henry VIII. There is a record, that in 1575 a payment was made to "George Gaver, serjeante painter, for painting the great dial at Hampton Court, containing the howrs of the day and night, the course of the sonne and mone, the xij signes with the characters of vij planates, envoironed into a circle, the sea, shippes, and territories," and the dial is all that now remains of the original clock. The works appear to have been repaired by Langley Bradley, of Fenchurch Street, in 1711. Further alterations and repairs were made between 1760 and 1800; but for many years in the early part of the present century the clock was idle, a condition which evoked the following from G. P. R. James:—

> "Memento of the gone-by hours
> Dost thou recall alone the past?
> Why stands't thou silent 'midst these towers,
> When time still flies so fast?"

There is still a clock at Hampton Court Palace; but it is one brought from Old Buckingham Palace in 1835, when that building was demolished.

Watches Invented, A.D. 1500.

Hele invents the Mainspring.

WEIGHTS dangling from ropes or cords being clearly inadmissible for portable timekeepers, some other means had to be devised for driving the mechanism, and, about 1500, the mainspring is said to have been invented for this purpose by Peter Hele, a clockmaker, of Nuremberg, though watches did not come into general use till many years after this date.

There is no doubt that at first the mainspring proved to be a very troublesome medium, on account of the difference in the power it exerted when fully wound and after a few hours' running. The stack-freed, a kind of spring brake, acting on an eccentric wheel or cam, so that a large radius was presented to the brake when the power was excessive, and a smaller radius as the power decreased, was among many early endeavours to provide a correction.

Zech invents the Fusee.
It remained for Jacob Zech, of Prague, to solve the difficulty, about 1525, by the invention of the fusee, a kind of conical pulley interposed between the barrel or circular box containing the mainspring and the train of wheels which the mainspring is to drive. The arrangement will be understood from Fig. 19.

The mainspring is a long ribbon of steel fixed at one end to an arbor, around which it is tightly wound. The arbor and spring are inserted in the barrel, the outer end of the spring being hooked into the inside of the edge of the barrel. The arbor is prevented from turning by a ratchet and click, and therefore the spring in its effort to uncoil causes the barrel to rotate.

A string of catgut is connected at one end to the circumference of the barrel, and wound around it, the other end being fixed to the larger end of the fusee, which is attached to the driving wheel of the watch or clock, by the intervention of a ratchet and click. To wind the spring the fusee is turned backwards by means of a key, and this draws the string from off the circumference of the barrel on to the fusee. The force of the spring causes the fusee to rotate by pulling the string off it, coil by coil, and so drive the train of wheels. But while the mainspring, when fully wound, turns the fusee by uncoiling the string from the smallest part of the fusee, it gets the advantage of the larger radius as its energy becomes lessened.

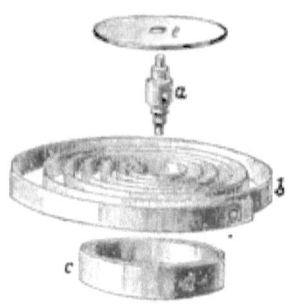

Fig. 19.—Mainspring and Barrel.

a, arbor; *b*, mainspring; *c*, barrel; *d*, hook; *e*, barrel cover.

The fusee is still used for marine chronometers; such clocks as have a mainspring and a pendulum, and occasionally for fine watches; but for watches it was really rendered unnecessary by the advent of the going barrel, although English watchmakers clung to the fusee for many years after the Swiss cast it aside and placed the teeth for driving the train direct on to the barrel.

Artistic Cases in the Sixteenth and Seventeeth Centuries. During the latter part of the sixteenth and first half of the seventeenth centuries, artists and mechanicians in Germany, France, and England vied with each other in producing watches and small table clocks of varied patterns to suit the public taste. Nearly all had wheels of steel and a fusee. The verge escapement was the only one available, and there was no spring to regulate the motion of the balance, so that the performance of all portable horological machines of the period was very irregular, compared with the precision exacted from timekeepers to-day; but as the only index of the time was one hand, which travelled around a circle on which the hours were marked, small variations from equal progression remained unnoticed. Indeed, the pulsations of the escapement and the motion of the hand sustained through the day and night were, in themselves, sufficient to induce many ignorant and superstitious people to regard these small timekeepers with awe, as supernatural creations. This feeling was often fostered by the form of the case, which was made purposely of some curious or fantastic design. Hele's first watches, and early ones made in Holland and other countries, had small plain oval cases of metal, and were occasionally known as Nuremberg eggs; afterwards larger oval and circular cases, imitation skulls, coffins, snuff boxes, and many small articles of furniture were made the receptacles of timekeepers, in answer to the dictates of fashion, or a morbid taste. Every conceivable material, including precious metals studded with gems, wood, ivory, alabaster, and marble, were in turn utilized to enshrine the handiwork of ancient horologists.

Portable Clock by Zech. There is a portable clock by Jacob Zech, belonging to the Society of Antiquaries, which was made in 1525. The case is a circular box of brass, gilt, measuring $9\frac{3}{4}$ inches in diameter by 5 inches in height.

Timekeepers often presented. A popular writer recently hazarded the opinion that most of the watches and clocks ever made were purchased for presentation, and there really does seem to be some ground for such an opinion.

There is poetical authority for supposing that lovers measure the flight of time by heart beats rather than by figures engraved on a dial; nevertheless, as long as mechanical timekeepers have been made some of the most chaste and costly of them have been devised as love gifts and treasured as pledges of affection. For conspicuous individual bravery at sea, chronometer watches were for many years a usual and coveted recognition from the Admiralty, though of late an economical policy seems to have substituted watches of humbler pretensions in many instances. Among the general community watches and clocks have ever been regarded as appropriate and favoured media for recording family regard and friendly esteem.

 The amounts spent by Henry VIII. for "orlogerie," were far beyond his individual requirements. There is a record that in July, 1530, £15 was paid to "the Frenchman who sold the King ij clocks at Oking." In the following month was paid to "a Frenchman called Drulardy for iij dyalls & a clokk for the King's grace" another sum of £15. In December of the same year more clocks were supplied to the king, £19 16s. 8d. being "paid to Vincent Keney, clok maker, for xj clokks & dialls." From the fact that the king paid for so many clocks in the space of only a few months, it may be assumed that most of them were intended for presentation. But he was also the recipient of offerings; it is related that John Poynet, Bishop of Winchester, gave his Majesty an astronomical clock, which also showed the ebb and flow of the tide.

Henry VIII.

 Sir Anthony Denny, keeper of the king's palace at Westminster, in 1542, presented to Henry VIII., as a new-year's gift, a very singular clock. It was designed by Holbein, whose drawing, purchased by Horace Walpole at the sale of Mariette's collection, was exhibited to the Society of Antiquaries, by Mr. Graves, in 1848. On the summit was a clock driven by wheelwork, and underneath were before and afternoon dials, showing time by shadows; and below these was a clepsydra, indicating the quarter hours.

Queen Mary. Among the new-year's gifts received by Queen Mary in 1556, mention is made of "a faire cloke in a case cover with blake vellat," from Nicholas Vrsin; and "a cloke with a lambe on it of copper guilt," from John Demolyn.

Queen Elizabeth's Timekeepers. Queen Elizabeth had a passion for horological toys, and possessed a very large collection, most of the items being presents either from foreign sovereigns or less exalted admirers. It is difficult to decide from a description of many of the articles whether they were table clocks or watches to be worn on the person. Clock was clearly used **Derivation of "Clock" and "Watch."** originally to distinguish any horologium or horologe that struck on a bell, whether the expression was taken from the Saxon *clugga*, the German *klocke*, the Teutonic *glocke*, or the French *cloche*. The word watch may have been derived from the Saxon *waccan*, to wake; or the Swedish *racht*, watch; or the Danish *ragt*; but in the time of Elizabeth most of the portable timekeepers either struck the hour or were furnished with alarms, and clock or watch was used indiscriminately in designation thereof.

In 1572 the Queen received from the Earl of Leicester, Master of the Horse, "a juell, being a chrsolite garnished with golde, flagon facyon, thone side sett with two emeraldes, thother side having in it a clocke."

Two years later is the following record of a new-year's gift from Margaret, Countess of Derby, " A white beare of gold and mother of perle holding a ragged staffe standing upon a tonne of gold whearin is a clocke."

Shortly after Mr. Hatton, captain of the guard, gave the Queen "a rich juell, being a clock of golde, garnished with diamondes rubyes emeraldes & perles, all ix oz iii q." Then there is "a tablet of golde being a clock fully furnished with small diamondes & rubyes; abowte the same are six bigger diamondes & a pendaunte of golde;" this was presented by the Earl of Leicester in 1578.

The same year the Earl of Russell gave to the Queen "A ringe of golde called a parmadas, set with diamondes & in the same backside a dyall." Following this is "a watche set in mother of pearle with three pendaundes of golde." This also was from Earl Russell.

Mr. Edward Stafford gave her Majesty "A little clocke of goulde with a cristall garnished with dyamondes."

Thomas Knevitt also gave the Queen "a small clocke, the case golde enamuled, with a small pelce."

Hentzner, a writer of the time of Elizabeth, says that the Queen had in her palace at Whitehall "a piece of clockwork consisting of an Æthiop riding upon a rhinoceros, with four attendants, who all make their obeisance when it strikes the hour; these are all put in motion by winding up the machine."

Queen Elizabeth's Clockkeeper. Queen Elizabeth seems to have had a clockmaker to keep her many watches and clocks in order. Under date 1590 there is a grant to Bartholomew Newsham of the office of clockmaker to the Queen, in place of Nicholas Ursean, deceased. This Bartholomew Newsham seems to have been a person of some importance, and like his royal mistress to have been the possessor of valuable timekeepers. In his will, dated 1586, he bequeathed to a friend "a sonne dyall of copper gylte;" to another "one cristall jewell with a watche in it garnished with goulde;" to another "one watche gylte to showe the hower;" to another "a strickinge clocke in a silken purse, and a sonedyall to stande upon a post in his garden;" and to another "a chamber clocke of fyve markes price." To his apprentice he left his "seconde clocke;" and to a relation his best vice, and to his son Edward Nowsham the rest of his tools.

Watch Bracelets in the Sixteenth Century. It is remarkable how many fashions of the present time are but revivals of our forefathers' conceits. In 1571, Queen Elizabeth received as a new year's gift from the Earl of Leicester, besides the items already mentioned, a richly jewelled armlet "haveing in the closing thereof a clocke." Again, Parker, Archbishop of Canterbury, by his will, which is written in Latin, and is dated April 5, 1575, makes the following bequest: "I give to my reverend brother Richard, Bishop of Ely, my stick of Indian cane which hath a watch in the top of it."

Also Watches in Walking-sticks.

Wearing two Watches an Old Custom. Jumping for a moment to a much later date, it may be mentioned that the practice of wearing two watches, one on each side, was a custom of over a century ago, when fashionable young sparks sported embroidered waistcoats. An anecdote is related of the Earl of Bridgwater, who, being stopped by a footpad near Windsor, was asked by the thief for a second watch after he had delivered one. "Why do you suppose I have another?" asked the Earl. "I know it," responded the other, "for I saw you cross your hand to your left fob when you gave me this."

In the *Universal Magazine* for 1777, among the constituents of a fop are stated to be

"A lofty cane, a sword with silver hilt,
A ring, *two watches*, and a snuff box gilt."

E. J. Wood says the foppery of wearing two watches was soon approved of and adopted by the ladies; but it was found to be too expensive to have two real watches, and accordingly a true watch was worn on the left side, and a sham one on the right side of the person. The latter was called a *fausse montre*, or a dummy watch. The false watches were sometimes of gold or silver, and occasionally enriched with jewels and enamelled miniatures at the back. Some had in front a dial plate, others a pincushion, and the most expensive ones had stars and devices set with stones which were made to revolve by means of internal wheelwork. Those who could not afford such costly articles, contented themselves with a dummy of gilt metal or of coloured foil. The recurrence of old ideas is accentuated by the recollection that a device for revolving jewels was presented but a very few years ago.

Elegant Timepiece, 1596. Fig. 20, dated 1596, is a curious form for a timepiece. The engraving is very beautifully executed. The minute hand, which is a subsequent addition, is out of keeping with the hour circle.

With strict utilitarians nothing is sacred that stands in the way of progress, but the interpolation of a minute hand in an old timekeeper really seems to show a strange disregard of the natural fitness of things. Such an interference with a portable timekeeper may be a small matter and of no concern to any one but the owner, but to attempt to modernize a clock attached to an ancient public building is more serious, for the additions are quite out of character and spoil the appearance of the whole structure.

"How Oxford folk can measure time 'tis hard to understand,
Since of their public clocks each one hath only got one hand."

This is the spirit that induces weak custodians to tamper with ancient monuments, and that metamorphosed Peter Lightfoot's unique old dial into its present grotesque patchwork state. One almost expects in the "silly season," to find a chorus of letters in the daily papers calling attention to the one hand on the Westminster Abbey clock as being sadly inefficient and unworthy of the nineteenth century.

Fig. 20.—Curious timepiece, 1596.

A HISTORY OF WATCHES

Neuwers, a Clockmaker, and Gilbert, Earl of Shrewsbury, 1599.

In the Sixth Report of the "Historical Manuscripts Commission," mention is made of an agreement, dated 1599, between one Michael Neuwers, a clockmaker, and Gilbert, Earl of Shrewsbury, for the construction of a clock. It is agreed that Michael should make a striking clock about the bigness of that which he made for the Earl six years past; it is to be made by the last of December next. "The cover or case of it to be of brass, very well gilt, with open breaking through all over, with a small fine hand like an arrow, clenly and strongly made, the . . . or white dial-plate to be made of French crown gold, and the figure to show the hour and the rest to be enamelled the fynelyest and daintyest that can be, but no other colour than blue, white, and carnalian, the letters to be somewhat larger than ordinary. The price of the clock must be £15, which makes with the earnest already given £16, but the circle I must pay for, beside the gold which shall make it. The sides of the brass case must not be sharp, but round, and the case very curiously made."

This same Earl of Shrewsbury appears to have been a connoisseur and general authority in the matter of time-keepers. The following letter from him, preserved in the Lansdown MSS. in the British Museum, is dated 1611, and is addressed to Sir Michael Hickes :—

Letter from Gilbert, Earl of Shrewsbury, to Sir M. Hickes, 1611.

"I preceived by you to-day that you understood My Lord Treasurer's design was to have a watch, but I conceaved he wysshed a strykynge clock, made lyke a watch, to stande oppon a cubbart, and suche a one (though no new one, and yet under a dozen years ould) I have found oute, and send you by this bearer, which I pray you deliver to his Lordship from me, and tell him that I am very well perswaded of the truth of it, or else I should be ashamed to send him so gross and rude a piece as this is, and if I hadd thought his Lordship could have well forborne it but for four or five dayes longer, I would have bestowed a new case for it, for this is a very bad one. If his Lordship would not have it stryke, either in the dayes or nights, the striker may be forborne to be wounde up, and so the watch being wounde up it will go alone. It will goe twenty-six heures, but I wysh it may be wounde up every mornyng or nyght aboute 8 or 9 o'clock, which will be sufficient untill the next day or nyght at the same tyme. I am weary with my longe journey to-day to Greenwich, and with waytinge on the Queen, overstandyng myself, and therefore I will hast to bedd, and ever remayne

"Y' very assured lov: frend,
"GILB. SHREWSBURY."

Skull-shaped Watch of Mary Queen of Scots. Fig. 21 represents a most interesting death's head or skull-shaped watch, which formerly belonged to Mary Queen of Scots, and was bequeathed by her to her maid-of-honour, Mary Setoun, on February 7, 1587. It afterwards came into the possession of Sir Thomas Dick Lauder. The case is of silver gilt, and on the forehead of the skull is a figure of Death, with his scythe and sand-glass. Around him is a passage from Horace: "Pallida mors æquo pulsat pede pauperum tabernas regumque turres." On the posterior part of the skull is a representation of Time devouring all things. He also has a scythe, and near him is a serpent, with its tail in its mouth, as an emblem of eternity. This is surrounded by another motto from Ovid: "Tempus edax rerum teque invidiosa vetustas." The upper part of the skull is divided into two compartments, on one of which are represented our first parents in the garden of Eden, attended by some animals, with the motto, "Peccando perditionem miseriam æternam posteris memore." In the other is depicted the crucifixion, with the thieves on each side of Christ, while the Marys are adoring below. The legend to this is, "Sic justitiæ satis fecit mortem superavit, salutem comparavit." Below, on both sides, is open work, to permit the sound to issue freely when the watch strikes. This pierced work forms emblems of the Passion and Crucifixion, such as the cross, swords, lantern used in the garden, spears, one having a sponge on its point, scourges, flagon and cup of the Eucharist, coat without a seam, dice thrown for it, hammer, nails, thongs, ladder, and crown of thorns. Under all there is the motto, "Scala cœli ad gloriam via." The watch is opened by reversing

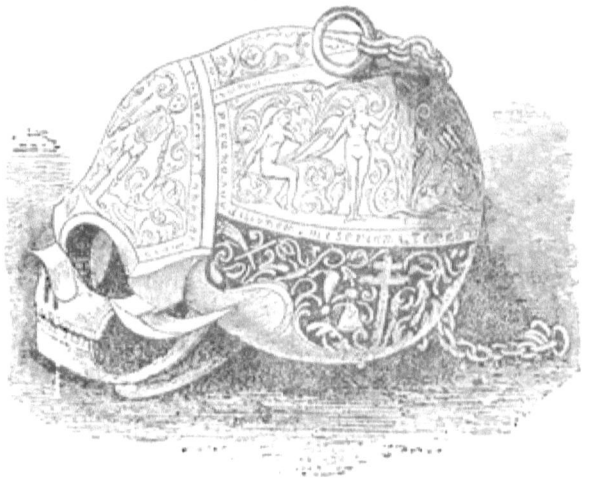

Fig. 21.—Mary Queen of Scots' skull-shaped watch.

the skull and placing the upper part of it in the hollow of the hand, then lifting the upper jaw, which rises on a hinge. Inside, on the plate or lid, is a representation of the holy family in the stable at Bethlehem, with the infant Jesus in the manger, and angels ministering to Him. In the upper part an angel is descending with a scroll, on which is written, "Gloria excelsis Deo, et in terra pax, hominibus bona volu." In the distance are the shepherds with their flocks, and one of the men is in the act of performing on a cornemuse. The works of this watch are as brains in the skull; the dial-plate of silver being on a flat where the roof of the mouth is to be found in a human being, and fixed in a golden circle richly carved in a scroll pattern. The hours are marked in large Roman letters, and within them is the figure of Saturn devouring his children, with this legend round the outer rim of the flat: "Sicut meis sic et omnibus idem." The movement is in perfect order, and said to perform astonishingly well. A silver bell of very musical sound fills the entire hollow of the skull, and contains the movement within it when the watch is shut. A small hammer, set in motion by a separate train, strikes the hour on it. The watch requires winding once a day. There is no date upon it, but the maker's name appears, "Moyso, Blois," to which place Mary went with her husband, the Dauphin of France, before his death. Although there is a chain attached to the watch, it is much too heavy to be carried about the person. Probably it was intended to occupy a stationary place on a *prie-dieu*, or private altar in a small oratory. A drawing of it is among the collection of the Society of Antiquaries of London, and it is engraved in Smith's "Historical and Literary Curiosities."

Splendid Watch with Cover, 1613. Fig. 22 shows the cover and dial of another curious watch, but of a slightly later period. The case is of silver, and is very highly ornamented with mythological subjects elaborately chased. On the inner rim is the following inscription: "From Alethea Covntess of Arvndel for her deare sone, Sir William Howad, K.B. 1629." Its extreme diameter is two inches and a half, and it is an inch and a half thick. It strikes the hours, is provided with an alarm, shows the days of the week, the age and phases of the moon, the days and months of the year, and the signs of the zodiac. On the inside of the cover there is a Roman Catholic calendar, with the date 1613. It also bears the name of the maker thus: "P. Combret à Lyons."

About 1620, or within a few years after this watch was made, glasses as a protection for watch-dials were introduced, and the metal covers were abandoned.

Fig. 22.

Ramsay, first English Watchmaker of Note. One of the earliest English watchmakers of any note was David Ramsay, whom Sir Walter Scott, in the "Fortunes of Nigel," has clothed with immortality. Though a creature of fiction with Scott, Ramsay was an entity of considerable importance in the horological world, as shown by the official records of the time. In an explanatory note, Scott styles him "Constructor of Horloges to His Most Sacred Majesty, James I.;" and in the novel referred to he is represented as having a shop in Fleet Street. His first appointment at the court of James I. appears to have been clockmaker and groom of the chambers to Henry Prince of Wales. These apparently incongruous offices he held till the death of the prince in 1612.

On the plate of a watch supposed to have been made for James I. is the inscription, "David Ramsay Scotus me fecit," and this, together with the fact that he had a grant of denization in 1619, shows that he was a native of Scotland. It has been suggested that he either attended or followed his royal master on his accession to the English throne. It is also conjectured that he may have been introduced to James by George Heriot, the goldsmith.

In the Audit Office, Somerset House, is the following entry: "Watches, three bought of Mr. Ramsay, the Clockmaker, lxj^{li}." [£61]. In the list of Guyftes and Rowardes in the same account will be found—"Mr. Ramsay, the Clockmaker, xj^s." [11s.]. In 1613, James, prodigal of promises, gave him a pension of £200 per annum, probably for his services as groom of the bedchamber to the late Prince of Wales, and in the same year a further pension of £50 per annum. In the grant he is styled Clockmaker Extraordinary. In 1616 a warrant was signed to pay him £234 10s. for the purchase and repair of clocks and watches for the king. On November 26, 1618, he was appointed to the office of "Chief Clockmaker" to his Majesty, with fees and allowances for workmanship. On September 30, 1622, he received £232 15s. for repairing clocks at Theobalds, Oatlands, and Westminster, and for making a chime of bells adjoining the clock at Theobalds.

Fig. 22.

In 1625, James I., his patron, died; but Ramsay appears to have retained his appointments, for in 1627 there is a warrant to pay to David Ramsay, page of the bedchamber, and clockmaker, £441 3s. 4d. for work done for his late Majesty, and £358 16s. 8d. in lieu of diet and bouche of Court. In 1628 a warrant was signed to pay him £415 for clocks and other necessaries for the king's service. In 1632 £219 were paid him.

Below are two views of a superb example of Ram-

Clock-watch and alarm by David Ramsay.

say's work, in the form of a clock-watch, with alarm, the property of Mr. Evan Roberts, an enthusiastic collector. The piercing of the case is, of course, to emit the sound; and the elegant design and skilful execution of this feature enhances the value of the relic. The fusee is cut for a twelve hours' run, so that the watch would require to be wound twice a day. On the hand-wheel, or hour-wheel, is a star-wheel having twelve teeth, which, by lifting up a brass arm connected with a silver locking plate, or count-wheel, allows the hour to be struck on a bell occupying the space between the movement and the case. Under the dial, and fixed to the alarm index, is a brass disc, with a notch in its edge. Attached to the verge of the alarm is an arm terminating in a V-shaped tongue, which, pressed by a spring, drops into the notch in the edge of the disc, and so lets off the alarm. The alarm is wound by a wheel and pinion, and in the wheel is a piece the thickness of two teeth, uncut to act as a stop when the pinion has made three turns. On the top plate is engraved—"David Ramsay, inv^t Fecit."

By the Charter of Incorporation David Ramsay was appointed as the first master of the Clockmakers' Company in 1631, a proof that his position at the Court was still maintained; but he does not appear to have taken any active part in the management of the company; and he was probably not in robust health for some time prior to his death, which occurred in 1650.

In the "Calendar of State Papers," temp. Charles I., is a petition from one William Partridge asking to be reinstated as king's clockmaker. At the foot of the petition is a note: "To succeed Da. Ramsay." No further record of Partridge having held such an office is to be found. But Edward East, a renowned horologist, did occupy the position of watchmaker to Charles I., even before David Ramsay's death, and this rather justifies the inference that Ramsay was incapacitated during the last years of his life. Edward East was one of the ten original assistants appointed by the Charter of Incorporation of the Clockmakers' Company in 1632; he filled the office of Warden in 1638 and 1639; was elected Master in 1645, and again in 1652. He was appointed Treasurer in 1637, and was the only occupant of that office in the history of the Company. At one time he resided in Pall Mall, near the Tennis Court. It is reported that Charles II., when Prince of Wales, frequently played at tennis, the stakes being an "Edwardus

Edward East.

East," or a watch of East's make. East appears to have afterwards removed to Fleet Street, for it is related of Charles I. that, annoyed at not being awaked to time one morning, he ordered his chamberlain to be provided with a gold alarm watch, and forthwith the Earl of Pembroke sent to the king's watchmaker, Mr. East, of Fleet Street, for such a watch. In the possession of Mr. Alfred Morrison is a warrant, dated June 23, 1649, from the Committee of Public Revenue to Thomas Fauconbridge, Esq., Receiver-General, authorizing him to pay "unto Mr. Edward East, watchmaker, the some of fortie pounds for a watch and a Larum of gould by him made for the late King Charles by directions of the Earle of Pembrooke by order of the Committee, and delivered for the late king's use the xvii. of January last." It is worthy of note that the watch was supplied but a fortnight before the execution of Charles I.

Fig. 23.—Clock-watch of German manufacture early in the seventeenth century.

Early Twenty-four Hour Watch. The engraving, Fig. 23, shows a German watch of the same period. It will be observed that there are two hour-circles, the inner one completing the notation from twelve to twenty-four, thus serving for a continuous reckoning of the hours for a complete day, in the manner now urged after the lapse of two centuries, and reminding one of the adage that there is nothing new under the sun.

Introduction of the Pendulum.

First Application of the Pendulum to Clocks.

UCH angry controversy has taken place over the claim to have applied the pendulum to clocks, which was the first great step towards accuracy of timekeeping. Galileo, the famous astronomer in 1582, when a student at Pisa, was struck by the synchronous vibrations of the swinging lamps in the cathedral, and afterwards discovered that the shorter the pendulum the less was the time of its vibration. It has been asserted that his son,

Galileo.
Vincent Galileo, adopted a pendulum to a clock in 1649. Richard Harris is credited by some with having made a turret clock with a long pendulum for St. Paul's Church, Covent Garden, in 1641. But it is known that Christian Huygens, a distinguished

Huygens.
Dutch mathematician, in 1657 devised a clock with a long pendulum, and to him most authorities ascribe the honour of having practically demonstrated the suitability of the pendulum as a controller for timekeepers.

Evelyn in his "Diary," under date May 3, 1661, records that he "returned by Fromantel's, ye famous clockmaker, to see some pendules." And in the *Commonwealth Mercury* of Thursday, November 25, 1668, there is an advertisement in which it is said, "There is lately a way found out for making clocks that go exact and keep equaller time than any made now without this regulater, examined and proved before his Highness the Lord Protector. . . . Made by Ahasuerus Fromantel, who made the first that were in England. You may

Fromantel.
have them at his house on the Bankside, in Mopes Alley, Southwark, and at the sign of the 'Maremaid' in Lokbury, near Bartholomew Lane End, London." Evelyn on another occasion says, "I went with some of my relations to Court to show them his Maj^{ties} cabinet

and closet of rarities. . . . Here I saw . . . amongst the clocks one that showed the rising and setting of the sun in y° Zodig, the sunn represented by a face and raies of gold upon an azure skie, observing y° diurnal and annual motion rising and setting behind a landscape of hills, the work of our famous Fromantel." Ahasuerus Fromantel's claim to have introduced the pendulum into England is probably well founded, for Derham, in his book published in 1696, conceding the invention of the pendulum to Huygens, says that " Mr. Fromantel, a Dutch clockmaker, came over into England, and made the first that were ever made here about the year 1662. One of the first pieces made in England is now in Gresham College, given to that Honourable Society by the late eminent Seth, Lord Bishop of Salisbury, which is made exactly according to Mr. Huygens's method."

Fromantel was admitted as a member of the Clockmakers' Company either in 1632 or in 1665. Mr. Overall, in his History of the Company, says 1632; but as a certain Ahasuerus Fromantel *was* undoubtedly elected in 1665, I am inclined to think it must have been the Dutch clockmaker who came over after making himself acquainted with Huygens's invention. This view is strengthened by the fact that, according to the same History, one Thomas Loomes, a member of the Company, resided at the "Mermayd" in Lothbury in 1649. *The* Fromantel may have succeeded to the business of Loomes.

Time of Pendulum Vibration. A pendulum drawn aside from its point of rest and then released, is impelled by gravity to fall at once to its lowest possible point, and, but for the momentum acquired in falling, it would remain there at rest; but its momentum carries it up as far on the other side as it fell at first through the action of gravity. The length of the pendulum determines the time occupied in its vibrations: a long pendulum moving slowly and a short one quickly, because with a long pendulum the curve described at the centre of oscillation is flat, and with a short pendulum it is steep. The course of the pendulum bob attached to a long suspending rod, and that of one attached to a short suspending rod, may be compared to rolling a ball first down a slight decline and then down a steep hill.

Length of Pendulums. The theoretical length in London of a seconds pendulum for mean solar time—that is, the distance between the point of suspension and the centre of oscillation—is approximately 39·14 inches; the length of pendulum for vibrating sidereal seconds in the same latitude is 38·87 inches.

As the force that gravity asserts on a body depends on the distance of the body from the centre of the earth, the length of a pendulum varies in different latitudes. A seconds pendulum is 39 inches long at the equator, and 39·206 inches at the poles.

At Rio Janeiro it is	..	39·01 inches.
„ Madras	.. ..	39·02 „
„ New York	.. ..	39·10 „
„ Paris	.. ..	39·13 „
„ Edinburgh	.. .. ..	39·15 „
„ Greenland	.. .. ..	39·20 „

Cycloidal Path for Pendulum. The long and short vibrations of a free pendulum will only be isochronous if the path described is a cycloid, which is a curve described by rolling a circle along a straight line. But a pendulum swung freely from a point travels through a circular path, and the long arcs are performed slower than the short ones. This divergence from the theoretical cycloid may be disregarded with the small vibration required by modern escapements, but when the arc described was large, as it was of necessity with the verge escapement, the error was considered to be of prime importance.

Pendulum clocks are usually regulated by means of the rating nut, which is screwed on to the bottom of the rod, and on which the bob rests. By screwing this nut up or down on the rod the bob is raised or lowered and the effective length of the pendulum altered as required. Some mantel clocks have an arrangement for lengthening or shortening the pendulum at the top by letting down or drawing up the chops that embrace the pendulum spring. For convenience, this regulation is accomplished by turning the squared extremity of an arbor at the top of the dial. The arbor runs through to the back of the movement, and carries a bevelled pinion which engages with a wheel fixed to the screw that traverses the pendulum chops.

Pendulums should be heavy. It is certain that Huygens clearly appreciated the principles which govern the motion of the pendulum, for he made it of a good length, with a heavy spherical bob, so that it might be insensible to variations in the force transmitted through the train which would be sure to arise from faulty engagement of the wheels, lumpy teeth, and other inaccuracies; yet the first pendulums applied to house clocks in England were miserably inadequate. They were fixed to the verge, very light, and but a few inches in length. Even when the long-case clocks were introduced with seconds or "royal" pendulums, the bobs were exceedingly light; and for a long time many clockmakers seemed to be imbued with the idea that a heavy pendulum would throw a great strain upon the clock, whereas by doubling or even quadrupling the weight of a pendulum, the extra force needed to maintain its vibrations is really infinitesimal. Old turret clocks may be found with pendulums thirty or forty feet long, this great length being to obtain a dominion over the clock, as the clockmakers expressed it. But such excessively long pendulums are very susceptible to the influence of the wind and other disturbing elements, and the requisite "dominion" is better obtained by a more reasonable length and heavier bob.

Suspension of Pendulums. The cord suspension of Huygens found favour with many generations of French clockmakers. Here the hanging shackle on which the pendulum was hooked in the old long-case clocks was continued for ordinary, and knife edges for fine work, till the introduction of a thin spring, which is now almost universally adopted as the means of suspending vibrating pendulums of every kind.

Though the pendulum as a regulator was such a marked improvement on the balance uncontrolled by a spring, it was found, as clocks were more carefully finished in answer to the demands for more perfect timekeepers, that the lengthening and shortening of the pendulum rod, **Compensation of Pendulums.** owing to changes of temperature constituted a serious drawback to good performance. And to neutralize this variation of length was the next step undertaken by scientific horologists. Graham, after many experiments with different metals, made the steel rod to terminate in a stirrup, on which he placed a glass jar of mercury to form the bob of the pendulum. Harrison chose an arrangement of brass and steel rods, known as the "gridiron" pendulum, with the same object. In recent years, the zinc tube compensation, as applied to the Westminster clock, is most favoured, although the mercurial pendulum still has its champions for use in fine clocks. Wood expands very much less than metal, and a cheap compensated pendulum may be formed of a wood rod and a lead or zinc bob of a proper length resting on the rating nut. I recommend this kind of pendulum for railway stations and other similar clocks, where good performance is required, but the absolute precision demanded by astronomers and watchmakers who use the seconds hand is not needed.

Beyond its service to the horologist as the most exact and unerring controller of timekeepers, the pendulum has other important uses. Kater, Sabine, Airy, and others made experiments as to the number of vibrations of a pendulum at different parts of the surface of the earth, with a view to ascertain the form and relative position of the parts of the earth. Foucault, in the last century, hung a pendulum 160 feet long in the Panthéon, with a view to determining terrestrial motion. With the same object, M. Mascart recently suspended a pendulum of no less a length than 377 feet from the Eiffel Tower. Professor Airy, some years ago, actually weighed the earth, or at least determined its average specific gravity, by means of pendulum experiments conducted at Hartley Colliery, South Shields. He compared the rate of a regulator at the bottom of a deep mine with that of one at the surface. At the bottom of the mine was an exact counterpart of the pendulum of the regulator at the surface, the beats of the two being maintained in unison by means of an electric current; so that the difference in the beats of the controlled pendulum and the one dependent on gravity could be readily noted.

Pendulum Experiments.

Conical or revolving pendulums, either single or double, like the governor balls of a steam-engine, are usefully employed where continuous motion is desired, as in clocks for driving equatorial telescopes.

Conical Pendulums.

Curious Clocks.

OF all horological machines, the successive clocks at Strasburg Cathedral have, perhaps, attracted the most attention as mechanical curiosities. The first of these, constructed about 1352, under the

First Strasburg Clock. direction of John, Bishop of Litchenberg, consisted of a calendar, like those in use at the period, with paintings relating to the principal movable feasts. An astrolabe whose pointers showed the movements of the sun and moon, and the hours, and figures of three wise men of the East, who bowed before a statue of the Virgin, while a cock on the top of the case was made to move its beak, crow, and flap its wings. There was also a small set of chimes composed of several cymbals.

Second Strasburg Clock. The second clock was certainly a triumph of ingenuity. It was projected in 1547, but though the designs appear to have been then ready, the execution went no further than the building of the chamber and the preparation of some of the heavier ironwork till 1570, when Conrad Dasypodius, a native of Strasburg, undertook to supervise the completion of the horologium. By his advice, the mechanical works were confided to Isaac and Josiah Habrecht, clockmakers of Schaffhausen in Switzerland, while Tobias Stimmer, of the same place, was employed to do the paintings and the sculpture which were to serve as decorations of the achievement.

Early in the present century it was evident that reconstruction was necessary, and this was, after considerable debate, entrusted to Charles Schwilgue, who entered on his task in 1838, and completed it about the middle of 1842. On the 2nd of October of that year the life of the resuscitated marvel was solemnly inaugurated. Although in some few cases only a restoration of the former mechanism was made, the greater part of the movements was the original design of Schwilgue. On the floor-level is a celestial globe, indicating sidereal time. In its motion round its axis the globe carries with it the circles that surround it, namely, the equator, the ecliptic, the solstitial and equinoctial colures, while the meridian

Third Strasburg Clock. and horizon circles remain motionless, so that there are shown the rising and setting as well as the passage over the meridian of Strasburg of all stars that are visible to the naked eye, and which

Fig. 24.—Clock at Strasburg Cathedral.

appear above the horizon. Behind the celestial globe is the calendar; on a metalic band nine inches wide and thirty feet in circumference, are the months, days of the month, dominical letters, fixed and movable feast days. The band is shifted at midnight, and a statue of Apollo points out the day of the month and the name of the saint corresponding to that day. The internal part of the annular band indicates true solar time; the rising and setting of the sun; the diurnal motion of the moon round the earth, and its passage over the meridian; the phases of the moon, and the eclipses of the sun and moon. Adjacent compartments are devoted to a perpetual calendar, solar and lunar cycles, and other periodic recurrences; solar and lunar equations, etc. Above the calendar appear allegorical figures, seated in chariots, and representing the days of the week. These chariots, drawn by such animals as are assigned as attributes of the divinities, run on a circular iron railway, and appear each in order. On Sunday is seen Apollo, drawn by horses of the sun. Diana, emblem of the moon, drawn by a stag, appears on Monday. She is succeeded by Mars, who in turn gives place to Mercury; Jupiter, armed with a thunderbolt, fills the space on Thursday; Friday is consecrated to Venus, accompanied by her boy Cupid. Saturday is the day of Saturn.

In the Gallery of Lions above is the dial for showing ordinary mean solar time. On each side of the dial is a genius. The genius of the left bears in one hand a sceptre with which he strikes the first note of each quarter-hour on a bell held in his other hand. The genius on the other side holds an hour-glass filled with red sand, which he reverses at each completion of sixty minutes.

The story above is occupied by a planetarium, in which the revolutions of the planets are represented upon a large dial plate.

Above the planetarium, and upon a star-decked sky, is a globe devoted to showing the phases of the moon.

Next come movable figures representing the four ages, one of which in turn appears and gives upon a bell the second stroke of each quarter of an hour. At the first quarter a child strikes the bell with a rattle; a youth in the form of a hunter strikes it with an arrow at the half-hour; at the third quarter the blows are given by a warrior with his sword; the fourth quarter an old man produces the notes with his crutch. When he has retired, a figure of Death appears and strikes the hour with a bone.

In the upper apartment is a figure of Christ, and when death strikes the hour of noon, the twelve Apostles pass before the feet of their Master, bowing as they do so. Then Christ makes the sign of the cross.

During the procession of the Apostles, the cock perched at the top of the weight-turret flaps his wings, ruffles his neck, and crows three times.

A remarkably handsome dome crowns the case or chamber of the clock. On the right is a spiral staircase, by means of which the various galleries are reached.

In addition to the mean-time dial in the gallery, there is one, seventeen feet in diameter, above the principal entrance to the cathedral.

In the course of the last Franco-Prussian war, Strasburg was subjected to a prolonged siege; but although the cathedral was several times struck by projectiles, the clock happily escaped injury.

Beauvais Cathedral. At Beauvais Cathedral is a clock very much on the lines of the Strasburg one. It is 36 feet high, 16 feet in breadth, and nearly 9 feet in depth.

There are no less than fifty dials pertaining to this extraordinary production. Among other epochs recorded on separate dials are—

The days of the week.
The movements of the planetary bodies.
Sunrise.
Sunset.
The seasons.
The signs of the zodiac.
The duration of daylight.

The duration of night.
The equation of time.
The dates.
The saints' days.
The months.
The phases of the moon.
The age of the moon.
The time at the principal cities of the world.
The solstices.
The movable feasts.
The age of the world.
The year of the century.
The bissextile years.
The longitudes.
The number of the century.
The tides.
The eclipses for all the world, both total and partial.

Complicated Clock by Habrecht in the British Museum. There is in the British Museum a most elaborate and complicated horological instrument, made in 1589 by Isaac Habrecht, one of the two ingenious brothers who have already been mentioned in connection with the famous clock at Strasburg. Although it is only from four to five feet in height, and can bear no comparison as to size with its gigantic prototype, yet in detail many of the parts betray the same hand. The general design is the same as that of the left tower of the Strasburg clock, and on the sides of both are figures of the three Fates—Clotho, Lachesis, and Atropos—and both are surmounted by a figure of the cock of St. Peter, which at the stroke of the hour flaps its wings and crows. The quarters are struck by four figures representing the ages of man, and the hour by a figure of Death. On a lower balcony is a seated figure of the Virgin and Child, before whom passes a circle of angels, who, as they are set in movement by the striking of the clock, are caused to make an obeisance in front of the Virgin. Below this the gods of the days of the week perform their circuit, each driving in a chariot, while two dials on the lower stages fulfil the more useful functions of indicating the hour, the phases of the moon, the feasts of the Church, etc. The case is of gilt copper, with well-engraved figures and ornamental designs, perhaps by Tobias Stimmer, who was employed to decorate the original clock at Strasburg. The history of this clever piece of mechanism is somewhat curious, though it rests upon slender foundations. It is stated that Pope Sixtus V. was so pleased with the Strasburg clock that he ordered Habrecht to make one of the same kind. This one was made and remained at the Vatican for two hundred years. Its next appearance was in Holland, where it was in the possession of the King; from Holland it came to London, and was exhibited about 1850. A pamphlet was printed giving a description and recounting this somewhat apocryphal history of the clock, which was purchased by the late Mr. Osborne Morgan, and by him bequeathed to the nation.

Closed Clock-case of the Sixteenth Century. Many clock-cases of the sixteenth century, prior to the introduction of glass coverings for the dial, were of metal, and in the form of a square tower, closed on all four sides. This style admitted of the most lavish decoration, and much of the work is of quite as high a quality as the silversmith's work of the same time, and, in fact, in some instances, proceeded from the same workshops in Augsburg or Nuremberg. Fig. 25 shows a choice case of this type, made of iron, damascened with precious metals.

Lyons Cathedral Clock. In the cathedral of Lyons is a clock very much on the lines of the Strasburg one. It was made about two hundred years ago by a mechanician named Lippius of Basle, and, as far as the internal work is concerned, was substantially remade during the last century by Nourisson, a well-known clockmaker of Lyons. A view of the exterior is given in

Fig. 25.—Closed clock-case, sixteenth century.

Fig. 26. On different dial-plates are exhibited the diurnal and annual motion of the earth, the course of the moon,

Fig. 26.—Clock at Lyons Cathedral.

the day of the year, with its length from sunrise to sunset, and a calendar of remarkable feasts. The hours are announced by the crowing of a cock after it has clapped its wings. When the cock has done crowing, angels appear, and, by striking various bells, perform the air of a hymn.

St. Dunstan's Clock.
The old Church of St. Dunstan in the West, in Fleet Street, was built in 990. It was a peculiar structure, with a row of small shops intervening between it and the street, except at the

Fig. 27.—Clock of St. Dunstan in the West, Fleet Street.

western end, where the grand entrance was. Here, high above the gateway, were erected in 1671 two gilt clock-dials, placed back to back, and mounted in a handsome square case, with circular pediment, which projected well out over the footway; the tube containing the rod for actuating the hands being supported by a well-carved figure of Time. An alcove was built on the roof of the gateway, and within were large gaudily painted and gilt figures of Gog and Magog, which struck "ting tang" quarters with clubs on two bells suspended above them. The clock and figures seem to have been put up at the instigation of one Thomas Harrys, a clockmaker, then living at Water Lane, Blackfriars, whose handiwork they were. Harrys submitted a statement of what he proposed to do, and, after describing the "two figures of men with pole-axes to strike the quarters," continues, "I will do one thing more, which London shall not show the like; I will make two hands show the hours and minutes without the church, upon a double dial, which will be worth your observation, and to my credit." This must have been one of the earliest applications of the concentric minute hand in England, and therefore worthy of notice; but the figures of Gog and Magog were undoubtedly the great attraction, for they speedily became one of the sights of London, and their removal in 1830, when the church was rebuilt, elicited many expressions of regret.

Early Application of Minute Hand.

When the old church was in course of demolition, the Marquis of Hertford, who was then building a residence at the north-west corner of Regent's Park, offered two hundred guineas for the clock, the quarter figures, and three old statues representing King Lud and his sons, which happened to be in possession of the churchwardens. This offer was accepted, so that "the pets of cockneys and countrymen," as a writer of the last century termed the Gog and Magog quarter clubmen, migrated a little way out of the City, and after a brief interval patiently resumed their office.

St. Dunstan's Lodge, as the Marquis of Hertford called his house, has now passed into the possession of Mr. H.

Hucks Gibbs, M.P.; but the clock and accessories are still in the grounds, and may be seen from Regent's Park. The dials are now in a circular case; but the movement, though it has, of course, undergone repair from time to time, is still substantially the one Harrys supplied over two centuries ago.

Cowper refers to those figures in his "Table Talk" as follows—

"When labour and when dulness, club in hand,
Like the two figures at St. Dunstan's stand
Beating alternately, in measured time,
The clockwork tintinnabulum of rhyme,
Exact and regular sounds will be;
But such mere quarter strokes are not for me."

The engraving (Fig. 27), taken from a print of old St. Dunstan's Church, represents the clock as it was in 1737.

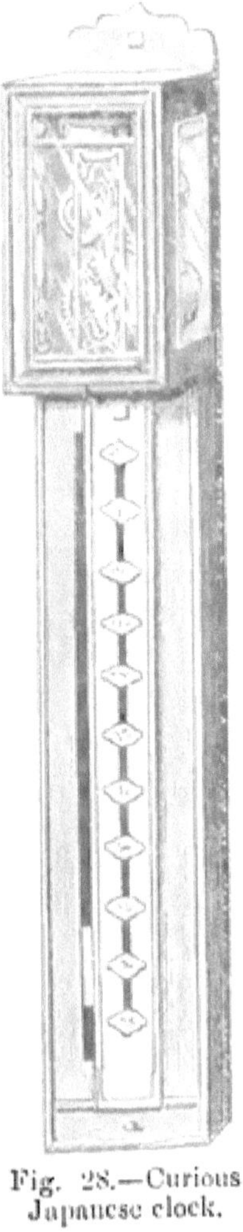

Japanese Clock for Varying Hours. Until the early part of the present century, the Japanese divided the interval between two successive transits of the meridian into twelve periods of time, six of which were appropriated to the darkness, and six to the light. The day being calculated from sunrise to sunset, there was a necessary variation in the length of the six day and six night hours. The timekeepers had, therefore, to be altered periodically to suit the seasons of the year. Fig. 28 represents an old Japanese clock, in which the time is indicated by the position of the weight which drives the movement. This is seen through a slit in the case; the hour indicators, of metal, each one bearing a symbol corresponding to its title, are made to shift closer together or further apart as may be required.

Fig. 28.—Curious Japanese clock.

94   A HISTORY OF WATCHES

Monumental Clock at Venice. Among the horological monuments erected in the seventeenth century must be mentioned the great clock tower of the Grand Piazza at

Fig. 29.—Monumental clock at Venice.

Venice. A view of this is given in Fig. 29. Above the large dial for showing the hours is a balcony of gilt lattice surrounding an image of the Blessed Virgin, seated between two doors overlaid with gold. Every year, on the Feast of the Ascension, and for fourteen days afterwards, as the hour struck, the door on the right hand opened, and an angel with a trumpet issued forth, followed by three Eastern kings, each of whom, as he passed the Virgin, raised his crown, bowed, and then disappeared through the other door. The edifice is capped by a large bell, on which the hours were struck by two bronze giants.

Head of Hans von Jena. As a specimen of what may be called grotesque horology of the seventeenth century, the famous *Head of Hans von Jena*, in Saxony,

Fig. 30.—Head of Hans von Jena clock in Saxony.

illustrated in Fig. 30, may be cited. Above the clock-dial is a large bronze head of surpassing ugliness. As the honr strikes the figure of an old pilgrim offers to the open mouth a golden apple, mounted on a stick, and suddenly withdraws it, while at the same instant the figure of an angel on the left raises her eyes from her book. The legend is that Hans von Jena was condemned to undergo this kind of tantalization for three centuries.

Perpetual Motion. Expansion and Contraction of Gases and Fluids. Many old clockmakers pursued that delusive *ignis fatuus*, perpetual motion, with wonderful pertinacity. Some of the most promising perpetual clocks have been those driven by the alternate expansion and contraction of gases and fluids exposed during the day to the rays of the sun. But in all these devices, even if the constancy of the medium could be assured over a lengthened period, there remains the lubrication of the moving parts of the machine, which has to be renewed, and so, however sanguine the inventors may be that their expectations are actually realized directly they behold their cherished theories worked out in practicable form, none of the perpetual-motion clocks are able to withstand the insidious attacks of the Old Destroyer, whose flight they measure for a brief period.

The Clockmakers' Company.

IN the year 1622 the clockmakers of London complained to James I. of the deceitful tricks of foreigners practising their trade, and begged that they might not be permitted to work except under English masters, and that no foreign clocks might be imported. In 1631 the Clockmakers' Company of London was incorporated by a Royal Charter from Charles I., under the title of "The Masters, Wardens, and Fellowship of the Art of Clockmakers of the City of London." Power was given to the Company to make by-laws for the government of all persons using the trade in London, or within ten miles thereof, and for the regulation of the manner in which the trade should be carried on throughout the realm. And in order to prevent the public from being injured by persons making, buying, selling, transporting, and importing any bad, deceitful, or insufficient clocks, watches, 'larums, sun-dials, boxes, or cases for the said trade, the Company could search vessels, warehouses, shops, or other places they suspected, and if entrance be denied they might effect it by force. This right of search was constantly exercised, and many instances are recorded of deceitful works being found and broken up.

According to the Charter, the officers were to be elected annually on the feast day of Saint Michael the Archangel. The Master to be chosen being a professed clockmaker at the time of his election. It would be interesting to know if this condition has been always respected. The Clockmakers' is a poor Company and has no Hall.

The first Court of the Company consisted of

DAVID RAMSAY, *Master.*

HENRY ARCHER,	
JOHN WELLOWE,	} *Wardens.*
SAMPSON SHELTON,	

Assistants.

JOHN SMITH,	SAMUEL LYNAKER,
JAMES VANTROLLYER,	JOHN CHARLTON,
FRANCIS FORMAN,	JOHN MIDNALL,
JOHN HARRIS,	SIMON BARTRUM,
RICHARD MORGAN,	EDWARD EAST.

David Ramsay and Edward East are the only ones of these who have left behind any considerable reputation, though John Midnall was evidently of the front rank, and is known as the maker of a watch for Oliver Cromwell. Of other members of the Company elected during the seventeenth century, the following may be mentioned as being above mediocrity.

Simon Hackett, "of the Royall Exchannge," who was elected a member of the Company in 1632, and served as Master in 1660, was a watchmaker whose works are still prized. He died in 1665.

Jeffry Baylie, who was elected in 1648, lived at "Ye Turn Style in Holburn," and was a noted maker of chamber clocks.

Clocks made by Peter Closson, "neare Holbourne Bridge," who was admitted as a brother of the Company in 1633, are occasionally met with.

David Bouquett, who was admitted as a member in 1632, was well known as a maker of high-class and costly watches, some of these with cases enamelled by French artists still exist, and are much prized. He died in 1665.

Nicholas Coxiter, admitted in 1648, was a very excellent clockmaker, who resided near Goldsmith's Hall.

Solomon Bouquett, admitted in 1650, was probably the successor of David.

Abraham Beckner, admitted as a brother in 1652, lived in Pope's Head Alley, and was a well-known watchmaker.

Ahasuerus Fromantel was admitted in 1655.

Thomas Loomes, who was admitted in 1649, appears to have resided at the Mermayd, Lothbury, where Fromantel afterwards carried on business.

Henry Jones, who was apprenticed to Edward East, and resided in the Temple, attained some eminence, and made clocks for Charles II. He was admitted in 1663, and served as Master in 1691.

Joseph Knibb, who made a clock for Windsor Castle, was admitted in 1670.

Charles Gretton, who was admitted in 1662, and served as Master in 1700, was also a celebrated maker of watches; he was the apprentice master of Henry Sully.

Daniel Quare was admitted as a brother in 1671, and served as Master in 1708.

Thomas Tompion was admitted as a brother in 1671, and served as Master in 1704.

Henry Aske, who was admitted in 1676, is worthy of mention as the apprentice master of George Graham.

John Ebsworth, who was elected in 1665, and served as Warden in 1695, lived in "New Cheap Side," and was a maker of many excellent clocks.

Joseph Windmills, who was admitted in 1671, was a celebrated maker of long-case clocks, who lived first at St. Martin's-le-Grand, and afterwards in Tower Street. He served as Master in 1702. Later clocks bear the inscription, "Joseph and Thomas Windmills." Thomas served as Master in 1718.

Henry Young, elected in 1671, carried on business in the Strand, and was a maker of bracket and other clocks.

Isaac Lowndes, who carried on business in Pall Mall, was also a well-known clockmaker. He was admitted in 1682.

Peter de Baufre, Church Street, St. Anne's, Soho, and who took a prominent part in the application of jewels in watches, was elected in 1689.

Simon de Charmes, who was eminent as a maker of repeaters, was elected in 1691.

Langley Bradley, of Fenchurch Street, the renowned maker of St. Paul's clock, Cripplegate Church clock, and some others in the City of London, was elected in 1694, and served as Master in 1726.

Jasper Taylor, elected in 1694, was a watchmaker living in Holborn, and accounted a fair craftsman in his time.

Charles Cabrier, elected in 1697, was a maker of good watches; specimens of his work in gold *repousse* cases are occasionally to be met with.

Daniel Delander, elected in 1699, was known as a watchmaker producing good sound work.

Clock at Windsor Castle.

At Windsor Castle is a clock which was made by Joseph Knibb, in 1677. Wood, in his "Curiosities of Clocks and Watches," says, "This artist issued the following token: Obverse, 'Joseph Knibb, clockmaker in Oxon' (in capitals, consisting of four lines); reverse, 'J. K.,' a clock face and hands; so that it seems clockmakers, like other tradesmen, issued their tokens in the seventeenth century." "In the 'Camden Society's Secret Services,' *temp.* Charles II. and James II., are various accounts of payments made on behalf of the king, some of which were for clocks supplied to him. In the account up to July 3, 1682, is an item, 'Paid to Mr. Knibb, by His said Majestie's command upon a bill for clockwork, £141.'"

Clockmaker's Token.

Foreign Clockmakers predominating till the Middle of the Seventeenth Century.

In the time of Henry VIII. it appears that most of the "orologes" were the production of foreign artists, and, judging from State Papers and other records, foreign clockmakers preponderated till about the middle of the seventeenth century, so that the three clockmakers imported by Edward III. do not seem to have increased and multiplied to any great extent. "A true Certificat of the Names of the Straungers residing and dwellinge within the City of London," dated 1618, states that "in the ward of Farringdon Within was then living Barnaby Martinot, clockmaker, b. in Paris; a Roman Catholicque." In Portsoken ward was living "John Goddard, clockmaker; lodger and servant with Isack Sunes in Houndsditch; b. at Paris, in France; heer 3 yeers, a papist; yet hee hath the oath of allegiance to the king's supremacy, and doth acknowledg the king of his soveraigne dureing his abode in England; and is of the Romish church."

Among the State Papers, *temp.* James I., there is an original letter, dated 4th of August, 1609, addressed by Sir Julius Cæsar to the clerks of the Signet, requesting them to prepare a warrant to pay £300 to Hans Niloe, a Dutchman, for a clock with music and motions. And on the 17th of the same month Sir Julius wrote from the Strand to Salisbury, stating that he was pressed by Hans Niloe for the £300 for his clock.

Fob Watches introduced.

IT will be observed that many of the early watches differed but little from table clocks; the smaller ones, when attached to the person, were originally on a chain worn round the neck. The fob, from the German *fuppe*, a small pocket, seems to have been introduced by the Puritans, whose dislike of display induced them to conceal their timekeepers from the public gaze; besides which, for men engaged in active pursuits, and who carried timekeepers for use rather than for ornament, the fob was decidedly more convenient. This conjecture as to the origin of the fob is borne out by the fact that a short "fob" chain belonging to a watch of Oliver Cromwell's, in the British Museum, is in point of date the first appendage of the kind to be found. The arms and initials of the Protector are engraved upon the seal end of the chain. The watch is a small oval one, in a silver case, and was made about 1625, by John Midnall, of Fleet Street, who was one of the first members of the Court of the Clockmakers' Company, and Warden in 1638. Mr. Evan Roberts has another watch said to have belonged to Oliver Cromwell. It is in a very plain round silver case.

French Enamelling on Watch Cases and Dials. The middle of the seventeenth century was marked by the introduction of beautiful decoration in enamel for watch cases and dials. The process of painting in opaque enamels is of French origin, and is said to have been the invention of Jean Toutin, a goldsmith of Château Surr, who was distinguished for painting in transparent enamels, and, about 1630, succeeded in applying to thin gold plates thick colours of different tints, which would melt with fire and yet retain their lustre. Others besides the inventor speedily devoted themselves to the new art. Among those who excelled in it, and whose work is now much prized by connoisseurs, may be mentioned Henry Toutin, a brother of the inventor, a goldsmith and enameller at Blois; Dubie, a court goldsmith, who worked at the Louvre; Paul Viet of Blois; Morlière, a native of Orleans, who worked at Blois; Robert Vauquer, a pupil of Morlière; Chartière of Blois, who was noted for his paintings of flowers; and Huand le Puisné, who was equally celebrated for figure-painting. Several examples, some of them of wonderful brilliancy of colouring and admirable drawing, are to be found in the British and South Kensington Museums, as well as among private collections. Among those in the British Museum are some that belonged to the late Osborne Morgan which are really worth inspection. A representation of some nymphs bathing, exquisitely executed in enamel by Jean Toutin; also an enamelled watch-case, very finely painted by Henry Toutin, illustrating the story of Tancred and Clorinda in "Orlando Furioso;" another by the same artist treats of the "History d'Apain." A watch by D. Bouquett, a well-known London watchmaker, the case being ornamented with flowers in relief, and enriched with diamonds; a very finely enamelled watch-case, illustrating the early life of Christ; two cases painted in enamel by H. le Puisné, and one by I. L. Durant, may be cited. The fragile surface of the enamel required the protection of an outer case, and upon this the goldsmith in his turn lavished all his skill.

From this time the practice of adding a loose outer case to watches, forming what are called "pair cases," continued to the early part of the present century. These

cases were often covered with a remarkably tough,
leather-like green covering called Shagreen.
Shagreen. It was, and in smaller quantities is still, made
at Astrachan from the strong skin that covers the crupper
of the ass or the horse. In its preparation a peculiar
roughness is produced by treading into the skin hard
round seeds, which are shaken out when the skin has
been dried; it is then stained green with copper filings
and sal-ammoniac, and the grains or warts are then
rubbed down to a level with the rest of the surface, which
thus presents the appearance of white dots on a green
ground. It was customary to insert in the outer case of
pair-case watches circular pieces of velvet, muslin, or
other material, adorned with fancy needlework, or "watch-
Verses in papers," having printed thereon sometimes
Pair-cased an advertisement of the watchmaker, and
Watches. occasionally admonitory or sentimental verses.
Some of these are worth reproducing. The following
lines I remember seeing over an old clock in Somerset,
though they are often to be met on old watch papers:—

> "Onward perpetually moving,
> These faithful hands are ever proving
> How quick the hours fly by;
> This monitory pulse-like beating
> Is oftentimes methinks repeating,
> 'Swift! swift! the moments fly.'
> Reader, be ready, for perhaps before
> These hands have made one revolution more
> Life's spring is snapped—you die!"

The same exhortation pervades many others, of which
another example may be given—

> "Time is—the present moment well employ;
> Time was—is past—thou canst not it enjoy;
> Time future—is not and may never be;
> Time present—is the only time for thee."

The next appears to be anything but complimentary to
the recipient—

> "To-morrow! yes, to-morrow you'll repent
> A train of years in vice and folly spent.
> To-morrow comes—no penitential sorrow
> Appears therein, for still it is to-morrow.
> At length to-morrow such a habit gain'd,
> That you forget the time by Heaven ordained;
> And you'll believe that day too soon will be
> When more to-morrow you're denied to see."

Content and benevolence are advised in a quaint, old, and apparently a favourite paper. It runs—

> "Content thy selfe withe thyne estat,
> And sende no poore wight from thy gate;
> For why, this councell I thee give,
> To learne to dye, and dye to lyve."

Watch papers occasionally breathed assurances of tender regard, and were probably prized accordingly. Here is one bearing the date 1730—

> "With me while present may thy lovely eyes
> Be never turned upon this golden toy,
> Think every pleasing hour too swiftly flies,
> And measure time by joy succeeding joy.
> But when the cares that interrupt our bliss
> To me not always will thy sight allow,
> Then oft with kind impatience look on this,
> Then every minute count—as I do now."

The next is quoted from the "Annual Register" for 1807—

> "For her who owns this splendid toy,
>   Where use with elegance unites,
> Still may its index point to joy,
>   And moments wing'd with new delights."

Transposition of Mementos in Watch Cases. The space between the outer and inner cases of watches has also been made the receptacle of some treasured memento of persons or events. A bit of ribbon, a lock of hair, a rose-petal, or a four-leaved clover is not infrequently discovered by the watchmaker who has the watch to clean or repair. Though they may be lightly thrown aside on the workbench, care must be taken to replace love-tokens so found, or trouble will ensue. Stories are told of angry feelings aroused and jealous recriminations caused by the disappearance, or, worse still, the transposition of these relics while the watch is in the hands of the repairer. It is said that one man insisted on having a written statement from his watchmaker to the effect that a lock of golden hair found by the suspicious wife of the customer in the place where one of her raven tresses had been wont to repose was due to an accidental exchange on the part of the workman.

Mysterious Clocks.

TIMEKEEPERS in which the motive-power is not apparent have always found admirers, and therefore people to devise them.

Nicholas Grollier, who was born at Lyons in 1689, con-

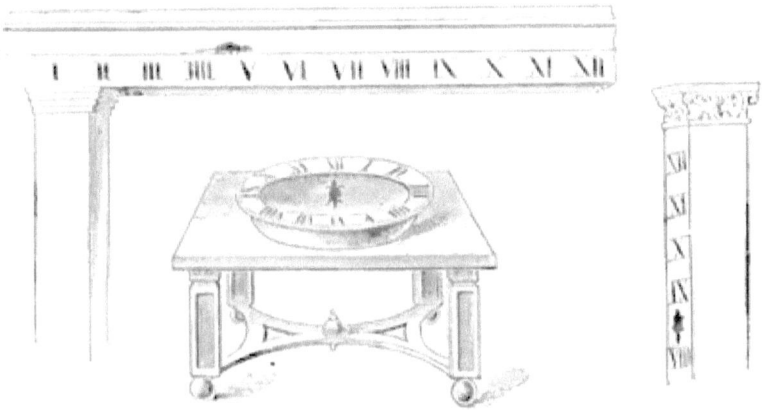

Fig. 31.—Mysterious clocks by Grollier.

trived many curious horological mysteries. One consisted of a metal dish containing water, and having the hours of the day marked round its edge. A small figure of a tortoise being dropped into the water would float round

Fig. 32.—Grollier's diagonal shoot clock.

and stop, and indicate the time; if not removed, would continue to advance as time elapsed, always keeping its nose to the proper hour. Though considered to be marvellous, and the cause of much conjecture at the time, the action of the tortoise would now be readily attributed to the guidance of a magnet revolving outside and under the rim of the dish. The figure of a mouse was by the same means made to move along a cornice, on which the hours were painted; a lizard ascending a pillar is but the same idea in another form. These devices are illustrated in Fig. 31. Fig. 32 shows a somewhat similar conception by the same artist, in which a ball descended diagonal shoots, or an inclined plane, and was carried up by a screw, which was hidden from view in the case. Grollier also made a machine in which time was measured by the descent of a ball in a metal groove twisted round columns supporting a dome; when the ball

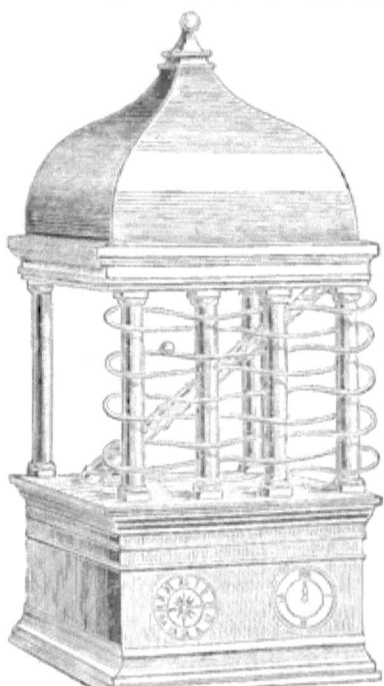

Fig. 33.—Grollier's Archimedean screw clock.

had finished its descent, its impetus, lifting a detent, discharged the wheelwork, and gave motion to an Archimedean screw, which raised the ball to its former position at the top of the metal groove. The action will be understood by reference to Fig. 33. Canon Cinqumani devised a clock on a very similar principle, which was exhibited in London in 1890. In the Canon's very ingenious arrangement the hours and quarters were sounded by bullets rolling down inclined shoots, and striking tubes and gongs. The bullets for both going and striking fell into pockets attached to endless webbing, which passed over rollers at the top; so raising

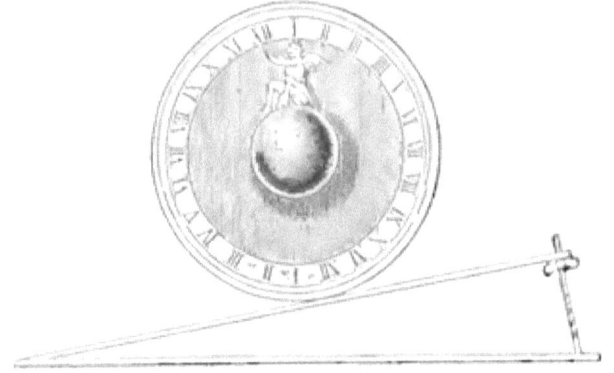

Fig. 34.—Grollier's inclined plane clock.

Clock rolling down Inclined Plane.

the bullets to their highest position, and discharging them again. Another of Grollier's conceptions was a clock which descended an inclined plane, as shown in the subjoined figure, 34; the working of this will be understood from the uncovered view of the front, Fig. 35. A weighted lever, b, in its present position, just keeps the clock in equipoise. It and the hour hand c, and the wheel a, are all fixed together. By means of an escapement and balance, to which the wheel a is connected by the intervention of the train of wheels shown to the left of the centre, the weight b is allowed to slowly descend, and so the clock rolls down while the hand points to the hour. By means of the screw and nut *g* the inclination of the plane, and therefore the speed of descent, can be regulated as required. There is neither weight nor spring to be wound, and therefore no casualty to be feared from the breaking of the cord or spring. This was advanced as a strong reason in favour of these clocks, many of which were made as curiosities till quite recently. Each morning or evening, as found to be most convenient, the clock, which would then be near the bottom of the incline, would be lifted bodily, and placed at the top. It is but fair to state that the invention of this inclined plane clock is also claimed for the Marquis

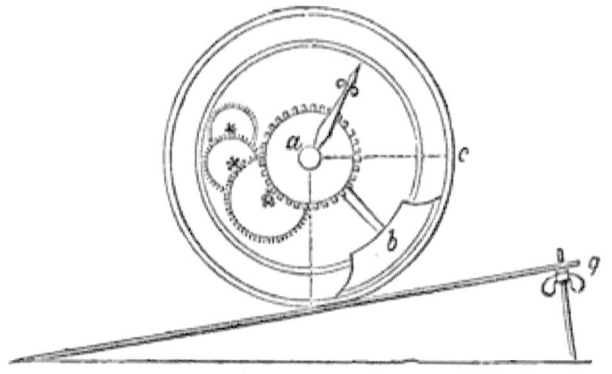

Fig. 35.—Mechanism of inclined plane clock.

of Worcester. One of Grollier's most useful inventions was a night clock, consisting of a transparent dial, which revolved in front of a slit illuminated by a lamp.

Magniac's Automata. About the middle of the eighteenth century, Colonel Magniac, a famous clockmaker, lived in an old mansion in St. John's Square, Clerkenwell, and had his workshops there. He made automaton clocks for many foreign potentates, and his reputation perhaps did much to render Clerkenwell noted as the clockmaking parish. Two of the most remarkable clocks manufactured by him for the Emperor of China were rare specimens of mechanical skill, and occasioned much interest when exhibited here prior to delivery. In addition to regiments of soldiers, there were musical performers, parading beasts and birds, all displaying appropriate action, and, *pace* a writer of the time, " were combined to show what various and graceful motions could be produced by wheels, pinions, and levers." Early in the present century the mansion was pulled down.

Cox's Museum, 1773.   John Cox, a watchmaker of Shoe Lane, Holborn, opened a museum of curious clocks, watches, and automata of his own contriving and manufacture in 1773. Half a guinea was the price of admission, and but few people were to be admitted at once, even if the demand were great, for fear of damage or loss; but the speculation proved anything but remunerative. This Cox was not only a skilful mechanician, but a man of taste; and he employed Nollekens, the sculptor, and Zoffany, a celebrated painter, to decorate the cases and accessories of his productions. The fifty-six pieces which composed his museum were valued at £197,500. He obtained an Act of Parliament, empowering him to dispose of the various articles by lottery, and the drawing took place at the Guildhall in 1775. Mention is made of an eight-day musical clock, with a moving procession of many of Shakespeare's characters; a cage of singing birds attached to another clock; and a timepiece similar to one made for the Emperor of China, in the embellishment of which a large number of diamonds, rubies, emeralds, and pearls was used. Some of Cox's clocks were wound by the opening and shutting of the door of the room in which they were placed. Others were connected with a square plate concealed under the mat at the entrance, and raised about a quarter of an inch above the flooring which surrounded it. As visitors trod upon the mat, the plate was slightly depressed, this motion often repeated being sufficient to recharge the motive-power.

Ball of Venice.
In the collection of M. Paul Garnier is a remarkably clever and elegant piece of seventeenth-century mysterious horology, known as the Ball of Venice, the author of which is unknown. In form it is a sphere, to be suspended from a bracket on the

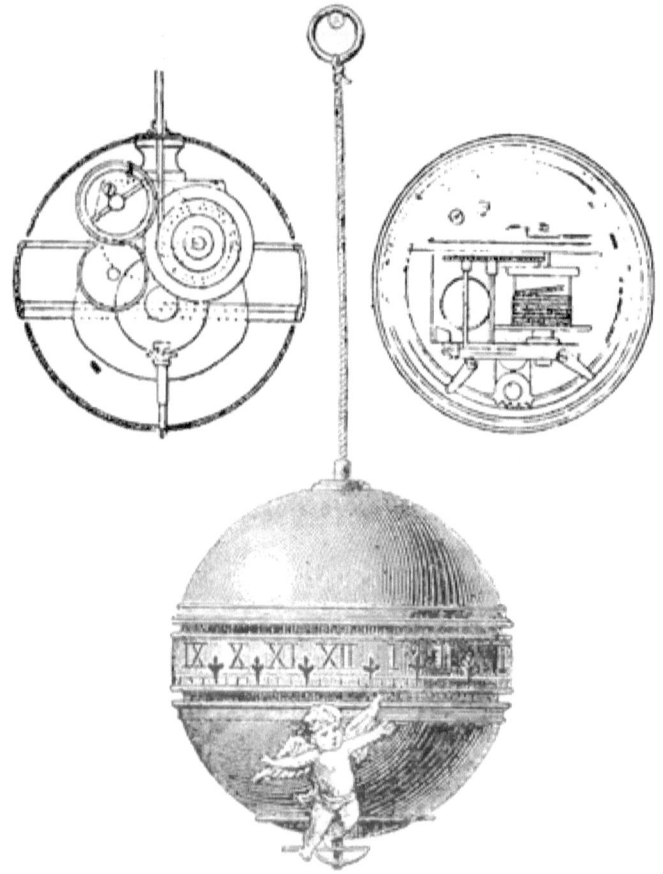

Fig. 36.—Ball of Venice.

ceiling of a room. The ball is of metal, the upper and lower portions being gilt, while around a silvered band in the middle are marked two series of roman numerals from I. to XII., and subdivisions for the quarter hours. The extremity of one of the wings of a cupid on the lower part of the ball points to the hour of the day or night. The internal construction will be understood from the vertical and horizontal section given in Fig. 36. There is a barrel round which the suspending cord is coiled, also a train of wheels, and a verge escapement with a heavy balance and no balance spring, that accessory not having been invented when the mechanism was devised. The upper and lower portions of the ball are fixed together, but the middle part is free to move, and by means of an internal circular rack attached to it, it is driven round once in twenty-four hours by a pinion. When the ball is lifted a light spring in the barrel turns it and causes it to coil sufficient of the suspending cord on to itself to cover its surface. But when the ball is allowed to hang freely on the cord its weight acts as the driving power. To rewind the mechanism all that is needed is to place the hand under the ball and raise it a little, which allows the barrel to gather up the cord in the way described.

Fig. 37.—Double globe timepiece.

Double Globe Timepiece. M. Henri Cunge, a French artist, devised the mysterious timekeeper shown in Fig. 37.

There are two clear glass globes. The figure with a wand points to the hour on the larger globe, while the minutes are indicated by a pointer on the smaller one. The movement is in the base with a driving arbor carried up the support, and by means of belted wheels to the bottom arbor of the large globe. In the cap on the large globe the motion work for the smaller globe is concealed.

Fig. 38 —Marie Antoinette's timepiece.

Fig. 39.—Falconet's Three Graces.

Vase and Urn Timepieces. Urn and vase timekeepers were a fancy indulged in by many wealthy people. In the original of Fig. 38, which belonged to Marie Antoinette, the movement was covered by the handsome carved marble pedestal, the urn was of porcelain with bronze mountings. A serpent curled round the foot of the vase had its head erect to point to the hour on the double polygonal band, which made a rotation in twelve hours.

Three Graces. Fig. 39 represents a magnificent design by Falconet, wherein the three graces are pourtrayed, one of whom indicates the hour with her finger. The vase is supported by a column standing on a handsome; plinth the panels of the plinth show very choice

Fig. 40.—Mysterious glass dial.

carvings of groups of children at play. As in the preceding example, the hour hand goes round.

Glass Dials. The glass dial shown in Fig. 40 is so common as to be no longer much of a mystery, and familiarity with its appearance has caused people to lose much of the curiosity which the arrangement awakened many years ago. In the collection of the late Mr. Napier, there was a very nice dial on this principle with but one hand. In the counterpoise of the hand was a semicircular weight and a watch movement, which carried this weight round once in twelve hours. Starting with the hand say at twelve o'clock, the weight would then be with the middle of its half-round edge towards the VI., and as the weight was carried upwards to the left, so the hand would travel downwards to the right so as to keep the hand and counterpoise, or the beam as it may be termed, in equilibrium.

Another form of transparent dial occasionally met with is what appears to be a sheet of glass fixed in a frame and mounted on a substantial wooden base. The base is really a box containing the movement, and the glass is double, the hinder sheet carrying a click which takes into a small ratchet attached to the hand, which is carried by the front sheet. The clock movement gives a reciprocating motion to one of the sheets, so slight as to be barely perceptible yet sufficient to cause the click to carry the hand forward the correct amount.

Tamborine and Bee. One of the prettiest conceits among mysterious timekeepers is the floral tamborine, Two bees, a large and a small one, creep round among the flowers, pointing the former to the hours and the latter to the minutes without any apparent connection with the movement. The explanation is simple, two magnets at the back of the tamborine skin travel round, and by their attraction carry the insects, which are of steel, with them.

Free Pendulum. A female figure holding in her outstretched hand what seems to be a free pendulum which is kept swinging by a small circular motion imparted to the figure by the movement contained in the base on which it stands was a popular form of mysterious timekeeper introduced a few years ago.

Fig. 41.—Clock at Palais de Justice, Paris.

Clock at Palais de Justice, Paris.

In many of the older French public clocks there is a delightful harmony between the dial and its surroundings that may well be commended to English architects of to-day. Take the clock of the Paris Palais de Justice, shown in Fig. 41. The whole effect is excellent, and there is a completeness about it sadly wanting in most of the timekeepers pertaining to our public buildings, or, to speak more precisely, attached to them; for in too many instances the dial seems to be an excrescence quite out of character with the building which it disfigures instead of completes.

Fig. 42.—Clock at Hotel de Ville, Paris.

Clock at Hotel de Ville, Paris.

The clock of the Hotel de Ville at Paris, Fig. 42, of a later date, is hardly so good. Though the design is well adapted for the reception of a timekeeper, the dial is obscured with ornament, besides being too small, which makes it seem subsidiary to the adjacent statuary, whereas it should be the centrepiece of the whole. The movement of this clock was made by Lepaute, in 1781. It has his pin-wheel escapement and a two-seconds pendulum, compensated with nine brass and steel rods on Harrison's principle.

Great Stride towards Perfection in Timekeepers, 1650-1700.

N the latter half of the seventeenth century many serious endeavours were made to improve the timekeeping qualities of watches and clocks. In 1658 Dr. Hooke discovered the particular suitability of the balance spring for rendering the vibrations of the balance isochronous, and balance springs were forthwith applied to watches by Tompion and other eminent makers. The pendulum was introduced for clocks by Huygens in 1657, and was followed a few years later by the anchor escapement, another of Hooke's conceptions. The fusee chain was substituted for catgut by one Gruet, of Geneva, in 1664. The concentric minute hand was added by Quare, and other English clockmakers, about the year 1670, and the horological trades were further stimulated through the revocation of the Edict of Nantes, in 1685, which was the means of driving many skilful watchmakers to this country. Tompion obtained a patent for the cylinder escapement in 1695. In the early part of the eighteenth century Graham devised the dead-beat escapement, and the mercurial pendulum was also evolved from the same master mind, while a further step towards perfecting watches was made by the introduction of jewels as bearings for the balance pivots by Nicholas Facio, a native of Geneva, who settled in

London, and for some time practised in secret the art of piercing holes in rubies and sapphires for the purpose.

Watch Jewelling. The following notice appeared in the *London Gazette* of May 11, 1704: " Her Majesty having granted to Mr. Nicholas Facio, gentleman, of the Royal Society, Peter Debaufres and Jacob Debaufres, watchmakers, her letters patent, &c., for the sole use in England, &c., for fourteen years of a new art, invented by them, of figuring and working precious or common stones, crystal or glass and certain other matters, different from metals, so that they may be employed in watches, clocks, and many other engines, as internal and useful parts of the engine itself, in such manners as were never yet in use. All those that may have occasion for any stones thus wrought, may be further informed at Mr. Debaufres', in Church Street, near St. Anne's. There they may see some jewel watches, and all belong unto the same art." The inventors, Facio and the two Debaufres, were not satisfied with their fourteen years' patent, and therefore they applied to Parliament for an extension of the term, and also for an Act for the sole monopoly of the art of clock and watch jewelling. This application was opposed by the Clockmakers' Company, and the matter was referred to a committee of the House of Commons, who decided against the applicants.

False Jewelling in Huggeford's Watch. There is a curious episode in connection with the opposition of the Clockmakers' Company, to Facio and Debaufres' application. Among the evidence brought against the Bill was "an old watch made by Ignatius Huggeford, that had a stone fixed in the balance cock." The production of this piece of anterior jewelling had great weight with the committee, and the Company bought the watch, which was placed in the master's hands. But subsequent examination disclosed the fact that the so-called jewelling was merely a dummy stone stuck on the surface of the cock.

Motion Work for actuating Hands. The motion work, sometimes called "dial work," which allows both the minute and the hour hand of timekeepers to travel from a common centre, will be understood by a reference to Fig. 43. The centre arbor of a watch or clock rotates once in an hour, and on it is fixed friction tight a pinion with a long boss or pipe, called the cannon pinion. The cannon pinion drives the minute wheel which, with the minute wheel pinion attached to it, runs loosely on a stud fixed to the plate of the watch or clock. The last-named pinion drives the hour wheel, which has a short pipe, and runs loosely on the pipe of the cannon pinion. The minute hand is fixed to the pipe of the cannon pinion, and the hour hand to the pipe or body of the hour wheel. Of course, in order for the minute hand to make the circuit of the dial twelve times while the hour hand goes round once, the product obtained by multiplying together the number of teeth in the minute and hour wheels must be twelve times the product obtained by multiplying together the teeth in the cannon and minute wheel pinions.

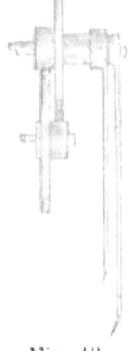

Fig. 43.

Repeaters of Especial Value before Lucifer Matches were invented. Another important improvement introduced during the latter part of the sixteenth century, was the making of watches and clocks so that the possessor could cause the number corresponding to the last completed hour to be repeated at will by strokes on a bell. Many of the early clocks and watches were either furnished with an alarum or striking work of the locking plate kind, as shown in the engraving of the fourteenth-century clock on page 53. In this the hours can only be struck in regular progression, and could therefore not be adapted for repeating. In those days, it must be remembered, lucifer matches were unknown, and the only means of obtaining a light was by striking together flint and steel until a spark ignited a piece of rag burnt to tinder, an operation occupying sometimes a quarter of an hour, and even failing altogether if the tinder happened to be damp, so that the addition of repeating work very much enhanced the value of timekeepers, and gave increased importance to the horological trades.

Horologists of Renown and their Inventions.

Thomas Tompion.

OREMOST among the horological artists of the seventeenth century must be placed Thomas Tompion, "the father of English watchmaking" as he has been termed, who was born in 1638. It is said that his father was a farrier, but there are no reliable particulars of his initiation into the horological arts. The first traces of his career show that he kept a shop in Water Lane, Blackfriars; and while yet a young man he is found to have been intimately connected with Dr. Hooke, the Rev. Edward Barlow, and other scientists of repute; while all the records of the time point to him as the leading watchmaker at the court of Charles II., and he appears to have been on good terms with many of the nobility. By favour of Mr. P. Webster, I am enabled to give in Fig. 44 a drawing of one of Tompion's earlier clocks. It has a light pendulum, six inches in length, fixed to the verge; the escapement for the alarum is behind the going train, the hammer striking the bell which forms the domical top of the clock. Tompion subsequently applied to clocks the anchor escapement of Hooke and the striking work of Barlow. But his greatest triumph was controlling the

motion of the watch balance by means of a spring, as suggested by Hooke. At first the springs were straight, then curved like a pothook; a volute, the form ultimately adopted, was evolved, we may be sure, only after much patient research and countless experiments.

Tompion undoubtedly patented the cylinder escapement in 1695, but no watches of his with the cylinder escapement have survived, and many people ascribe the invention to his assistant, Graham, who most probably worked the design into a practicable shape.

The distinguishing characteristic of Tompion appears to be the facility with which he embodied new ideas in sound and enduring mechanism. That his ordinary clocks and watches should be of good proportion and well executed is to be expected, but the admirable and tasteful arrangement of his later works, including repeating clocks and watches, stamp him as a master of his art.

Fig. 44.

There is in the Horological Institute a fine portrait of Tompion, painted in oils, which represents him showing the movement of a watch. It is said he was so jealous of his reputation, that upon one occasion, when a person consulted him respecting a watch on which the name of the great horologist had been fraudulently placed, Tompion broke the spurious article with a hammer, and presented the inquirer with a genuine one, with the remark, "There, sir, is a watch of my making." If such generous treatment were the practice nowadays, it is to be feared that a good many imitations would be submitted to watchmakers of surpassing skill.

It was stated that Tompion was attacked by the Plague, and fled to the continent, where he breathed his last; but this may be erroneous, for in the Pump Room at Bath is a record of his having presented a clock to that city, and the probability is that when the Plague broke out he migrated with friends to the "Queen of the West," then a most fashionable resort. However, he died in 1713, and his remains met with the exceptional honour of interment in Westminster Abbey, of which more will be said when speaking of Graham.

Balance Spring. Fig. 45 shows a balance spring in the form usually applied to watches. The inner end of the spring is attached by means of a collet to the arbor of the balance, and the outer end is held in a stud which is fixed to the plate or cock of the watch. The balance, impelled by the escapement, makes a rotary motion, winding up the spring as it goes. Just as the energy of the balance is exhausted the potential stored up in the spring is utilized to help the balance on its return vibration. If greater im-

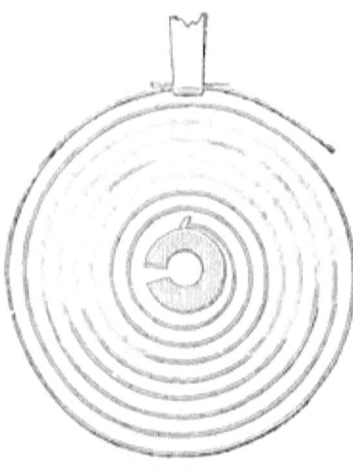

Fig. 45.—Balance spring.

pulse is given by the escapement the balance takes a longer excursion, but it is met by increased resistance of the spring, and the extra potential of the latter when expended on the balance enables it to attain a higher velocity on its return, and so, within reasonable limits, the time of vibration is the same whether the vibrations are of greater or lesser extent, or, as watchmakers express it, the long and short arcs are isochronous.

The strength of the balance spring is adapted to the moment of inertia of the balance as nearly as possible; but for bringing the watch exactly to time, the spring near its outer end is lightly clasped by two fingers on an arm which may be moved to and fro, thus lengthening or shortening the effective length of the spring as may be required.

The cylinder escapement is a conception of great merit. Though it belongs to the frictional as distinguished from the detached class, it is by no means obsolete, and is especially suited for many kinds of watches.

Cylinder Escapement. The vibrations of the balance are not so much affected by inequality in the force transmitted and other faults as when a highly detached escapement and very fine pivots are used. It is certainly remarkable that English watchmakers should have been so baffled by a constructional difficulty as to throw aside the horizontal escapement. Mudge and other eminent English makers used hard brass for the escape wheel and ruby for the cylinder, but without overcoming the tendency to cutting and excessive wear of the acting surfaces. It remained for the Swiss to bring the problem to a successful issue by making both wheel and cylinder of steel and hardening them.

Fig. 46 is a plan of the cylinder escapement, in which the point of a tooth of the escape wheel, a, is pressing against the outside of the shell of the cylinder, b. As the cylinder, on which the balance is mounted, moves round in the direction of the arrow the wedge-shaped tooth of the escape wheel pushes into the cylinder, thereby giving it impulse. The tooth cannot escape at the other side of the cylinder, for the shell of the cylinder at this point is rather more than half a circle, but its point rests against the inner side of the shell till the balance completes its vibration and returns, when the tooth which was inside the cylinder escapes, and the point of the succeeding tooth is caught on the outside of the shell. The teeth rise on stalks (see *f*) from the body of the escape wheel, and the cylinder is cut away just below the acting part of the exit side, leaving only one-fourth of a circle in order to allow as much vibration as possible.

Fig. 46.—Cylinder escapement.

The cylinder escapement was formerly more generally spoken of as "the horizontal escapement," because the teeth of the escape wheel lie in a horizontal plane, whereas the teeth of the verge escape wheel stand vertically; but this title is no longer definitely descriptive, for all modern watch escapements have escape wheels lying horizontally.

George Graham. George Graham, "honest George Graham," worthy coadjutor of and successor to Tompion, was born at Kirklinton, Cumberland, in 1673, and was apprenticed to Henry Aske, a clockmaker, in the city of London. On completion of his apprenticeship he became an assistant of Tompion, and remained his friend and fellow-worker until the death of the latter in 1713.

Graham married a relative of Tompion, and afterwards, under the sign of "The Dial and one Crown," opened a shop opposite the "Bolt and Tun," Fleet Street.

Graham's dead-beat escapement is shown in Fig. 47. Comparing this with the anchor escapement of Hooke, shown in Fig. 53, which was the best hitherto available for clocks, it will be observed that when the wheel is at rest a tooth bears or locks on a curved face which is struck from the centre of motion of the pallets, so that there is no recoil of the wheel. When by the motion of the pendulum the tooth is allowed to leave the locking face, it slides on an inclined plane, which intercepts the path of the wheel tooth, and the pressure exerted gives impulse to the pendulum.

To counteract the effect of changes of temperature on the length of the pendulum, Graham, after experimenting with various substances, used a steel rod for

Fig. 47.
a, Escape wheel; b, Pallets.

the pendulum and formed the bob of a glass jar containing mercury, the mercury being of such a height that, as the pendulum rod lengthened with a rise of temperature, the mercury expanded upwards just sufficient to keep the distance between the point of suspension and the centre of oscillation of the pendulum constant. With a fall of temperature the action was of course reversed. It says much for his genius, that the dead-beat escapement and the mercurial pendulum are still employed for clocks of extreme precision, such as are used in observatories and as regulators by watchmakers. Graham died in 1751, and was buried in Westminster Abbey. A large slab of black stone was placed in the nave of the sacred edifice, with an inscription of which the following is a reduced *facsimile*.

Tomb of Tompion and Graham in Westminster Abbey.

HERE LIES THE BODY
OF M^R THO TOMPION
WHO DEPARTED THIS
LIFE THE 20TH OF
NOVEMBER 1713 IN THE
75TH YEAR OF HIS AGE

ALSO THE BODY OF
GEORGE GRAHAM OF LONDON
WATCHMAKER AND F.R.S.
WHOSE CURIOUS INVENTIONS
DO HONOUR TO Y^E BRITISH GENIUS
WHOSE ACCURATE PERFORMANCES
ARE Y^E STANDARD OF MECHANIC SKILL
HE DIED Y^E XVI OF NOVEMBER MDCCLI
IN THE LXXVIII YEAR OF HIS AGE

In 1838 this commemorative slab was removed, and a couple of small lozenge-shaped stones bearing merely name and year of demise substituted. No reason whatever appears to have been at any time assigned for this wanton desecration, but there has always been a feeling that some little-minded person in authority considered a panegyric to mere mechanicians out of place, and this really intensified the natural outburst of wrath on the part of horologists and other admirers of these eminent men, who, as a writer, referring to the indignity, remarked, were "greater benefactors to mankind than hundreds whose sculptured urns impudently emblazon merits that never existed." However, in response to many protests as to the injustice that had been done, the late Dean Stanley, with much good feeling, ordered the slab to be restored in 1866. Let us hope that when time has obliterated the inscription there will yet remain horologists sufficiently jealous of the honour of their craft to see that the memory of the two masters of their art is perpetuated in the way their contemporaries desired.

Christian Huygens. Christian Huygens was a distinguished Dutch mathematician, who was born at the Hague in 1629. His reputation induced Louis XIV., in 1665, to invite him to found a Royal Academy of Sciences in Paris. Huygens resided in the French capital till 1681, when he returned to Holland, and died there in 1695. He was the author of "Horologium Oscillatorium," etc., published in Paris in 1673, and to him is due the credit of first applying the pendulum to clocks.

The long and short vibrations of a free pendulum will only be isochronous if the path described at the centre of oscillation is a cycloid. But a pendulum swung freely from a point travels through a circular path, the long arcs occupying more time than the shorter ones. With such small arcs as clock pendulums describe now the divergence from the theoretical cycloid is very small, and is disregarded, but it was of more importance with the necessarily large arcs demanded by the verge escapement. Accordingly, Huygens devised cycloidal cheeks to lead his pendulum through a cycloidal path, but experience showed that such devices were quite impracticable, and the invention of the anchor escapement rendered further effort in that direction unnecessary. Nevertheless, Huygens's clock was in its way a triumph, for up to his time there had been no provision for driving the clock while it was being wound, for, of course, as the barrel is turned the reverse way, in order to raise the weight, the driving power is then withdrawn, and if the operation of winding was conducted slowly, and the length of cord to be wound was considerable, not only would the timekeeping of the clock be affected, but there would be danger of its stopping altogether. Huygens's arrangement of cords for driving the clock, and maintaining the power while winding, was a stroke of genius, and though his elegant conception is rarely used now, it has never been eclipsed for simplicity and effectiveness.

Huygens's Clock. A drawing of Huygens's clock, copied from his folio work published in 1673, is shown in Fig. 48. It will be seen that the upper part of the pendulum is formed of a double cord hanging between two cheeks of metal, against which the cord presses as the pendulum swings, to give a cycloidal path to the bob. Fig. 49, showing the cycloidal cheeks in perspective, gives a better idea of this device.

The other feature of Huygens's clock is the arrangement of the cord of the driving weight, which also acts as maintaining power. This will be understood by a reference also to Fig. 48, and to Fig. 50, where the cord and weights are shown away from the clock. P is the driving weight, supported by an endless cord passing over the pulley D, attached to the great wheel, and also over the pulley H, which is provided with ratchet teeth, and pivoted to the inside of the clock case. The cord m is pulled down to wind the clock, and the ratchet wheel H then runs under its click, so that while winding, as in going, one-half of P, minus one-half of p, is driving the clock. The pulleys D and H are spiked to prevent slipping of the cord.

When this ingenious maintaining power is applied to a clock with a striking train, the pulley with the ratchet is

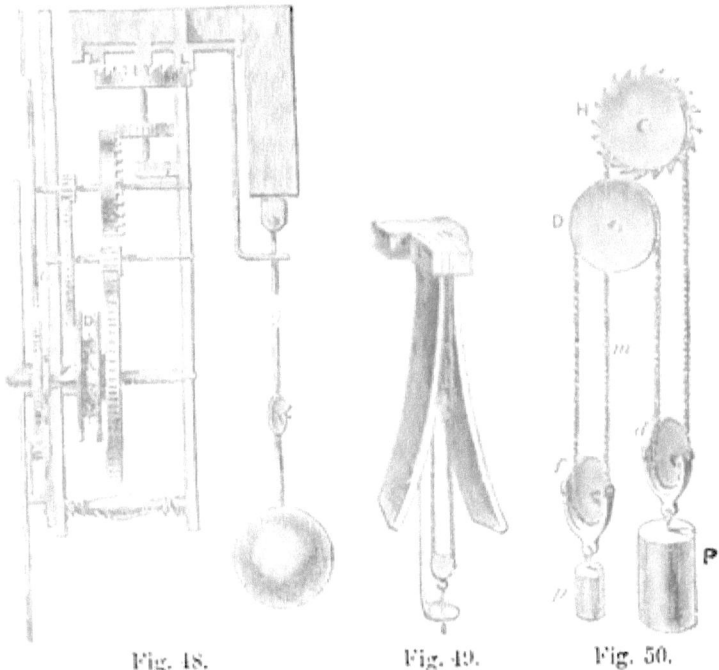

Fig. 48.　　　　Fig. 49.　　　Fig. 50.

attached to the great wheel of the striking part; one weight thus serving to drive both trains.

As far as I have been able to trace, this is the earliest record of any clock having a minute hand moving from the same centre, and therefore concentric with the hour hand.

Daniel Quare. Daniel Quare, who was born in 1632, and became a clockmaker of considerable note, must be credited with the invention of repeating watches. There is no doubt that he designed mechanism for such watches before 1680, and it is said that the first of Quare's repeaters was presented by Charles II. to Louis XIV. of France; but in the year 1686, the Rev. Edward Barlow, whose claim to be the originator of the rack repeating or striking work for clocks must also be admitted, applied for a patent for "the making of all pulling repeating clocks and watches." The Clockmakers' Company petitioned James II. not to grant this patent, and the king decided that the reasons against it should be heard before the Privy Council, which was done on March 2, 1687, the day appointed for the hearing. The result was that Barlow's application was refused; and the king, after a trial of a repeater made by Quare and one on Barlow's plan, gave the preference to the former, the fact being notified in the *Gazette*. The watch made for the king to try is described as being but little above the ordinary size, but very thick. It was in a handsomely embossed gold case, with the king's head in a medallion surrounded by emblems of war and power. Quare afterwards made a highly finished repeating watch for William III., as well as a twelve-month clock, which latter is still at the head of the bed in what was the bedroom of William III. at Hampton Court Palace. Quare has also been credited with the invention of the motion work for watches and clocks about 1680, whereby the minute and hour hands may be placed so as to revolve from the same centre, but this is doubtful, for the device appears on Huygens's clock of a prior date. It is quite possible that Quare introduced the motion work into England, and applied the concentric minute hand to many of his later timekeepers. He was a Quaker, and at his death in 1724, he was buried in the Quakers' ground at Bunhill Fields; many celebrated horologists testified to his respect by their presence on the occasion. Many records state that Tompion was among the company, but either a wrong date is given for Quare's death, or the statement must be incorrect, for Tompion died in 1713.

Edward Barlow. The Rev. Edward Barlow, who was born in 1634, invented as repeating work the "rack" mechanism, now almost exclusively used as striking work for clocks, except those of large size, was a man of remarkable attainments, and is much lauded by Dodd in his "Church History." He died in 1676.

Rack Striking and Repeating Work for Clocks. Fig. 51 is a view of the front plate of an English striking clock on the rack principle. The going train occupies the right and centre, and the striking train the left hand on the other side of the plate. The position of the barrels is indicated by their ratchets, and the position of the fusee by the winding squares, which are on the same level as the centre arbor. The connection between the going train and the striking work is by means of the motion wheel on the centre arbor, and connection is made between the striking train and the striking work by the gathering pallet, which is fixed to the arbor of the last wheel but one of the striking train, and also by the warning piece, which is shown in white on the boss of the lifting piece. This warning piece goes through a slotted hole in the plate, and during the interval between warning and striking stands in the path of a pin in the last wheel of the striking train, called the warning wheel. The motion wheel on the centre arbor, turning once in an hour, gears with the minute wheel, which has an equal number of teeth. These two wheels are indicated by dotted circles. There are two pins equidistant from the centre of the minute wheel which in passing raise the lifting piece every half-hour. Except for a few minutes before the clock strikes, the striking train is kept from running by the tail of the gathering pallot resting on a pin in the rack. Just before the hour, as the boss of the lifting piece lifts the rack hook, the rack, impelled by a spring at its tail, falls back until the pin in the lower arm of the rack is stopped by the snail. This occurs before the lifting piece is released by the pin in the minute wheel, and in this position the warning piece stops the train. Exactly

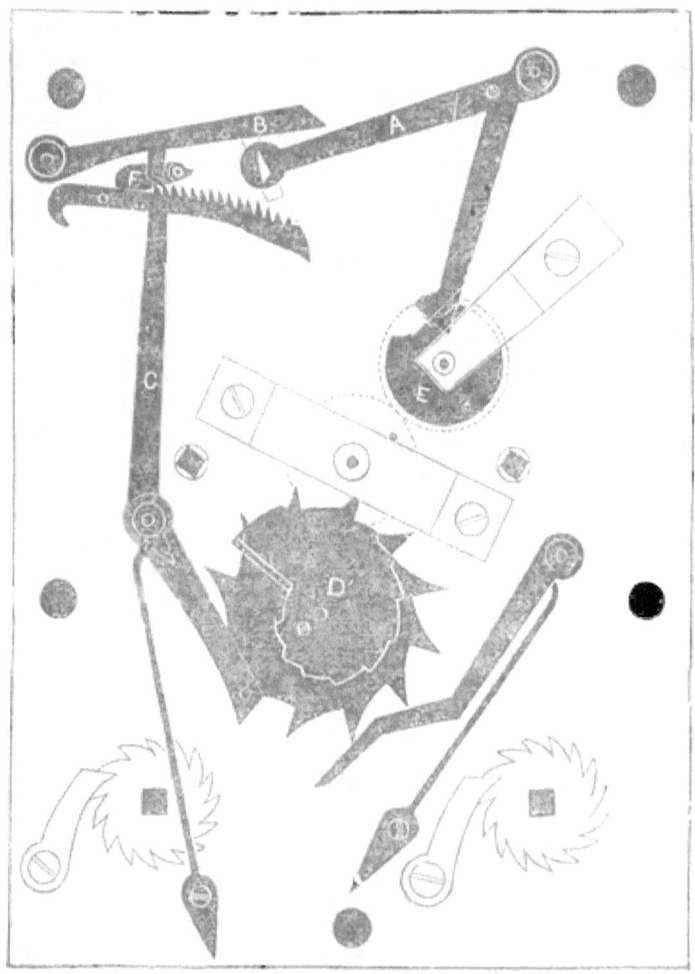

Fig. 51.—Rack striking work.

A, Lifting piece ; B, rack hook ; C, rack ; D, hour snail ; F, tail of gathering pallet.

at the hour the pin in the minute wheel gets past the lifting piece, which then falls, and the train is free. For every hour struck, the gathering pallet, which is really a one-toothed pinion, gathers up one tooth of the rack. After it has gathered up the last tooth, its tail is caught up by the pin in the rack and the striking ceases.

The snail is mounted on a star wheel placed so that a pin in the motion wheel on the centre arbor moves it one tooth for each rotation of the motion wheel. The pin, in moving the star wheel, presses back the click or jumper, which not only keeps the star wheel steady, but also completes its forward motion after the pin has pushed the tooth past the projecting centre of the click. The steps of the snail are arranged so that at one o'clock it permits only sufficient motion of the rack for one tooth to be gathered up, and at every succeeding hour additional motion equal to one extra tooth. The lower arm of the rack and the lower arm of the lifting piece are made of brass, and thin, so as to yield when the hands of the clock are turned back; the lower extremity of the lifting piece is a little wider, and bent to a slight angle with the plane of the arm, so as not to butt as it comes in contact with the pin when this is being done. If the clock is not required to repeat, the snail may be placed upon the centre arbor instead of on a stud with a star wheel as shown; but the position of the snail is not then so definite owing to the backlash of the motion wheels, and, besides, a smaller snail must be used, unless it is brought out to clear the nose of the minute-wheel cock.

Robert Hooke. Robert Hooke was born at Freshwater, Isle of Wight, in 1635, and was educated at Westminster School and Christ Church, Oxford. He suggested the application of the balance spring about 1660, and a few years later invented the anchor escapement for clocks. That Hooke was a clever mathematician and most ingenious mechanic there can be no doubt, yet it is curious there is not one of the improvements connected with horology with which his name is associated but what his claim to the authorship has been challenged. It may be accounted for in this way. He was essentially an investigator, and would examine a subject, write of it, talk of it, and then leave it for something else which caught his fancy; so that the attention of others would be directed to matters that had engrossed his attention, and in reference to which he had made discoveries to be elaborated at leisure; while they, fired by a spark from him, would plod on to the end, and so anticipate his results. His researches respecting the balance spring cannot be impeached. He promulgated the theory *Ut tensio sic vis* ("As is the tension so is the force"), which is the kernel of the whole thing. Variations in the motive force, which occurred even with the fusee, caused the excursions of the balance to be longer or shorter in extent, and thereby affected the time of its vibration. He proved that the excursions of the balance *should* be isochronous, if it were regulated by having a long spring attached to it, so that, with an increase of the motive force, though the extent of the vibration would be increased, the energy expended in winding up the spring would be utilized in increasing the velocity of the balance on the return vibration. And though the isochronous property of the balance spring was not fully developed in Hooke's time, skilful springers of watches to-day have so far triumphed over variations in the motive force that a marvellously near approach to absolute perfection in timekeeping is attained, even when the equalizing intervention of the fusee is dispensed with. I was always under the impression that Hooke obtained the D.C.L. degree at Oxford, though the Rev. H. L. Nelthropp speaks of his having been created M.D. by Archbishop Tillotson in 1691. On the death of Oldenburg, in 1677, Hooke was elected as Honorary Secretary of the Royal Society. He also occupied the post of Cutlerean Lecturer at Gresham College, where he died, and was buried at St. Helen's, Bishopsgate, in 1703.

AND OTHER TIMEKEEPERS.

Anchor Escapement. The anchor or recoil escapement, which is shown in Fig. 52, is the one most generally used for the ordinary run of dials and house clocks. There is no rest or locking for the pallets, but directly the pendulum in its vibration allows a tooth, after giving impulse, to escape from the impulse face of one pallet, the course of the wheel is checked by the impulse face of the other pallet receiving a tooth. The effect of this may be seen on looking at the drawing (Fig. 52), where the pendulum, travelling to the right, has allowed a tooth to fall on the left-hand pallet. The pendulum, however, still continues its swing to the right, and in consequence the pallet pushes the wheel back, thus causing the recoil which gives the name to the escapement. It is only after the pendulum comes to rest and begins its excursion the other way, that it gets any assistance from the wheel, and the difference between the forward motion of the wheel and its recoil forms the impulse.

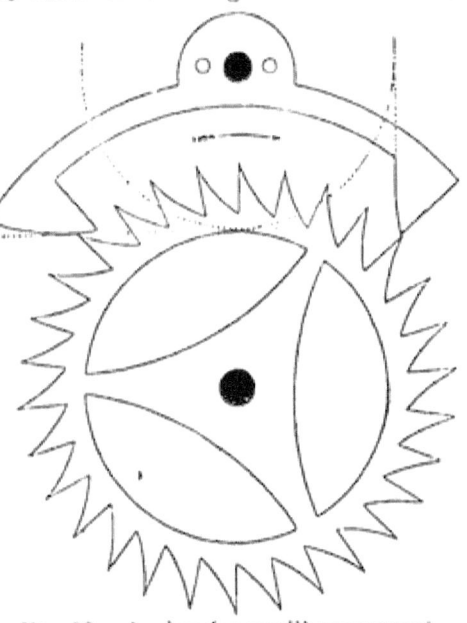

Fig. 52.—Anchor (or recoil) escapement.

The invention of the anchor escapement is claimed for William Clement, a London clockmaker, who applied it to clocks in 1680; but there is ample evidence that Hooke had made diagrams and pointed out the merits of it years before.

Among other things attributed to Hooke by many are

the application of the pendulum to clocks, the invention of an engine for cutting the teeth of wheels, and the duplex escapement, which latter, though thought much of forty years ago, is now obsolete.

So remarkable was Hooke's habit of cogitating that it is said Sir Isaac Newton dubbed him "the considerer."

John Harrison. John Harrison, who was born at Faulby, Yorkshire, in 1693, was the son of a carpenter, and devoted his life to the improvement of timekeepers.

Harrison was stimulated in his efforts by the announcement that the English Government would give a reward of £20,000 to any one who would produce a chronometer that would determine the longitude at sea to within half a degree. After surmounting enormous difficulties, he succeeded in fulfilling the conditions, and received a portion of the reward; but he had to convince the committee appointed that others could make similar instruments to his, and was subjected to other annoyances before he obtained the balance of the reward, which he did shortly before his death. His timekeeper, which is usually kept at the Royal Observatory, Greenwich, and was exhibited at the Naval Exhibition in 1891, is in a silver case in the shape of a watch case, and has a centre second hand. It has a verge escapement, driven by a *remontoire*, or small subsidiary spring, and is furnished with a "going fusee," that is, a fusee with a maintaining spring, to drive the watch while it is being wound. This device, which is now fitted to all fusees, and which Harrison invented about 1750, has proved to be the most lasting of his conceptions. Harrison is also credited with the invention of the "gridiron" pendulum, composed of a number of brass and steel rods, arranged to neutralize the effects of changes of temperature. But pendulums of this kind, though still used to some extent for fine clocks on the continent, never came into very general use here on account of the liability of the rods to move by jumps. Harrison died at his house in Red Lion Square in 1776, and was buried in the south side of Hampstead churchyard, where his tomb, restored a few years ago by the Clockmakers' Company, may still be seen.

William Derham. William Derham, D.D., and Canon of Windsor, an eminent philosopher and divine, took a remarkable interest in the details of horology, and wrote the first English technical work of any note relating to the art. It was a little book of 120 16mo pages, entitled "The Artificial Clockmaker, or a Treatise of Watch and Clockwork;" showing to the meanest capacity the art of calculating numbers to all sorts of movements, the way to alter clockworks to make chimes, and set them to musical notes, and to calculate and correct the motion of pendulums. Also numbers for divers movements, with the ancient and modern history of clockwork and many instruments, tables, and other matters never before published in any other book. It was first issued in 1696, and was republished in 1700; subsequent editions appeared in 1734 and 1759. Derham was born near Worcester, in 1657, and died in 1735.

Henry Sully. Henry Sully, who was born in 1680, and apprenticed to Charles Gretton, a London watchmaker, distinguished himself as a horologist and horological writer in France, where he spent most of his short manhood. He died in Paris in 1728. He is credited with having invented the duplex escapement, although an escapement very similar in principle was patented here by Thomas Tyrer in 1782. The action of the duplex escapement will be understood from Fig. 53.

Duplex Escapement. Like the chronometer, it is a single-beat escapement, that is, it receives impulse at every other vibration only. The escape wheel has two sets of teeth. Those farthest from the centre lock the wheel by pressing on a hollow ruby cylinder or roller fitted round a reduced part of the balance staff, and planted so that it intercepts the path of the teeth. There is a notch in the ruby roller, and a tooth passes every time the balance, in its excursion in the opposite direction to that in which the wheel moves, brings this notch past the point of the tooth resting on the roller. When the tooth leaves the notch, the impulse finger, fixed to the balance staff, receives a blow from one of the impulse teeth of the wheel. The impulse teeth are not in the same plane as the body of the wheel, but stand up from it so as to meet the impulse finger. There is no action in the return vibration. In the figure the detaining roller travelling in the direction of the arrow is just allowing a locking tooth of the wheel to escape from the notch, and the pallet is sufficiently in front of the tooth from which it will receive impulse to ensure a safe intersection. The balance is never detached, but the roller on which the wheel teeth rest is very small and highly polished, so that there is but little friction from this cause, and the alteration in its amount is, therefore, not of such consequence as might be imagined.

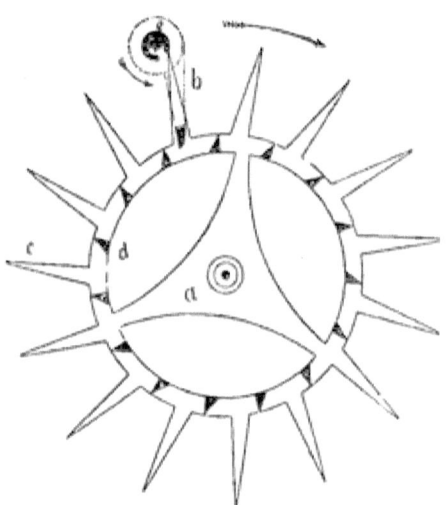

Fig. 53.—Duplex escapement.
a, escape wheel; b, impulse pallet; c, locking teeth; d, impulse teeth; e, ruby roller.

The idea of this escapement is seductive, and at one time it was considered an excellent arrangement, but it has proved to be quite unreliable. The best proportion of its parts and the finest work are insufficient to prevent it setting. On the introduction of the lever it declined, and is very rarely made now.

Poor Nicholas Forster, the watchmaker, in Captain Marryatt's novel, was, it will be remembered, going to do wonderful things when he had perfected his improvement of the duplex. As he never reached his goal, but retained his abstracted and melancholy condition to the last, it may be assumed that even he found the inherent defects of the duplex to be insurmountable.

John Ellicott. John Ellicott, born in 1706, carried on the business of a clockmaker for many years in Sweetings Alley, Cornhill, which was situated close to the spot where the statue of Rowland Hill now stands, and was abolished after the old Royal Exchange was destroyed by fire. He wrote one or two pamphlets on the construction of pendulums, and was the inventor of a compensation pendulum, in which the bob rests on the longer ends of two levers of which the shorter ends are depressed by the superior expansion of a brass bar attached to the pendulum rod. The device has not proved to be of practical value, though there is a clock to which it is attached still going at the London Institution in Finsbury Circus. As an instance of the substantial prices obtained for the best watches in the last century, it may be mentioned that Horace Walpole, writing to Sir H. Mann at Florence, on June 8, 1759, with regard to a commission to purchase a watch, states that for one of Ellicott's the price was 134 guineas, and the seal 16 guineas more, in all 150 guineas. Ellicott was elected a member of the Royal Society, and died in 1772.

Thomas Mudge. Thomas Mudge was born in 1715. He was apprenticed to the celebrated George Graham, and from 1750 to 1777 he carried on business at Graham's old shop in Fleet Street, at first in partnership with Dutton, another apprentice of Graham. Mudge devoted himself more particularly to the improvement of the marine chronometer. His chronometers were admirable as specimens of fine work and correct proportion of details; but though clearly a man of inventive genius, he unfortunately clung to the principles on which Harrison's timekeeper was constructed, and allowed Earnshaw and Arnold to solve the problem by the introduction of the spring detent escapement.

In 1793 a claim for reward for improvements in chronometers having been made by Mudge and opposed by the Board of Longitude, it was brought by petition before the House of Commons and referred to a Select Committee, who called to their assistance a sub-committee consisting of some of the most celebrated scientists and mechanicians of the day, including Atwood (who wrote a treatise on the isochronism of the balance spring), Ramsden, Troughton, and De Luc. This committee reported favourably on Mudge's claim, declaring it was "admitted on all hands that Mr. Mudge is one of the first watchmakers this country has produced," and thereupon Mudge was awarded £3000. He invented the lever escapement, which he applied to a watch for Queen Charlotte about 1765. He removed to Plymouth in 1771, where he died in 1794.

Lever Escapement. In the drawing (Fig. 54) a tooth of the escape wheel is at rest upon the locking face of the entering left-hand pallet. The impulse pin has just entered the notch of the lever and is about to unlock the pallet. The action of the escapement is as follows: The balance, which is attached to the same staff as the roller, is travelling in the direction indicated by the arrow which is around the roller, with sufficient energy to cause the impulse pin to move the lever and pallets far enough to release the wheel tooth from the locking face and allow it to enter on the impulse face of the pallet. Directly it is at liberty, the escape wheel, actuated by the mainspring of the watch, moves round the same way as the arrow and pushes the pallet out of its path. By the time the wheel tooth has got to the end of the impulse face of the pallet its motion is arrested by the exit or right-hand pallet, the locking face of which has been brought into position to receive another tooth of the wheel. When the pallet was pushed aside by the wheel tooth it carried with it the lever, which in its turn communicated a sufficient blow to the impulse pin to send the balance with renewed energy on its vibration. So that

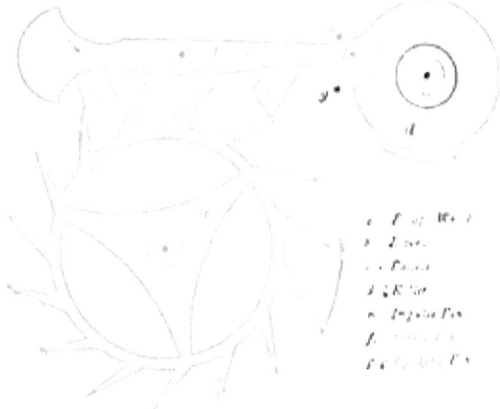

Fig. 54.—Lever Escapement.

the impulse pin has the double office of unlocking the pallets by giving a blow on one side of the notch of the lever and of immediately receiving a blow from the opposite side of the notch. The balance proceeds on its excursion, winding up as it goes the balance spring, until its energy is expended. After it is brought to a state of rest its motion is reversed by the uncoiling of the balance spring, the impulse pin again enters the notch of the lever, but from the opposite direction, and the operation already described is repeated. The object of the safety pin is to prevent the pallets leaving the escape wheel except when the impulse pin is in the notch of the lever.

The banking pins keep the motion of the lever within the desired limits.

Sometimes the escapement is planned so that the centre of the wheel, the centre of the pallets, and the centre of the roller are all in a line. Other variations in the construction and alterations of details are made at the judgment of the manufacturer, but the principle remains unchanged.

Perhaps the most remarkable episode in connection with the construction of timekeepers is that the lever escapement, which has proved to be the best for pocket watches, was, after trial, discarded by Mudge, who spent years afterwards in futile endeavours to improve the verge and the cylinder. In 1794 Peter Litherland patented a "rack lever," on which principle considerable numbers of watches were made at Liverpool. But Mudge's original conception was superior to the rack arrangement, and it was eventually reintroduced by the efforts of George Savage and others in the beginning of the present century. The engraving shows the lever escapement in its modern form.

Christopher Pinchbeck. Christopher Pinchbeck, who in 1721 lived at St. George's Court, Clerkenwell, on the spot now occupied by Albion Place, was not only a celebrated maker of clocks and musical automata, but the inventor of a metal named after himself, of which many watch cases and various ornaments were wrought. He is said to have exhibited a collection of his horological and musical instruments in a booth at Bartholomew Fair. The "Pinchbeck" metal was an alloy of silver and copper. Edward Pinchbeck, the son of Christopher, appears, from an advertisement in the *Daily Post* of July 9, 1733, to be then carrying on business at the "Musical Clock in Fleet Street."

Alexander Cumming. Alexander Cumming, who was born at Edinburgh about 1732, and died at Pentonville in 1814, was the author of an excellent treatise on clockwork, which was published in 1766. He kept a shop in Leadenhall Street, and was justly esteemed for the excellence of his work. Among the fine and curious clocks at Buckingham Palace is one Cumming made for George III., which registers the height of the barometer every day throughout the year. He had £2000 for the clock, and £200 a year for looking after it.

J. Le Roy. Julien Le Roy, a scientific French watchmaker, who was born 1686, and died 1759. He improved on Quare's repeating watch by introducing the "all or nothing" piece, which prevented the striking from beginning till the rack was pushed home to the snail, and this ensured correctness in the number of blows struck.

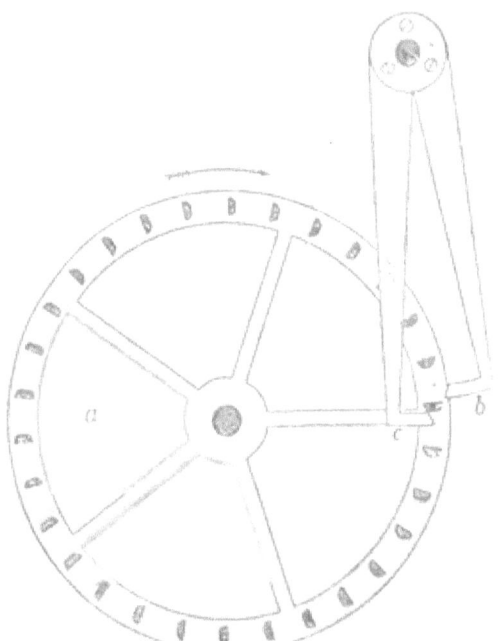

Fig. 55.—Pin-wheel escapement.
a, Escape wheel; *b* and *c*, pallets.

J. A. Lepaute. J. A. Lepaute, born 1709, died 1789. He was a French clockmaker, and the inventor of the pin-wheel escapement, a modification of the Graham, much favoured for turret clocks, till the advent of Denison's double three-legged gravity. Lepaute constructed several fine turret clocks, including that at the Hotel de Ville, and clocks for the Louvre at Paris, wound by means of an air current and fan, a method reinvented recently.

The pin-wheel escapement is shown in Fig. 55. The pressure of the pins on both pallets is downwards, and therefore the shake in the pallet staff hole does not affect the action of the escapement. The chief objection to it practically is the difficulty of keeping the pins lubricated, the oil being drawn away to the face of the wheel. To prevent this a nick is sometimes cut round the pins, close to the wheel, but this weakens the pins very much. Lepaute made the pins semicircular, and placed alternately on each side of the wheel so as to get the pallets of the same length. This requires double the number of pins, and there is no real disadvantage in having one pallet a little longer than the other, provided the short one is put outside, as shown in the drawing. Sir Edmund Beckett introduced the practice of cutting a piece off the bottoms of the pins, which is a distinct improvement, for if the pallet has to travel past the centre of the pin with a given arc of vibration before the pin can rest, the pallets must be very long unless very small pins are used.

P. Le Roy. Pierre Le Roy, son of Julien Le Roy, born 1717, died 1785, surpassed his father in inventive genius. Among his conceptions was a form of duplex escapement and an escapement on which the present chronometer escapement is founded. He also invented a compensation balance formed of tubes containing mercury.

Thiout l'Ainé. Thiout l'Ainé, a clever French watchmaker. Inventor of many ingenious forms of repeating work, curious clocks, etc., described in his "Traité d'Horlogerie," published 1741.

AND OTHER TIMEKEEPERS.

James Ferguson. James Ferguson, a master astronomer and mechanician, who was born in 1710, and died in 1776, designed many curious timekeepers. His astronomical clock is illustrated on pp. 167 and 168. The clock by him, which is shown in Fig. 56, contains **Clock with only Two Pinions.** only three wheels and two pinions. The hours are engraved on a plate, fitting friction-tight on the great wheel arbor; the minute hand is attached to the centre wheel arbor, and a thin

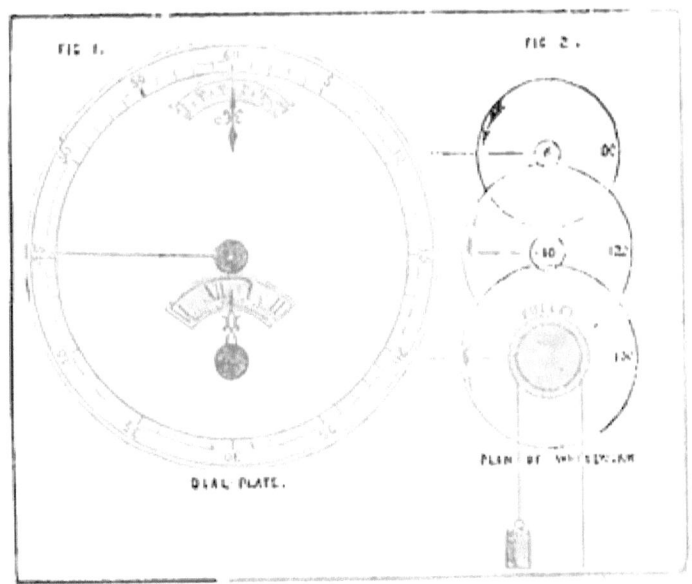

Fig. 56.

plate divided into 240 equal parts is fitted on the escape wheel arbor, and shows the seconds through a slit in the dial. The clock has a seconds pendulum. The number of teeth in the escape wheel is higher than is desirable, and the weight of the thin plate or ring in the escape wheel arbor is objectionable, though it might now be made of aluminium, vulcanite, or other very light material.

Peculiar Personality.   Ferguson, who rose from the position of a shepherd lad by dint of natural ability added to dogged industry and perseverance, lived in Fleet Street for some years, and travelled about the country giving lectures on astronomy and mechanics. As he passed along the streets he was singularly oblivious to all surroundings, and taking a walk one evening with his only daughter on his arm, when he returned home he did not notice in his abstraction that she was absent, nor could he remember where they parted, nor did he for years learn what had become of her. He was a widower, and as a matter of fact she had eloped, finding nothing congenial in the dry studies or unsympathetic home of her father.

Ferguson's Paradox.   Ferguson, in a letter to the Rev. Mr. Cooper, of Glass, in Banffshire, related how that one evening, being at a club held at a tavern in Fleet Street, he was so disgusted with the blatant pertinacity with which a watchmaker among the company denied the possibility of the Trinity, that he requested permission to put to him a question more nearly related to his own trade. Ferguson then asked if the watchmaker would believe in the Trinity if he could see three thin wheels all gearing with one thick one, and of the three thin wheels one should turn to the right, one should turn to the left, and one remain stationary. As the watchmaker derided this proposition also, Ferguson promised to bring a model of such a device in a week's time, and forthwith constructed what is known as Ferguson's paradox, which does certainly comply with these conditions. Ferguson says he kept the model for many years, and no one succeeded in finding out how it was done, and then he adopted the principle of it for showing the motion of the sun and moon in an orrery. The secret of the paradox is really this. The thin stationary wheel is fixed to an arbor, on which the other two thin wheels ride loosely. Whatever number of teeth there were in the stationary wheel, one of the other thin ones had one tooth more and the other one tooth less, although all three were of the same diameter. It will thus be seen that the teeth were a little out of pitch, and as the stationary wheel acting as a driver caused the thick wheel to revolve like a planet round the three thin ones, it continually pushed one of the loose wheels forward and drew the other back a bit in order to get the spaces in a line with its own teeth.

Simple Moon Train. The action will be understood by examining the engraving, Fig. 57. Here the thick wheel with fifty-seven teeth turns once in twenty-four hours, as does also the sun hand with the same

Fig. 57.

number of teeth, while the moon hand, having two extra teeth, loses a little each rotation, its divergence amounting to a complete revolution in a lunation nearly. By adding a pair of mitre wheels, as in Fig. 58, the rotation of the moon might also be indicated.

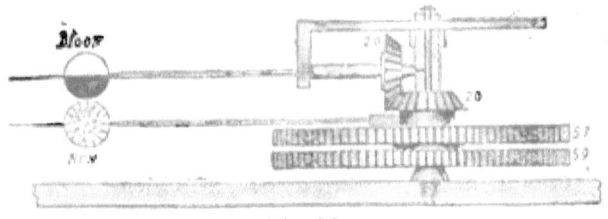

Fig. 58.

Ferdinand Berthoud. Ferdinand Berthoud, who was born 1745, and died 1807, was an eminent French watchmaker, author of "Essai sur l'Horlogerie,"

"Traité des Horloges Marines," "Histoire de la Mesure du Temps," and other works, containing a mass of useful information concerning the history, theory, and practice of the horological art, dealing with Harrison's, Sully's, and Le Roy's inventions; and, indeed, everything known in Berthoud's time.

A. L. Bréguet. Abraham Louis Bréguet, born 1747, died 1823, a French watchmaker of rare attainments and inventive power. His name is best known in connection with English horology by the balance spring used in fine watches. The outer coil of the volute, instead of being at once attached to the stud, is lifted above the plane of the spring and carried by a bold curve towards the centre.

Caron, *alias* Beaumarchais. Among the French horologists of the eighteenth century, mention must be made of Pierre Auguste Caron, who was a clever watchmaker. In 1752, when he was only twenty-two years of age, he made a keyless watch for Madame de Pompadour, which gained him a prize from the Academy of Sciences, and led to his introduction to the court, where he became a favourite of Louis XV. This is his description of the watch. "It is in a ring, and is only four lignes in diameter and two-thirds of a ligne in height between the plates. To render this ring more commodious, I have contrived, instead of a key, a circle round the dial, carrying a little projecting hook. By drawing this hook with the nail two-thirds round the dial, the ring is rewound, and it goes for thirty hours." Caron was an accomplished musician, and is well known under the name of Beaumarchais, as the composer of Le Barbier de Seville and Le Mariage de Figaro. He dropped the profession of watchmaking with his patronymic, and it is related that when at Versailles a nobleman, wishing to humiliate him by reminding him of his former calling, loudly asked him to see what was amiss with a watch which his tormentor produced. In vain Beaumarchais protested that his hand had lost its cunning. The nobleman insisted on the examination, and passed the timekeeper to the ex-watchmaker for the purpose. It had hardly reached the hand of Beaumarchais before he dropped it on the marble floor and smashed it, when he turned away with the remark, "You see, I know my awkwardness better than you your man."

Matthew Stogdon.
Matthew Stogdon was the inventor of the half-quarter repeating mechanism. He died in abject poverty, about 1770, at an advanced age.

John Arnold.
John Arnold, who was born in Cornwall in 1744, and died at Well Hall, near Eltham, Kent, in 1799, devised and patented in 1775 a chronometer escapement very closely resembling the one now in use. He also invented the helical form of balance spring now used in all marine chronometers, and a compensation balance. The reason the helical spring is preferred for chronometers is that it allows both ends to be taken in towards the centre by a bold curve which can be readily altered in character to ensure the concentricity of the spring, or to vary its controlling power. There would not be room in a watch for a helix of many turns, and therefore the volute is retained for pocket timekeepers.

It is but just to say that both Arnold and Earnshaw appear to have almost simultaneously hit upon almost the same form of escapement and balance. Arnold carried on business at 84, Strand, and was succeeded by his son, John R. Arnold, who was joined in partnership by E. J. Dent.

Thomas Earnshaw.
Thomas Earnshaw, who shares with Arnold the honour of inventing the escapement and compensation balance, both substantially as applied to the marine chronometer of to-day, was born at

Ashton-under-Lyne, in 1749, and carried on business in Holborn, near the turning now called Southampton Row. The chief points in which Earnshaw's escapement differed from Arnold's were the form of the wheel teeth and the direction in which the detent was moved to unlock, and in both of these particulars Earnshaw's design is adopted in the modern escapement. He died at Chenies Street, Bedford Square, in 1829.

Both Arnold and Earnshaw applied to the Board of Longitude for recognition of their improvements in timekeepers. Sir Joseph Banks warmly espoused the cause of

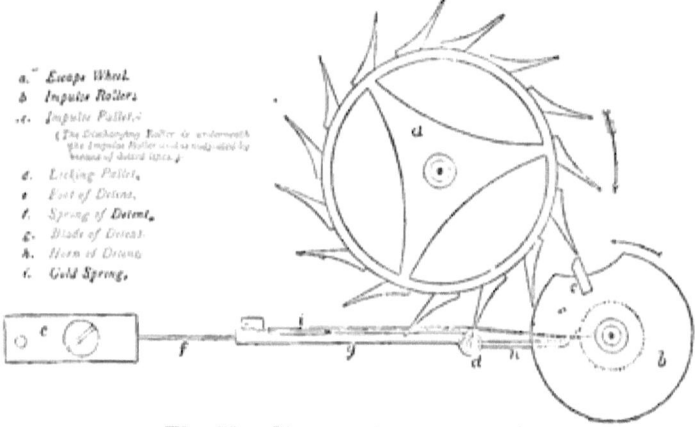

Fig. 59.—Chronometer escapement.

Arnold, and Dr. Maskelyne supported the claim of Earnshaw. Eventually each of the claimants was awarded £3000.

The Chronometer Escapement. The Spring-detent or Chronometer Escapement, which is unexcelled for timekeeping, is represented in Fig. 59. A tooth of the escape wheel is at rest on the locking pallet. The office of the discharging pallet is to bend the detent so as to allow this tooth to escape. The discharging pallet does not press directly on the detent, but on the free end of the gold spring, which in its turn presses on the tip of the horn of the detent. The balance, fixed to the same staff as the rollers, travels in the direction of the arrow around the rollers, with sufficient energy to unlock the tooth of the wheel which is held by the locking pallet. Directly the detent is released by the discharging pallet it springs back to its original position, ready to receive the next tooth of the wheel. There is a set screw to regulate the amount of the locking on which the pipe of the detent butts. This prevents the locking pallet being drawn further into the wheel. It is omitted in the drawing, to allow the locking to be clearly seen. It will be observed that the impulse roller is planted so as to intersect the path of the escape wheel teeth as much as possible, and by the time the unlocking is completed the impulse pallet will have passed far enough in front of the escape wheel tooth to afford it a safe hold. The escape wheel, impelled by the mainspring in the direction of the arrow, overtakes the impulse pallet and drives it on until the contact between them ceases by the divergence of their paths. The wheel is at once brought to rest by the locking pallet, and the balance continues its excursion, winding up the balance spring as it goes, until its energy is exhausted. After the balance is brought to rest, it is started in its return vibration by the effort of the balance spring to return to its state of rest. You will notice that the nose of the detent does not reach to the end of the gold spring, so that the discharging pallet in this return vibration merely bends the gold spring without affecting the locking pallet at all. When the discharging pallet reaches the gold spring the balance spring is at rest; but the balance does not stop, it continues to uncoil the balance spring until its momentum is exhausted, and then the effort of the balance spring to revert to its normal state induces another vibration; the wheel is again unlocked and gives the impulse pallet another blow. Although the balance only gets impulse in one direction, the escape wheel makes a rotation in just the same time as with a lever escapement, because in the chronometer the space of a whole tooth passes every time the wheel is unlocked. By receiving impulse and having to unlock at every other vibration only, the balance is more highly detached in the chronometer than in most escapements, which is a distinct advantage. No oil is required to the pallets, and another disturbing influence is thus got rid of. If properly proportioned and well made, its performance will be quite satisfactory as long as it is not subjected to sudden external motion or jerks. For marine chronometers it thus leaves but little to be desired, and even for pocket watches it does well with a careful wearer, but with rough usage it is liable to set, and many watchmakers hesitate to recommend it on this account. It is much more costly than the lever, and would only be applied to very high-priced watches, and in these the buyer naturally resents any failure of action. Its use in pocket pieces is therefore nearly confined to such as are used for scientific purposes, or by people who understand the nature of the escapement, and are prepared to exercise care in wearing the watch. There is another reason why watchmakers, as a rule, do not take kindly to the chronometer escapement for pocket work. After the escapement is taken apart, the watch does not so surely yield as good a performance as before. In fact, it is more delicate than the lever.

E. J. Dent, who carried on business in the Strand, at first in partnership with J. R. Arnold, and best known as the maker of the Westminster clock, was born in 1790, and died in 1853.

Benjamin L. Vulliamy. Benjamin Lewis Vulliamy, who was born in 1780, and died in 1855, succeeded his father as a watch and clock-maker in Pall Mall, and established a high reputation for the excellence of his work. He was the maker of the large clock at the General Post Office, and published a pamphlet on the construction of the dead-beat escapement for clocks, besides other small technical works. His son was for many years architect to the Board of Works.

Charles Frodsham. Charles Frodsham, who was born in 1810 and died in 1871, was a skilful and successful watchmaker, who succeeded J. R. Arnold in the Strand. He conducted many experiments with a view of elucidating the principles underlying the action of the compensation balance and the balance spring.

Grandfathers' Clocks. Long-case or "Grandfathers'" clocks, so common in the halls and kitchens of country houses during the last century, are a development of the very earliest form of chamber clock in general use. There is an excellent representation of the movement of one in the biographical note of Tompion, on p. 121, but that is hardly the oldest pattern, which, it is conjectured, was introduced even before the pendulum was adopted as a controller. At first the hour circle was narrow, with stumpy figures, and the frets round the bell at top usually had a shield for the crest or initials of the owner. About 1665 came the Tompion pattern with wider band, having bold numerals, and the frets round the bell with crossed dolphins, as shown. Sometimes the movement was simply placed on a bracket, with the pendulum and weights hanging below; but for the more wealthy people the movement was enclosed in a case, with a trunk to conceal the weights.

About 1680 the long or "royal" pendulum, hung from a cock by means of a shackle, and connected with the verge by a crutch, came into use, and with it the veritable long-case eight-day clock. The early cases had but very narrow waists, through the sides of which vertical slits were cut, so that the pendulum "bobbed" in and out. They were on this account often called bob pendulums.

The dials of these long-case clocks were square, but "chamber" clocks, with the annular form of dial, continued to be made for many years, though in the later ones the dial was enlarged, and often projected two or three inches on each side of the frame. These are now known among collectors as "sheeps' head" clocks. A great number of them were produced in the latter part of the reign of William III. and in the time of Queen Anne, and are still to be met with in the country, with a wooden hood as a protection from dust.

The "bob" pendulum variety of long case speedily gave place to others with wider waists. Sometimes a "bullseye" of glass was let into the door opposite the pendulum bob, the bob presenting a peculiar appearance, being magnified and distorted when viewed through the glass. The cases were frequently covered with marquetric work, most likely executed by Dutch workmen, many of whom were settled in London at the end of the seventeenth century. The corners of the earliest dials had gilt ornaments, consisting of the heads of cherubs or angels, and at the front angles of the hood were corkscrew pillars. The latter feature, though, can hardly be taken as a distinguishing mark of the period, for it was continued for many years, and is often seen in specimens produced during the reign of Queen Anne. The cherub-head dial corners were succeeded by more elaborate ornaments, such as two cupids supporting a crown in the midst of scroll work, and a crown with crossed sceptres and foliage. In the early part of the eighteenth century came the arch over the dial, a most becoming addition, which speedily became popular, and was utilized in a variety of ways. Besides representations of a ship tossing upon the billows, and other fanciful movements, the phases of the moon were occasionally exhibited in a pictorial way. This was done by means of a disc, which rotated once in two lunations, and had two representations of a full moon painted on it, as will be shown further on when a perpetual calendar is described. Simple calendar work for showing through slits in the dial the day of the week, the day of the month, and the name of the month, was often added to these clocks. A good form of this mechanism is shown in Fig. 60.

Calendar Work. Gearing with the hour wheel is a wheel having twice its number of teeth, and turning therefore once in twenty-four hours. A three-armed lever is planted just above this wheel; the lower

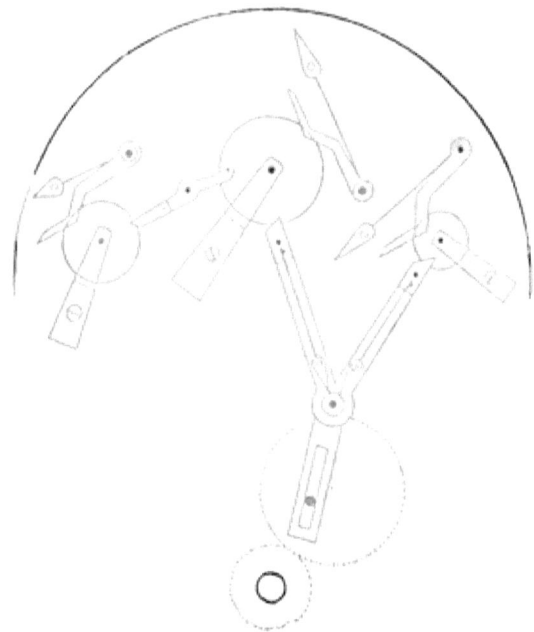

Fig. 60.—Simple calendar work.

arm is slotted and the wheel carries a pin which works in this slot so that the lever vibrates to and fro once every twenty-four hours. The three upper circles in the drawing represent three star wheels. The one to the right has seven teeth corresponding to the days of the week; the centre one has thirty-one teeth for the days of the month; and the left hand one has twelve teeth for the months of the year. Every time the upper arms of the lever vibrate to the left they move forward the day of the week and day of the month wheels each one tooth. The extremities of the levers are jointed so as to yield on the return vibration and are brought into position again by a weak spring as shown. There is a pin in the day of the month wheel which, by pressing on a lever once every revolution, actuates the month of the year wheel. This last lever is also jointed and is pressed on by a spring so as to return to its original position. Each of the star wheels has a click or jumper kept in contact by means of a spring.

For months with less than thirty-one days the day of the month ring had to be shifted forward by hand.

Attached to a long-case clock made in the seventeenth century was the following :—

> "Here I stand both day and night,
> To tell the hours with all my might;
> Do you example take by me,
> And serve thy God as I serve thee."

These lines, with slight variations, have been reproduced for several timekeepers of a later date.

Some of the earliest, and many of the eighteenth-century long-case clocks bore the inscription, *Tempus Fugit*. A story is told to the effect that an auctioneer in a provincial town, descanting on the merits of a household treasure he was submitting for sale, remarked, "This clock is not the production of an unknown man, gentlemen, but is one of the best examples of that eminent maker Thomas Fuggit"!

Legislative Enactments relating to Horology.

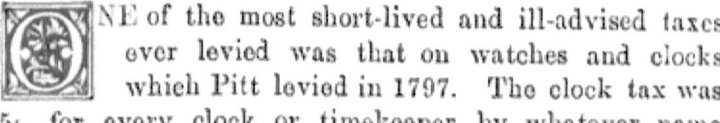NE of the most short-lived and ill-advised taxes ever levied was that on watches and clocks which Pitt levied in 1797. The clock tax was 5s. for every clock or timekeeper, by whatever name called and used in or upon any dwelling-house.

Tax on Watch and Clock Owners.
The watch tax was (1) for every gold watch, watch enamelled on gold, or other gold timekeeper worn or used, by any person, 10s.; and (2) for every silver or metal watch, 2s. 6d.

The tax was secured by elaborate provisions, and was charged, after the method of the assessed taxes, in respect of the greatest number of clocks and watches used in the year ending April 5th.

As may be supposed, this impost was strenuously resisted, not only by those on whom the tax was levied, but by the watch and clockmakers, who saw that the extent of their business would be seriously affected; and so it turned out, for the demand for timekeepers at once fell off to such an extent that thousands of people were thrown out of employment. So much pressure was brought to bear on the Government, that the tax was repealed in April, 1798, having existed but for one year, the amount realized from it being £48,820. In *Notes and Queries*, a few years ago, was a note in which the writer mentioned that he had met with a receipt on a printed form for half a year's taxes due from a small farmer in Essex, in which occurred the item, "For clocks and watches, 5s. 7½d." The receipt was dated April 10, 1798, the month in which the tax was removed.

Act of Parliament Clocks.
"It's an ill wind that blows no good," and, paralyzed as the horological trades were generally during the short life of this Act, there was a crumb of comfort, for the publicans, with that unity of action which is still their characteristic, began with one accord to fix in their taprooms a clock *pro bono publico*. These clocks were mural timepieces, most of them of a similar pattern, having a very large black painted wood dial without a covering glass, gilt numerals, and a long trunk to allow of a second pendulum. A few of the "Act of Parliament" clocks, as they were called, are still to be seen in old City taverns.

As a result of the inquiry which led to the repeal of the tax on watches and clocks, watch cases were exempted from the incidence of the plate duty, which though originally a war tax imposed in 1719, continued in operation till 1890.

Merchandise Marks Act. The horological trades were comparatively unfettered by the legislature in recent years till 1887, when the Merchandise Marks Act ordained that watches should bear some indication of their place of origin. This was to put a stop to fraudulent misrepresentation, which some unprincipled traders had been guilty of; and, so far, the object was a laudable one. But compliance with the Act has been in many instances inconvenient and difficult, because a watch is not a natural growth which must have been produced in some particular place. In some varieties of watches, many of the parts are either not made in England at all or else at a price far beyond that demanded by some of the specialists in Savoy or the mountains of the Jura, where whole families are engaged in agricultural pursuits in the summer, and in the production of certain pieces of watchwork during the winter. So that whereas formerly manufacturers of enterprise and judgment could with advantage select his material from the markets of the world, he must now confine himself to one country for the whole of one watch, and the consequence is that for many of the grades where formerly the English worker obtained a share of the work, the exigencies of trade now compel the manufacturer to depend wholly on the cheaper labour of Switzerland, although there are many parts for which he would prefer to employ native artificers were he free to do so. Of course, for the highest class of plain watches, England is still able to compete with the world, and is in fact supreme; but for chronographs, repeaters, and other complicated mechanism, even of the highest class, the lower wages paid in Switzerland is found to be a serious obstacle.

The London Chamber of Commerce has recently considered the possibility of obtaining some relaxation of the Merchandise Marks Act, so far as it relates to watches; but the legislature is always averse to altering an Act if it can be avoided, and so I think we shall have to be content with the law as it stands, and conform to it as best we may.

Personal Associations.

Charles V. of Germany.  CHARLES V., Emperor of Germany, had a genuine admiration for horology. He gave every encouragement to the production of portable timepieces, which was then a new art, and spent much time in examining the principle on which they were constructed. Judging by the splendid collection of timepieces and other scientific instruments which he left, he was not wanting in discrimination, but the only reward he obtained in his investigations and devotion was that people declared he was mad. Disgusted with the world, he retired to the monastery of St. Juste, and it is related that he was at great pains to keep his watches and clocks all going to time; but, as may be imagined, considering the state of the art in the sixteenth century, his efforts were not crowned with perfect success. A visitor having by accident overturned the table on which his horologes were supported, the monarch with a sigh of relief remarked, "Well, I have for years endeavoured to make them all go together without succeeding, but you have managed it in a moment."

Henry VIII. Henry VIII. of England spent a lot of money on the acquisition of horological devices, but his interest appears to have been merely a fashionable hankering after something new and curious.

Queen Elizabeth. Although Queen Elizabeth owned so many timekeepers, it would be a stretch of language to call her passion for the jewelled gew-gaws and other costly accessories of the primitive mechanism a love of horology.

George III. George III. had a fancy for dabbling in scientific pursuits, and the Kew observatory, in the Old Deer Park at Richmond, was built for him and gave some encouragement to horologists. Cumming and other artists received from him many marks of royal appreciation.

Leopold and Princess Charlotte. It is related of Leopold, husband of the amiable Princess Charlotte, daughter of George IV., that when, after the death of his first wife, he became King of Belgium, and married Louise, daughter of the King of France, he had a watch specially made so that he could form the space between the case and movement into a kind of reliquary in memory of the departed Charlotte. In this he placed her miniature, a small painting on ivory of her tomb, a lock of her hair, and a chip of the coffin in which she and her dead child lay. His frequent and long contemplation of his watch did not escape the notice of his wife, who also observed that whenever she approached her husband at these times he abruptly closed his timekeeper and returned it to his pocket. During one of Leopold's illnesses she obtained possession of the watch, and by perseverance found the secret spring which held the cover close. Like many others who give way to curiosity, she suffered much misery from her discovery, for on acquainting Leopold with her knowledge, he in great anger upbraided her for meddling with the souvenirs he held sacred, refused to be nursed by her, and when he recovered told her she had estranged herself from him for ever by her impertinent prying. Though the pair were afterwards cordial, no real reconciliation ever took place. The queen, when dying in 1851, said that from the day she forced the secret spring of the watch she always felt as though the corpse of the Princess Charlotte lay between herself and Leopold. In sign of her too demonstrative jealousy she called her eldest daughter, the now insane ex-Empress of Mexico, Charlotte, after the first wife of Leopold.

Jerome Buonaparte. A somewhat similar anecdote is told of Jerome Buonaparte, King of Westphalia, who secreted in his watch a portrait of Elizabeth Patterson, whom he had secretly married, but whom his uncle compelled him to abandon in order to wed his queen Catherine. The finding of the likeness by Catherine and subsequent explanations did not increase the happiness of the royal lady, or improve her relations with her lord.

Duke of Sussex. The Duke of Sussex, one of the sons of George III., took a keen and constant interest in all that pertained to horology, and possessed a fine collection of clocks and watches.

Prince of Wales. His Royal Highness, the Prince of Wales, though he cannot be said to deeply investigate the science of horology, is a stickler for punctuality, and insists upon an abundance of timekeepers throughout his establishments.

Marquess of Worcester. That versatile genius, Edward, Marquess of Worcester, who is credited with having invented the steam-engine, gave some attention to horology, and in 1661 was granted a patent " to make a watch or clock without stringe or chaine, or any other kind of winding up, but what of necessity must follow if the owner or keeper of the said watch or clocke will

M

know the houre of day or night, and yett if hee lay it aside severall dayes and weeke without looking or medling with it, it shall goe very well, and as justly as most watches that ever were made." This is supposed to have been the inclined-plane clock ascribed to Grollier, illustrated on page 107.

Sir Isaac Newton. Sir Isaac Newton investigated the action of the pendulum, and demonstrated the law governing its time of vibration. He had several clocks constructed under his direction. In 1708 he presented to Dr. Bentley, the Master of Trinity College, Cambridge, a clock for the observatory over the great gateway. This clock now stands on the staircase at the master's lodge, but has had a metal tubular compensated pendulum substituted for the original one, which had a wood rod and a heavy iron bob.

The Royal Society have a gold watch presented to Sir Isaac by Mrs. Conduit. The chasing on the outer case is well executed, and represents Britannia pointing to a medallion on which is shown a bust of the philosopher.

Voltaire. Voltaire's reputation is certainly not dependent upon his association with mechanism, but he thoroughly appreciated the details of timekeepers, and took an active part in the establishment of a watch manufactory at the little village of Ferney, situated about a league from Geneva, but on French soil. In a letter to a friend he says, "At my place here better watches are made than in Geneva are produced, and the Sieur Lepine, the king's watchmaker, has his establishment and workmen among us. We manufacture for Paris and for Bengal. Send me your orders, and you shall be supplied; you shall have very fine watches and very indifferent verses whenever you please to send for them." After the death of Voltaire the factory fell away in a few years. Its numerous and clever staff were dispersed to Geneva, Locle, Neuchatel, and Chaux de Fonds, to the great benefit of these localities.

In another communication Voltaire propounded the following riddle: "What is the longest, and yet the shortest thing in the world; the swiftest, and the most slow; the most divisible and the most extended; the least valued and the most regretted; without which nothing can be done; which devours everything, however small, and yet gives life and spirit to everything, however great? Answer—TIME."

Paley's Admiration for a Watch. Paley, in his treatise on "Natural Theology," selected a watch as the product of human skill which most embodied design and contrivance, and contrasted it with a stone, as a body seemingly without structure or definite form; though it must be confessed that if since his time the watch has advanced far towards perfection, mineralogy and geology have given meaning to what was then uninterpreted in the mineral world.

Nelson's Watch. In the museum of Greenwich Hospital is preserved the watch worn by Nelson when he received his death wound at the battle of Trafalgar. It is plainly cased in gold, and has a chronometer escapement. A modest verge, in a battered silver case, which accompanied him in many of his earlier voyages, is also preserved.

Napoleon Buonaparte. Napoleon Buonaparte had a watch which was wound by the action of the wearer in walking. Watches of this kind have been many times reinvented, and the mechanism also used for a pedometer, or step-counter, to register the distance walked. The principle of the pedometer watch will be understood from Fig. 61. There is a weighted lever, G, kept in its normal position by a long curved spring, so

Self-winding Watch. weak that the ordinary motion of the body in walking causes the lever to fall; the spring then returns it, and so an oscillating motion is kept up. The lever carries a pawl (*a*), which engages with the fine teeth of a ratchet wheel and turns it. Through other toothed wheels the ratchet wheel is connected with the mainspring, so that the spring is

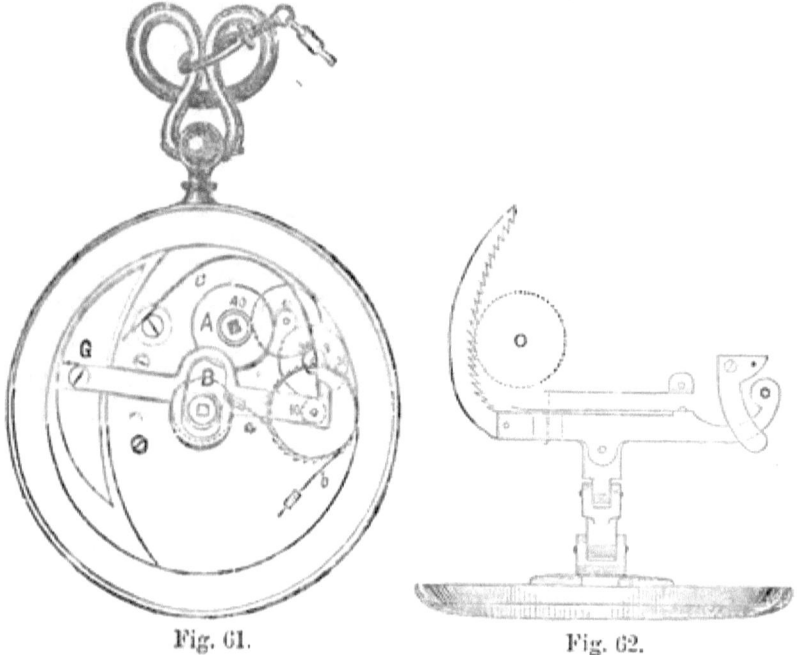

Fig. 61.   Fig. 62.

slightly wound at every step taken by the wearer of the watch.

Another Self-winding Watch. Among other devices for self-winding may be mentioned one applicable to a hunting watch, and shown in the engraving, Fig. 62. Every time the hunting cover is closed the scythe-shaped lever, which is attached to the hinge of the hunting cover, moves a little way round a wheel fixed to the mainspring arbor. If the hunting cover is opened and closed after the spring is fully wound, the spring slips round in the barrel.

Duke of Wellington. The great Duke of Wellington was extremely fond of watches, and liked to have at least half a dozen within reach. Fearing some ill might befall those just under his eye, orders were given, whenever the great man travelled, to have as many more stored away in a portmanteau made to fit his carriage. One timepiece was above all others his acknowledged favourite; it was of old-fashioned English construction, and had once been the property of Tippo Sahib.

The duke generally wore a touch watch, by which he could ascertain the hour when he merely seemed to be "just fumbling in his pocket."

Charles Dickens. Charles Dickens's marvellous power of imagination led him to regard a timekeeper almost as a sentient being, and he often declared that the ticking of a favourite clock was to him as the voice of a companion and a friend.

He never pretended to understand horological mechanism, and the absurd description Montague Tigg gives of Martin Chuzzlewit's watch must not be taken seriously; at the same time, it answers perfectly well as a voluble adventurer's transparent attempt to obtain credit for befriending his acquaintance and gulling the pawnbroker at the same time. In Captain Cuttle's panegyric on his famous timekeeper it is noticeable that there is a skilful avoidance of all reference to the construction of the watch, the old mariner contenting himself with recounting the slight bi-diurnal adjustments needed to establish its character as "a watch that'll do you credit."

Even into the most prosaic affairs of everyday life Dickens managed to introduce his quaint and inimitable humour in his own peculiar way, as is shown by the following characteristic note received from him:—

"MY DEAR SIR,

"Since my hall clock was sent to your establishment to be cleaned it has gone (as, indeed, it always had) perfectly well, but has struck the hours with great reluctance, and after enduring internal agonies of a most distressing nature, it has now ceased striking altogether. Though a happy release for the clock, this is not convenient to the household. If you can send down any confidential person with whom the clock can confer, I think it may have something on its works that it would be glad to make a clean breast of.

"Faithfully yours,
"CHARLES DICKENS."

Watch-wearers. As a rule, clergymen, doctors, engineers, military men, and sailors are considerate and gentle with timekeepers; while poets, actors, and painters are often distressingly careless of their watches.

Hooke and Mudge. It is curious that, of two great lights connected with horology, one, Dr. Hooke, should have been intended for a painter, a profession he abandoned because he disliked the odours inseparable from the oil and other materials used by artists; and the other, Thomas Mudge, had a passion for painting, and longed to follow the footsteps of Sir Joshua Reynolds, with whom he had more than a passing acquaintance.

Ferguson's Astronomical Clock. Formerly clocks to show the motions of the heavenly bodies were much prized, and, as a horological curiosity, the astronomical clock by James Ferguson, which is shown in Figs. 63 and 64, will doubtless be of interest. Fig. 63 is the dial, which is made up of four pieces: (1) The outer ring, divided into the twenty-four hours of a day and night, and each hour subdivided into twelve, so that each subdivision represents five minutes of time. (2) The age-of-the-moon ring, lying in the same plane as the hour ring, is divided into 29·5 equal parts, and carries a fleur-de-lis to point out the time on the hour circle. A wire, A, continued from the fleur-de-lis supports the sun, S. (3) Within, and a little below, is a plate, on the outer edge of which are the months and days of the year; further in is a circle containing the signs and degrees of the ecliptic. Further in, on the same plate, the ecliptic, equinoctial, and tropics

Fig. 63.—Ferguson's astronomical clock.

are laid down, as well as all the stars of the first, second, and third magnitude, according to their right ascension and declination, those of the first magnitude being distinguished by eight points, the second by six, and the third by five. (4) Over the middle of this plate, and a little above it, is a fixed plate, E, to represent the earth, around which the sun moves in 24 hours 50·5 minutes, and the stars in 23 hours 56 minutes 4·1 seconds. The ellipse, H, which is drawn with a diamond on the glass that covers the dial, represents the horizon of the place the clock is to serve, and across this horizon is a straight line, even with the XII.'s, to represent the meridian. All the stars seen within this ellipse are above the horizon at that time. Fig. 64 shows the astronomical train, which is

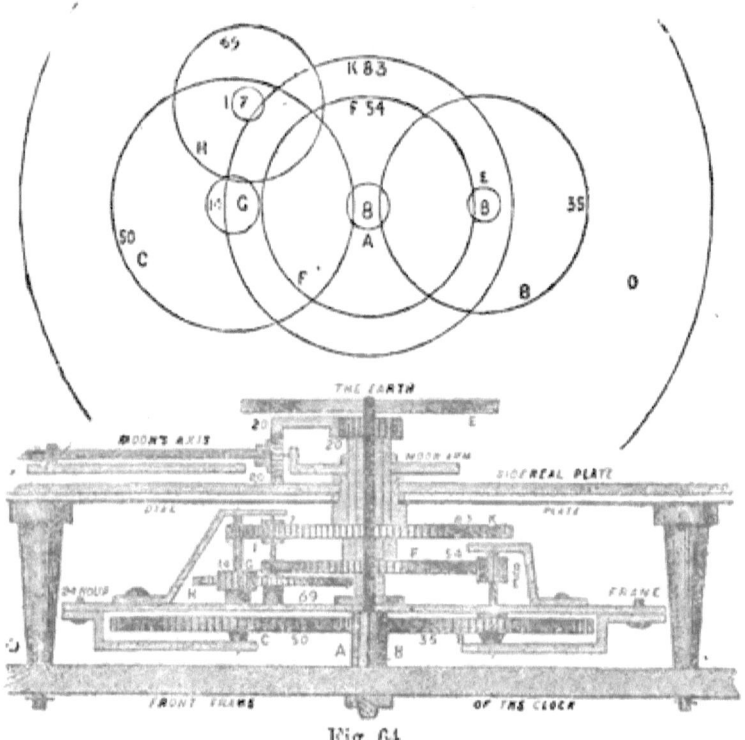

Fig. 64.

between the front plate of the clock and the dial. The earth, E, is stationary, and is supported by a stalk fixed to the front plate. The hollow axis of the frame that turns once in 24 hours works on this stalk. Fixed to the stationary stalk is a pinion of 8, A, which gears with a wheel of 35, B, and with a wheel of 50, C. On the top of the axis of B is a pinion of 8, E, which turns a wheel of 54, F, running on the pipe of the 24-hour frame, and carrying the moon round by the wire, B, in Fig. 63. This wire has a support fitted to the arbor of E. On the top of the pipe of the 24-hour frame is a wheel of 20, gearing with a wheel of 20, having two sets of teeth, one on the edge and the other on the face. It is pivoted to the moon wire support, and the face teeth gear with another wheel of 20 that carries the moon wire. On the axis of C is a pinion of 14, B, that turns a wheel of 69, H, on whose axis is a pinion of 7, I, turning a wheel of 83, K. This wheel is pinned to the sidereal plate of the dial. The age-of-the-moon ring is attached by pillars to the 24-hour frame, and turns with it. The moon is represented by a round ball, half black and half white.

Ferguson afterwards devised a simpler arrangement for showing the motion of the moon, which has been already described.

Westminster Abbey. The exterior clock dial at Westminster Abbey is very appropriately made with an hour hand only, and many people fancy the clock is of great antiquity. This is not so; for although the nave and chapels of the Abbey have existed for several centuries, the towers were built by Sir Christopher Wren in 1730. As the towers were to be in keeping with the rest of the building, he did not sanction the introduction of such an anachronism as a minute hand, which at that date was usually applied to clocks.

The clock itself was made by John Smith of St. James's, and possessed no remarkable feature. The movement of it was replaced in 1860 by a modern one.

Large Spring-Clock. There is, however, one horological curiosity which the Abbey possesses, and that is the interior clock in Poet's Corner, which is probably the largest clock in the world driven by springs instead of weights. It strikes "ting-tang" quarters, but not the hour, a peculiarity which many worshippers in the sacred edifice may have remarked. It was formerly a weight clock, and the weights hung down in St. Blaize's Chapel on the other side of the wall against which the dial is fixed. As the weights were found to be inconvenient, it was decided to alter the movement, and drive both the going and the quarter part with springs. The main wheels are eight inches in diameter; the barrels over seven inches in diameter, and the fusees at their superior ends the same size.

St. Paul's Clock and Bells.

FOR more than a century the St. Paul's clock held a recognized place among the sights of London, and till quite recently was an item not to be neglected by those indefatigable and untiring provincial trippers who climb to the top of the Monument, flit from Westminster Abbey to the Tower of London, and generally manage, in one short week, to more completely explore the metropolis than a born cockney finds time to do during the whole course of his life. It is true that the superior proportions of the great clock at the Houses of Parliament have latterly rather detracted from the importance of the City of London timekeeper, still there are many points of interest in the arrangement at St. Paul's that render the "former horological standard of the metropolis" attractive even in presence of its more modern rival.

Old St. Paul's. Dugdale's "History of St. Paul's," speaking of the old Cathedral which was destroyed in the Great Fire of London, says, "I now come to the dial belonging to the clock in this church, of which there was care taken in the 18th Ed. III., that it should be made with all splendour that might be; which was accordingly performed, having the image of an angel pointing at the hour both of the day and night, the charge for which workmanship then amounted to 6 lib."

It is clear by the design of the towers that Wren considered the clock should be a feature of the new building, but the later edition of Dugdale and other histories are silent respecting the timekeeper. Though it is difficult to obtain any precise information as to the circumstances that guided the Commissioners for re-building the Cathedral in selecting a design for their clock, it is probable there was as much squabbling and heartburning over the matter as arose when the question of the Westminster clock was discussed. At one time Tompion was evidently looked upon as the proper man to undertake the work, for in the year 1700 the following notice was published: "Mr. Tompion, the famous watchmaker in Fleet Street, is making a clock for St. Paul's Cathedral, which it is said will go one hundred years without winding up; will cost £3000 or £4000, and be far finer than the famous clock at Strasburg. Whether this represented the intention of the authorities, or whether the paragraph was inserted by Tompion's friends as a feeler, or was merely idle gossip, cannot now be ascertained, but it is certain the threatened extraordinary effort of Tompion, with its tremendous accumulation of driving power, was never put in hand, as four or five years afterwards the production of the timekeeper was entrusted to Langley Bradley,

Langley Bradley.

of Fenchurch Street, who was to be paid £300 for the work. It was fixed in the south-west tower about 1709, and an examination of his clock to-day proves that a more capable man could hardly have been selected.

Frame.

The frame of the St. Paul's clock consists of a cast-iron rectangular base-plate, from which rise cast-iron columns, supporting an entablature of the same metal. The going train occupies the centre of the space between the base and entablature, the wheels being arranged vertically; while the gun-metal bushes for the pivots are carried in wrought-iron straps bolted to the base and entablature. On one side of the going train is the quarter part, and on the other side the hour striking part similarly arranged. All the wheels are of gun-metal, the great wheels being 2 ft. 8 ins. in diameter, 1 in. pitch, and an inch and three-quarters wide.

Escapement. For the original recoil escapement was substituted the present half-dead one in 1805, when, as recorded on a brass plate fixed to the framing, the clock underwent substantial repair; but, with the exception of the escapement, it may be said that the whole of the mechanism is Bradley's. The two-second pendulum has a wooden rod and a cast-iron bob, weighing nearly 180 pounds. The striking work is on the rack principle already described. The mitre-wheels for driving the dial works are commendably large, being twenty inches in diameter; and for supporting the dial end of the minute-hand arbor there are three friction wheels, placed at equal distances apart,

Striking Work.

Dial Work. round the outside of, and carried by, the hour-hand tube. Slits are cut into the tube to allow a portion of the circumference of the friction wheels to enter, and the wheels are of such a size that they project into the tube just sufficient to meet the minute-hand arbor.

Dials. This ingenious contrivance is also applied to the Westminster clock, and is generally supposed to have been invented for it. As is well known, there are two dials, one facing down Ludgate Hill, and the other looking towards the south side of the church-yard. They are formed by black bands painted on the stonework on which the hour circles and the numerals are engraved and gilt. Each dial is a trifle over 17 ft. in diameter, and the central opening measures about 10 ft.

6 ins., the hour numerals being about 2 ft. deep. The clock is a thirty-hour one, and therefore requires winding daily. Though but two sets of dial-work are used, the stonework of the four faces of the tower is alike, and on the eastern side, which faces down Cannon Street, although the dial is not painted, the hour numerals are cut in the stone; this suggests the inference that it was at one time intended to show the time there. It was probably found that the pediment over the southern entrance to the Cathedral so obscured the view as to render the third dial comparatively useless. On the roof just outside of this dial aperture is a horizontal sun-dial, with a plate over two feet in diameter. This was fixed, it is said, for the purpose of regulating the clock by the sun.

Belfry. From the clock-room the upper part of the belfry is approached by a stone staircase formed in the wall of the tower itself, which is five feet thick, composed of two stone shells with a space of fifteen inches between them. Here, forty feet from the clock floor is hung the celebrated hour bell, which, in addition to its primal duty of recording the hours, is tolled when the Sovereign, the Bishop of London, the Dean of St. Paul's, or the Lord Mayor of London passes away. It is 6 ft. 9¼ ins. in diameter at the mouth, and **Hour Bell.** weighs 5 tons 4 cwt. Round the waist is the inscription, "Richard Phelps made me, 1716," and though the clock is said to have been completed in 1709, these figures may be taken to fix the date when the clock and bells were dedicated to the public service. For tolling, it has a clapper weighing 180 pounds. The hammer-head which strikes the hours on the outside of the sound bow weighs 145 pounds. Just below the hour **Quarter Bells.** bells are two bells, on which the "ting-tang" quarters are struck; the larger of these weighs 1 ton 4 cwt., and the smaller 12 cwt. 2 qrs. 9 lbs.

First Hour-Bell Cracked. The Commissioners appear to have had just as much trouble with their hour bell as was experienced over the casting of Big Ben for the Houses of Parliament. In the year 1700, when the Cathedral was approaching completion, they purchased for 10d. a pound, from the churchwardens of St. Margaret's, Westminster, the celebrated Great Tom, which formerly hung in a clock-tower facing Westminster Hall, and which appears to have been given to the churchwardens by William III. They then entered into a contract with William Whiteman to recast the bell, and when the work was done the bell was temporarily hoisted into the north-west tower of St. Paul's, and exhibited to the public, Whiteman being paid £509 19s. for his labour. But lo! after sustaining many blows for the delectation of the ears of the citizens, Great Tom the second exhibited a crack, which rapidly developed, so that the bell was pronounced to be useless. What was now to be done? The Commissioners suggested that of course Whiteman would make good his work by recasting the bell. "Not so," rejoined Whiteman; "I delivered to you a sound bell, for which I was paid, and since it has been in your possession it has been cracked." So, to make the best of a bad job, a very stringent agreement was entered into with another founder—Richard Phelps, to wit—in which he covenanted for a certain consideration to cast a bell of similar dimensions to the fractured one, of all new metal, deliver the same to the Commissioners, and when they expressed themselves satisfied he was to be paid; then, and not till then, removing the old bell and allowing the value thereof. This accident with the first hour bell accounts for the difference between the date of the finishing of the clock and the time when the present hour bell was cast.

Great Paul. In the clock-tower is the monster bell, Great Paul, which, although hung on a level with the clock, has no connection whatever with the timekeeper. It was cast in 1881, placed in position in 1882, and is the largest bell in Europe which is mounted for swinging. Its exact weight is 16 tons 14 cwt. 2 qrs. 19 lbs., thus exceeding Big Ben in weight by more than three tons.

There are four or five heavier bells that are simply chimed, without mentioning the broken Russian casting of 200 tons, which has never been mounted at all. The actual dimensions of Great Paul are 8 ft. 10 in. in perpendicular height from base to top of cannons; diameter at base, 9 ft. 6¼ in.; height inside to crown, 6 ft. 11¼ in.; thickness near the base where the clapper strikes, 8¼ in. The clapper is 7 ft. 9 in. long, and weighs 4 cwt. 20 lbs. The centre of suspension, or axis of the gudgeons, is 7 ft. 9 in. from the lip. The gudgeons or trunnions of the headstock are of wrought iron 5¾ in. in diameter working on gun-metal bearings. Instead of lubricating with oil, little holes are drilled in the gun-metal, into which are placed pellets of metalline—a substance resembling plumbago or black lead—to act as a lubricant. The head-stock, which is formed of three balks of oak bolted together, with half-inch plates of iron between, is 2 ft. 6 in. deep by 18 in. across. The note of the bell is E flat. At its waist, under the arms of the dean and chapter, are the words "Vae mihi si non evangelisavero;" around the crown, "John Taylor and Co., founders, Loughborough." The alloy of which it is cast consists of thirteen parts copper to four parts tin. From the headstock spring out horizontally two long wooden levers, one on each side of the bell. Attached to the extremity of one, is a lead weight of about half a ton, which rests on the floor when the bell is stationary. By means of the other lever the bell is swung, the rope passing over a pulley to obtain a greater purchase. The object of the lead weight seems to be to check the motion of the bell so that the clapper shall strike the hour with a very small swing of the bell. Few people are aware that this monster blares out its note every afternoon from five minutes to one to one o'clock. It must be confessed that the effect is very disappointing. Lord Grimthorpe clearly states that "tucking up," as the placing of the trunnions below the crown of the bell is called, is detrimental to the sound of a bell, and either from this or from the small arc of vibration given to the bell or from some other cause, the volume of the sound is meagre, and cannot be heard any distance away, while the striking of the hours on the five-ton bell is wonderfully clear. Read, the clockmaker, declared he heard St. Paul's clock strike when he was at Windsor, twenty-two miles away.

Peal of Bells. In the north-western tower, which corresponds to the clock tower, there was, till 1875, but a single bell, which was tolled for prayers. In that year a peal of twelve bells of John Taylor and Co., was provided and hung at the cost of some of the Corporation, the City companies, Lady Burdett Coutts, and some other subscribers.

Fee to see Clock. The twopence fee which visitors used to pay for the privilege of inspecting the clock and bells was, for many years, the perquisite of the clock-winder, who, from attending every morning to wind the clock, gradually extended his visits over the rest of the day; and it is said that in the year of the Great Exhibition of 1851, he collected as much as £1100 from this source. Shortly after, the Dean and Chapter included the clock in their official scale of charges till the dynamite scare of a few years ago, when this portion of the building was closed to visitors, as it still remains.

Westminster Clock and Bells.

BOTH exteriorly and interiorly the great clock of the Houses of Parliament is one of which the nation may well be proud. The grand clock tower is a lasting tribute to the genius of the architect, the late Sir Charles Barry, and affords evidence that it is possible to have large dials distinct, without appearing to be merely excrescences stuck on the building; while the excellent arrangement and timekeeping properties of the clock reflect the greatest credit on its designer, Mr. E. B. Denison (now Lord Grimthorpe).

Clockmakers objected to Stipulations. The parliamentary papers referring to the clock extend from 1844, when the new Houses of Parliament, which the destruction of the old building by fire rendered necessary, were in course of construction, till 1862. In 1851 Mr. Denison, then a barrister holding a good position at the parliamentary bar, was requested by the government to act as referee in conjunction with Mr. G. B. Airy, Astronomer Royal. Vulliamy and other leading clockmakers, who were invited to tender for the work, all demurred to a stipulation that the clock should be guaranteed to perform within a margin of a second a day, which they declared to be too small. Eventually it was decided to entrust the work to the late E. J. Dent. Shortly afterwards the Astronomer Royal declined to act further, and it was left for Mr. Denison to furnish the plan of the clock, which was finished in 1854, fixed in the tower in 1859, and permanently set going in 1860.

Dials and Hands. Its four dials are 180 feet above the ground-level; each of them is 22½ feet in diameter, or nearly 400 square feet in area. They are formed of cast iron framework giving the divisions and figures, the spaces being filled in with opalescent glass. The hour figures on the dials are two feet long and the minute spaces one foot square. The hour hands are solid, and cast of gun metal. For lightness the minute hands are tubular; they are of copper, the shells being thin, but strengthened by diaphragms at intervals. The copper tubes are tapered and closed at the tips; their open ends being fitted to gun-metal centres, which also form the outside counterpoises. Each minute hand measures eleven feet from the centre to the point, besides the counterpoise of three feet, so that the load on the clock when the hands are subjected to a high wind or covered with snow can be appreciated.

Illumination. Between the backs of the dials and the walls of the clock-room is a passage about three feet wide, and here are fixed a number of gas-jets to illuminate the dials at night. The passage is very hot when the gas is burning, but the clock room is so isolated that the heat and products of combustion cannot enter. There is no stint of gas, yet though the time can be seen very plainly at night if the observer is but a little distance away, it must be confessed that a little greater brilliance would allow the position of the hands to be more distinctly discerned from afar. Still it must be remembered that the glass is not fully transparent, and the dead whiteness that is such an admirable ground by day militates against the success of artificial illumination from within. As a matter of fact, I believe the best effect is produced that is possible. The electric light has been tried, but it was found to be not so suitable for this purpose as a number of gas-jets.

The driving weight of the clock being sufficiently heavy to carry the hands round, even under the most adverse circumstances, the force transmitted to the escapement would clearly be excessive when the wind or snow happened to be helping instead of retarding the hands in their course. Hitherto the practice had been in such cases to interpose a *remontoire*, consisting of a small spring which was wound by the train and discharged at intervals. However great the force which wound the spring, its pressure in unwinding would be constant, so that by using this spring to drive the escapement the impulse given to the pendulum could be maintained nearly at the required amount. Mr. Denison discarded this kind of *remontoire*, and used the double three-legged gravity escapement shown in Fig. 65, which he invented for the purpose.

Double Three-legged Gravity Escapement. This escapement consists of two gravity impulse pallets pivoted as nearly as possible in a line with the bending-point of the pendulum spring. The locking wheel is made up of two thin plates having three long teeth or "legs" each. These two plates are squared on the arbor a little distance apart, one on each side of the pallets. They are connected by means of three pins or a three-leaved pinion. In the drawing one of the front legs is resting on a block screwed to the front of the right-hand pallet. This forms the locking.

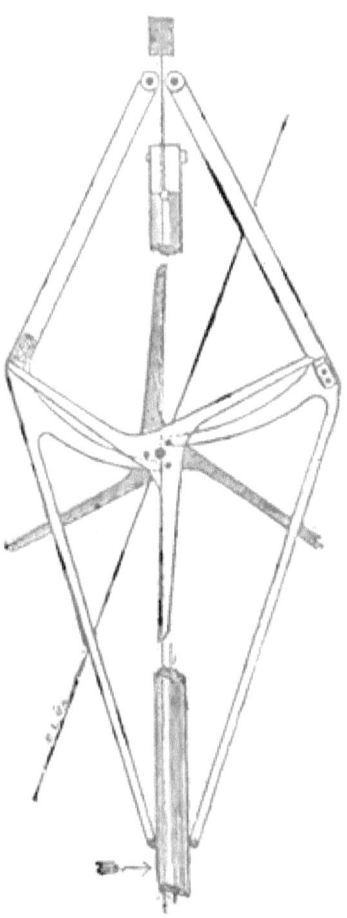

Fig. 65.—Double three-legged gravity escapement.

There is a similar block screwed to the back of the left-hand pallet for the legs of the back plate, which is shaded in the drawing, to lock upon.

Projecting from each of the pallets is an arm. The tip of the one on the right-hand pallet is just in contact with one of the leaves of the three-leaved pinion. The pendulum is travelling in the direction indicated by the arrow, and the left-hand pallet is delivering impulse across the line of centres. The pendulum rod in its swing will push the right-hand pallet far enough for the leg of the front locking plate, which is now resting on the block, to escape. Directly it escapes the left-hand pallet is lifted free of the pendulum rod by the lowest leaf of the pinion. After the locking wheel has passed through 60° a "leg" of the back locking plate is caught by the locking block on the left-hand pallet. As the three-leaved pinion always lifts the pallets the same distance, the pallets in returning give a constant impulse to the pendulum. The friction in unlocking would, of course, vary with the pressure transmitted through the train, but the effect of such variation is found to be practically of no moment. To avoid any jar when the locking leg falls on the block there is a fly kept, by a spring, friction-tight on an enlarged portion of the arbor. This fly causes the legs to fall smoothly and dead on the blocks, and thus avoids all danger of tripping.

Up to the time that Mr. Denison designed the "works" of the Westminster clock the usual custom had been to make the frame by screwing together loose bars of wrought iron, very much after the fashion shown in the engraving of De Vick's clock, and not the least important of Denison's improvements was the providing of a rigid self-contained support for the whole of the arbors.

The Movement. The movement of the Westminster clock is contained in a frame made up of two cast-iron girders fifteen and a half feet long, placed side by side four feet apart, and braced together. There are three trains or sets of wheels, each one driven by a separate weight. The "going" or "watch" train that drives the hands, and is controlled by the escapement and pendulum, occupies the centre of the frame; on the left hand is the hour-striking train, which only moves once an hour when it is released by the going train, and locks itself after it has struck the number of blows corresponding to the hour of the day; on the right is the quarter train, which is released by the going train every fifteen minutes, and chimes either one, two, three, or four quarters as required, and again locks itself.

As it has less to do, the going train is lighter than either of the striking trains, and in all three the strength of the wheels and other parts is greatest near the weight barrels, and is gradually diminished as the velocity of the parts increases. In the going train the parts near the escapement can hardly be too light, for it is necessary that they should get into action quickly, directly they are unlocked, and to give as light a blow or shock as possible when they are locked again. The four pairs of hands are driven by four horizontal minute arbors placed high above the movement, and leading each one to the centre of one of the dials. Each dial has separate motion wheels for reducing the rate of travelling of the hour hand, the motion work being carried on the walls of the clock room. It will be seen from the drawing, Fig. 66, that connection between the movement and the minute arbors is made by means of the oblique shaft, *a*, and the mitre wheels, *b*, *c*, *d*, and *e*.

Quarter Striking. The four-armed cam or snail, *g*, turns once in an hour. It is gradually pressing down the lever *h*, and allows it to escape once every fifteen minutes. The quarter train is held by the locking lever *i*, which rests on the upper one of two blocks on the lever *k*. The lever *h* acts on the lever *k*, and as the quarter hour approaches the lever *k* rises and allows the locking lever *i* to escape from the first locking block to the second one, which is rather lower on the lever; this allows the train to move a little and causes the noise

182 A HISTORY OF WATCHES

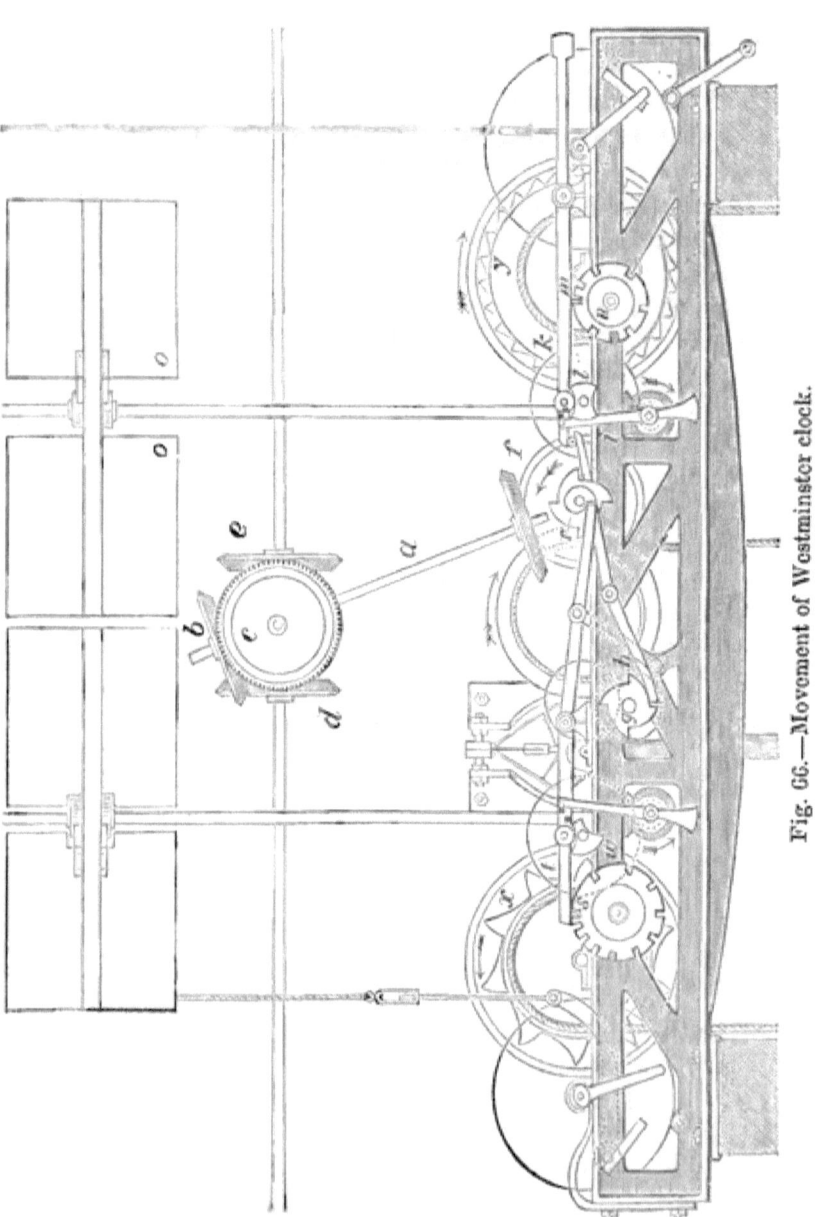

Fig. 66.—Movement of Westminster clock.

generally known as warning. Exactly at the quarter the
lever k falls free of the locking lever i, and the train of
wheels begins to run, the lever k being lifted sufficiently
high by the cam l to disengage the tongue m from the
notch of the locking plate or count wheel n, in which it is
resting. If one chime only is to be struck the tongue m
descends into the same notch of the locking plate, for that
notch is wide enough to receive the tongue again after
the small angular movement made by the plate, and the
upper block on the lever k catches the locking lever i as
it comes round. But at the next quarter, after one chime
has been sounded, the tip of the tongue rests on the
periphery of the locking plate till another chime is struck,
when it falls into the next notch. The locking plate
makes one rotation in three hours, and it will be observed
that it is spaced out to allow of three sets of quarters.
The intervals between the quarters is kept constant by
the resistance of the air against the revolving fly o, which
is composed of two large blades of sheet iron.

Lord Grimthorpe states that the four-armed snail g,
close to the escapement, was provided to ensure greater
regularity in the quarter striking than could be obtained
by the customary plan of placing the snail on the arbor
of the wheel f, that turns once in an hour and drives the
hands; but it involves an extra lever for discharging the
quarter train, and I am not sure that the gain is worth
the extra complication.

Hour Striking. The action for letting off the hour striking
is very similar to that for discharging the
quarters. The hour-striking train is held by
a stop on the locking lever w, resting against the upper of
two blocks on the lever t. A few minutes before the
hour the locking lever falls on to the lower block and is
released exactly at the hour by the snail r, which revolves
once in an hour. At one o'clock the tongue on the lever,
t, descends into the wide notch of the locking plate, s; at

two o'clock it is retained on the edge of the plate till two blows have been struck, and so on, the locking plate, which turns once in twelve hours, being divided so as to allow all the hours to be struck in rotation.

For lifting the hammers of the bells Mr. Denison had curved cams attached to the great wheels, x and y, of the hour and quarter striking trains, instead of the usual round pins, which answer very well for small clocks, but would have absorbed too much of the power in friction when dealing with such large weights. The cams press down levers, which are connected with the bell hammer levers by means of steel wire ropes.

About two seconds elapse between the unlocking of the train and the striking of the first blow of the hour. As one of the conditions of the specification required that the first stroke of the hour should be given within a second of true, fears were entertained that the ordinary method of letting off the striking train by a snail turning once in an hour would not be sufficiently accurate, and special striking work devised by Mr. Denison was in use for some time. The ordinary lever raised by the hour snail was retained, but it carried the warning stop only. The second stop was on another lever, let off every fifteen minutes by a snail on the wheel next to the escapement. Three times during the hour the second lever, though let off by its snail, merely rocked and returned to its position, but, after the warning, it held the locking lever till the two-second pendulum beat the fifty-eight second of the last minute of the hour, when it was again let off and discharged the train.

The clock frame is not in the centre of the room, but placed so as to allow a space of about two feet clear from one of the walls, to which a very strong cast-iron bracket is fixed, and from this bracket the pendulum is hung.

Pendulum The pendulum, thirteen feet and half an inch long from the point of suspension to the centre of oscillation, makes one vibration every two seconds. It weighs nearly 700 lbs., and is compensated so as to neutralize the effects of varying temperature by means of a zinc tube in a way that will be understood by reference to the drawing, Fig. 67. Screwed to the bottom of the iron pendulum rod is the rating nut, and on that is placed a zinc tube ten feet long. From the top of the zinc tube an iron tube depends, and on the bottom of this the castiron bob rests. When a rise of temperature occurs, the iron rod and the iron tube both expand downwards, while the zinc tube, with a superior co-efficient of expansion, lengthens upwards just sufficient to keep the distance from the point of suspension to the centre of oscillation constant. In the Westminster clock the bob rests on its bottom. I rather prefer it suspended from the middle of its length, as shown, for the bob is then neutral as a factor in the componsation, and as by reason of its great bulk it answers much more slowly to changes of temperature than the other parts of the pendulum, this is an advantage.

With a decrease in the pressure of the air and consequent fall of the barometer, the pendulum increases its arc of vibration; with an increase in the pressure of the air and consequent rise of the barometer, the pendulum diminishes its arc of vibration. In the Westminster clock the pendulum vibrates 2·75° on each side of zero, and Lord Grimthorpe points out that with this large arc the circular error just componsates for the barometric error.

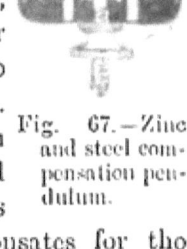

Fig. 67.—Zinc and steel compensation pendulum.

Maintaining Power. To maintain the vibration of the pendulum during the twenty minutes or so that it takes to wind the going part of the clock, Mr. Denison invented a special kind of maintainer. The back bearing of the winding-pinion arbor is carried in a loose link slung from the barrel arbor. To obtain a resisting base so that the winding pinion should not run round the wheel with which it gears, a click presses against the ratchet-teeth on the side of the great wheel, and so drives the clock. But as the great wheel travels on, the back end of the winding arbor in following it is taken out of the horizontal line and soon becomes so oblique that the winder has to stop and let it down to its normal position again; so that, on the whole, though this maintaining work is decidedly ingenious, it is not in my judgment so good as the continuous sun and planet maintainer invented by John Harrison. For clocks of moderate size that take but a few minutes to wind, I would prefer a spring maintainer.

"Big Ben" the First Cracked. It was decided to call the hour bell, which was to weigh fourteen tons, "Big Ben," out of compliment to Sir Benjamin Hall, who was First Commissioner of Works when the order for the clock was given. When cast it actually weighed sixteen tons, and shortly after the clock was started it cracked, from using too heavy a hammer as the founder of it averred, though the clock authorities declared that only a hammer of sufficient weight to bring out the tone had been used. However, the founder declined to cast another bell except on such terms that the authorities would not accede to, and so the production of the second and present Big Ben **Present "Big Ben" also cracked.** was entrusted to another founder. It was duly hung and approved, but after a few months' use the tone altered, and it was found that this bell had also developed a crack on the inside of it three inches deep. For three years afterwards the hours were struck on the largest of the quarter bells—a most miserable makeshift—and then some one suggested turning "Big Ben" round, so as to present a fresh place for the hammer to strike on. This was done, and a lighter hammer than was before used provided. The result was perfectly satisfactory, for the fissure does not seem to have increased during the twenty-six years which have elapsed, and "Big Ben" still blares out the hour so as to be heard at different points round the metropolis, sometimes for a distance of ten miles, according to the direction and intensity of the wind. Many people take the first stroke of the bell as a regulator for their time-keepers; allowing for the interval which has elapsed since the bell was struck. Big Ben's voice can often be distinctly detected at Greenwich Park, the sound taking twenty-six seconds to reach there. A curious error prevails with some, who fancy that the wind affects the accuracy of the time so heard, but the fact is, that the velocity of sound is unaffected by the direction of the wind. Sound travels at the rate of 1110 feet per second, and if the note of the bell is heard at all it always reaches the same spot in the same time, whether the wind is with or against it. There is, it is true, a very slight difference in the velocity of sound from variation of temperature, but this is so small that it may be disregarded.

"Big Ben" as a Regulator.

Hour and Quarter Bells.

The bells are arranged in a chamber above the dial, and hung from massive wrought-iron framing. The hour bell is 9 feet in diameter; is 8¾ inches thick at the sound bow, and it weighs 13 tons 11 cwt. It is struck by a hammer with a cast-iron head weighing 4 cwt., which is lifted 9 inches vertically and 13 inches altogether from the bell before it falls. There are four quarter bells weighing respectively 78 cwt., 33½ cwt., 26 cwt., and 21 cwt. The hammers for the quarters are each about one-fortieth of the weight of the bell it strikes. To prevent the hammers jarring on the bells, they are kept from contact by indiarubber buffers, on which the shanks fall.

Not the least attractive feature of the clock are the charming Cambridge Chimes. They are founded on a phrase in the opening symphony of Handel's air, " I know that my Redeemer liveth," and were arranged by Dr. Crotch for the clock of Great St. Mary, Cambridge, in 1793. They run as follows :—

Cambridge Chimes.

Cost of Clock and Bells. Altogether, from first to last, about £22,000 were spent on the clock and bells. The clock movement cost about £4000; £5500 were paid for the dials and hands; the bells absorbed £6500, including £750 for re-casting "Big Ben;" and the iron framing for the bells, which was at first too weak, and had to be strengthened, took the remaining £6500.

The weight for the going part of the clock is comparatively light, and it requires winding once a week only. But both the hour and the quarter parts have to be wound twice a week, the operation taking five hours in each case. The weight for the quarters is just upon a ton and a half, and the hour weight is over a ton.

Winding. To obtain a sufficient purchase in winding the hour and quarter parts there is an intermediate wheel and pinion to each, and the bearing of the arbor of the intermediate pinion is formed of an eccentric bush, so that the pinion may be readily disengaged from the wheel when the time for striking approaches, or when the winding is completed. The action of these eccentrics will be understood from the drawing. The hour pinion is out of gear, the lever attached to the eccentric being pushed away from the spring catch, while the one for the quarter winding is shown in gear ready for winding.

While the clock was in progress various suggestions were made to dispense with hand labour for winding. A steam-engine, windmill, water-engine, a float to rise and fall by the action of the tide in the adjacent river, were among the devices proposed, but disregarded, for it was considered that so large a machine required for keeping exact time should not be left to haphazard regulation, and was more likely to get proper periodical lubrication and other attention if the men attended at frequent intervals to wind.

Electrical Connection. There is electrical connection between the Westminster clock and Greenwich Observatory, not for the purpose of controlling the clock, as some people suppose, but merely that the timekeeping of it may be ascertained. Two signals a day are sent automatically by the clock, one at 11 a.m., and one at 1 p.m., and from the general reports of the Astronomer Royal, the error of the clock is rarely over one second in a week.

Clock stops. Three times during its career the clock has been stopped by an abnormally heavy fall of wet snow lodging and freezing on the hands.

Strikes One Hundred. In December, 1861, just before the lamented death of the Prince Consort, London was startled by a long-continued striking of the Westminster clock, at least a hundred blows being given in quick succession; and when the fatal termination of Prince Albert's illness was known, many people declared the erratic behaviour of the clock was an omen of the sad event; but an easy solution of the phenomenon is to be found in the fact that some experimental striking work, that had been attached, failed, and allowed the striking train to run down.

On April 9, 1886, the day that Mr. Gladstone made a great speech in unfolding his Home Rule for Ireland Bill, the clock suddenly stopped. This was due to the binding of the dial work for want of lubrication, but again credulous souls, who delight to search in the region of metaphysics for explanations of purely natural occurrences, accepted the inaction of the clock as a sign that the Bill would fail to pass, and we may be sure their faith in the supernatural was not weakened when, in due course, the measure was rejected. I think I have now mentioned every one of the few occasions when the clock has deviated from its usual regularity.

Westminster Clock the Largest. In spite of many challenges it must be conceded that the Westminster clock is still the largest in the world. Mechlin boasts of a public clock with a single dial forty feet in diameter. But mere size of dial is not an absolute criterion in estimating the size of clocks; many other features demand consideration. The heaviest pendulum in the world is claimed for a church in St. Albans, and there is a church clock in Bristol with a heavier pendulum than the Westminster clock has. Still, taken all round, the Westminster clock, with its four dials, each of 22½ feet in diameter, its striking work for four quarter bells weighing collectively 8 tons, and for an hour bell of over 13 tons, is still unique, and worthily entitled the King of Clocks. The clock of Shandon Church, Cork, has four dials, each of 16 feet in diameter. The dials of St. Paul's clock measure 17 feet each across, as already stated, but there are only two of them.

Large Figures Objectionable. Lord Grimthorpe insists that large and heavy figures, instead of making it easier to see the time, as many people suppose, really obscure the position of the hands, and he advocates the substitution of dots or short radial lines for numerals. By his advice the dial of the exterior clock of the dining-hall of Lincoln's Inn was so made, and it certainly is very distinct, although one may glance at it many times without noticing the absence of the numerals.

Many Dials of Turret Clocks too small. However plain the dials of turret clocks may be, they will not indicate the time clearly unless they are large in proportion to their height from the observer. Their diameter should not be less than one foot for every ten feet they are raised. Many otherwise good public clocks are obscured through the dials being too small in relation to the height, but it is very rare to find a dial too large. The architects, and not the clockmakers, are usually the sinners in this respect, for if the architect does not provide the room the clockmaker is helpless.

Curious Hour Allegories. Among curious departures from the usual divisions of clock dials may be mentioned one in which, instead of the usual numerals, twelve small but distinct scenes are delineated. The first, corresponding to one o'clock, represents a woman with a very young child in her arms, the infant being in long clothes. At two o'clock mamma is still there, but the child is represented as a boy just emerging from babyhood. At three o'clock he gambols alone. At four o'clock he goes to school for the first time. At five o'clock he is older and bigger. At six o'clock he may be seen with his college gown and mortar board, standing by his mature but happy mother. At seven o'clock his eye rests with loving glance on the maiden by his side and foreshadows eight o'clock, where he stands with her at the altar. At nine o'clock his own children gather round him. At ten o'clock is a death-bed scene where he parts with his beloved parent. At eleven o'clock he is a man over whom the snows of many winters have passed. At twelve o'clock an old and decrepit specimen of humanity praying for a better land.

Single Dial to indicate 12 and 24-hour Time. Many different forms of dials have been devised in view of the proposal to count hours of the day in succession from one to twenty-four. The simplest way, of course, is to mark the hour circle into twenty-four, and cause the hand to complete the circuit in a day, as is the case with astronomical clocks; but there is a general feeling that something must be done to gradually accustom the public to so great a change—to let them down easy as it were—and this has led to several ingenious propositions. Perhaps the very simplest device for indicating the time in the present and the proposed new style on one dial is that of Kendal and Dent, which was applied to the large clock erected by them in the central avenue of the International Inventions Exhibition, 1885. The special feature is that the hour hand is double the usual length, and extends equally on both sides of the centre instead of one side only; so that at say eighteen hours after the day began, one extremity would be pointing to eighteen and the other to six. Eighteen hours after the beginning of the day is, of course, according to our present reckoning, six in the afternoon.

Double-dialled Watch. The same firm exhibited a watch which attracted considerable attention. It had two dials placed back to back with the movement between them. On one dial were marked the old divisions of twelve hours; and on the other the suggested hour circle with twenty-four divisions. Causing one hour hand to revolve in twelve hours, while the other took double the time to traverse its path, presented little difficulty; but under ordinary conditions the hands, being actuated from the same centre arbor, would revolve in opposite directions. This was ingeniously obviated without increasing the bulk of the watch.

Striking Work under the 24-hour System. Lord Grimthorpe, the president of the Horological Institute, who is one of the most influential opponents of the proposed alteration in the counting of the hours, makes a point of the difficulty that would arise with the striking. Apart from the many practical difficulties of altering public clocks for the striking to correspond with the indicated hour, it must be admitted that to have to listen to and count twenty-three measured strokes on a bell would be intolerable. But it does not follow that because the hours of the day are counted continuously, the striking should be arranged on the old plan of one blow for every unit. A combination of bells or numbers might be made to represent the different hours. Or the old striking work could even be retained without inconvenience. Four blows would then be struck at four, and also at sixteen o'clock, and there need not be the slightest fear of any one mistaking one hour for the other. It is, therefore, clear that the striking does not present an insuperable barrier.

House Clocks.

Quarter Clocks.

F modern house clocks there are many varieties. Quarter clocks, as those which sound every quarter of an

Fig. 68.—Eighteenth-century clock case.

hour are called, may be divided into two classes, "ting tang" and "chiming." The title of each is expressive the former strikes one blow on each of two bells, having dissimilar notes for each quarter; while the latter runs through a series of notes, generally either on four or eight bells or on gongs. The Cambridge chimes, which are given in the description of the Westminster clock, are the favourite. When struck on gongs, the sound resembles the tones from large bells; some prefer the

Fig. 69.

Cambridge chimes to be sounded on bells, and the hour struck on a deep-toned gong. There are three trains, one for the gong, one for striking the hour, and one for the quarters. When the quarters are chimed, the hammers are lifted by pins projecting from a barrel similar to a musical-box barrel.

Quarter-chime clocks are essentially an English production, though the French and Germans have both essayed the manufacture of them. For the vestibule, staircase, or landing they are usually in carved wood cases, having but little enrichment, and with a bracket *en suite*.

Dining-room, library, and drawing-room clocks are, as a rule, enshrined in a more costly manner, and present a

Fig. 70.

wider field for decoration. Fig. 68 is a very choice design of the early part of last century, and probably of French origin. It must be admitted that for a long time many of the English striking and chiming clocks were encased in a very unworthy manner; the finials too often out of upright and ready to fall off on the slightest provocation. Under such circumstances it was, thereforo, not to be wondered at that people of wealth and taste availed themselves of the artistic feeling exhibited by many of the French clock-case makers. But the attention recently bestowed here on the cultivation of art, has enabled our designers to produce much better patterns. The artistic mind shudders at the hateful word "patterns;" but *que voulez vous?* An original conception even for a clock case by the best men, and therefore the men most sought after, costs a good deal more money than one purchaser in a thousand would care to pay; and when that one willing purchaser has been found, the matter is far from settled. He has notions of his own, or he wants something to harmonize with his furniture; then the high and mighty designer is not to be dictated to, or he lets the thing slide for the work of less exacting customers; or else, in deference to the ideas given him, he sketches something very beautiful in the abstract, and in accordance with all the canons of art,

Designs for Clock-cases.

Fig. 71.—Marble clock case.

but alas! quite unsuitable as the case of a clock if the dial is to be distinct, of adequate size, and the one feature which all the rest supports and embellishes, as it should be. But conceding "patterns," very appropriate cases for different situations and apartments are now to be obtained. Figs. 69 and 70 present a choice. They are only examples of which the material and treatment may be varied almost as desired. Oak, rosewood, walnut, ebony, and wood stained black in imitation thereof, mahogany, with or without bronze mountings, or with original paintings, offer a wide range for individual indulgence. Dials as well as cases afford scope for a variety of tastes. Many people like the plain dead-silvered dials, others prefer the richer appearance obtained by having a silvered band for the figures, surrounded by a matted gilt surface and carved or engraved corners.

French Clock Cases The French have for over a century excelled in ormolu cases, which were very popular a few years ago, and though latterly many, especially the low-priced ones, have shown a sad falling off in taste, good examples, worthy of the best days of the art, are to be had. Most of the cases now used for the cheaper kinds of dining-room and library clocks are of marble or alabaster, such as are shown in Figs. 71 and 72.

Fig. 72.—Marble clock case.

Pin-pallet Escapement The pin-pallet escapement shown in Fig. 73 is much favoured for portable short pendulum clocks, and when well made is very suitable. The fronts of the teeth of the escape wheel are sometimes made radial, as shown; sometimes cut back so as to bear on the point only, like the "Graham;" and sometimes set forward so as to give recoil to the wheel during the motion of the pendulum beyond the escaping arc. The pallets, generally of cornelian, are of semicircular form.

In some clocks this escapement is planted in front of the dial, so that its action may be visible; but this attraction is counterbalanced by the increased difficulty of discerning the hands some distance away.

Bedroom Clocks. For bedroom timepieces, clocks which either do not strike or have an alarum attachment are mostly preferred; the cases are small, with but little decoration, as in Figs. 74 and 75.

Lamp Clocks. Lamp clocks, in which the globe with hours painted thereon revolves, already mentioned as an invention of Grollier two centuries ago, have been introduced as bedroom timepieces, and are particularly acceptable to many invalids and others suffering from insomnia.

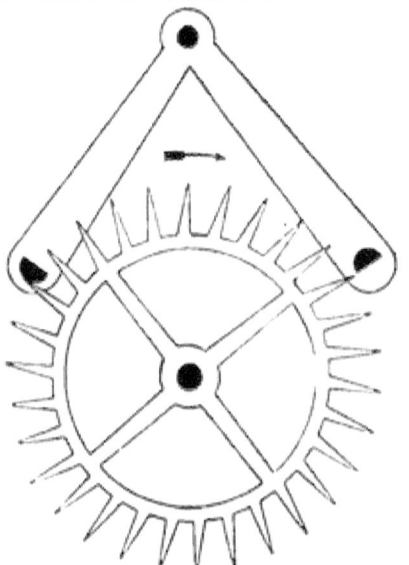

Fig. 73.—Brocot's pin-pallet escapement.

Fig. 74.—Bedroom clock.

Most clocks for the mantelpiece are made to go for fourteen days from winding to winding, though it is better to wind them once a week; for if a certain day is fixed for the operation, it is more likely to be remembered than a day once a fortnight is; besides which, the main-

Fig. 75.—Bedroom clock.

springs, however good, are sure to relax their elasticity in course of time, and this, added to the thickening of the oil, renders it prudent not to depend upon the clock running to the extreme limit.

Simple Idea of winding Eight-day Clock.

It is curious that one-week clocks, which always have an extra day's run in the springs to counteract forgetfulness, should have got to be called "eight-day" clocks. Of course it is generally understood they are to be wound once a week; but there is a record of a punctilious individual who entered a watchmaker's shop bearing a heavy parcel, which he proceeded to untie, with the remark, "I wish you would change this clock for me; it is an eight-day clock, and I am continually letting it run down, because the day for winding always changes. Now, I think if I had a seven-day clock, which I could wind every Saturday, I should be sure to remember it." "Well, but," said the shopkeeper—"but why not wind this one every Saturday?" "What!" rejoined the other, "do you mean to say that an eight-day clock may be wound every seven days?" "Oh, certainly; at any time within the eight days." Not another word was spoken; but, with a determined expression, the caller tied up his clock again, and went off to experience the felicity, let us hope, of finding his clock ticking satisfactorily, as he gave it renewed life on each succeeding Saturday.

Electric Clocks.

Classification of Electric Clocks.

ELECTRIC clocks may be divided into three classes—(1) Clocks in which electricity is used to impel the pendulum and turn the hands, so that periodical winding of a spring or weight is dispensed with; (2) Clocks that are driven by a weight or spring, and wound in the usual way, but in which the vibrations of the pendulum are controlled by currents transmitted automatically from a standard timekeeper; and (3) Clocks in which the mechanism is quite uncontrolled, but the proper position of the hands is ensured by periodical electric currents from a standard. It is clear that if the current fail in clocks of the first class, not only do they cease to register, but on the resumption of the current they start with the error accumulated during its cessation. The late Alexander Bain and the late Sir Charles Wheatstone spent much time and ingenuity in elaborating systems of electrically driven clocks in circuit; but however well they appeared to perform at first, none of them have secured a lasting place.

Bain. Wheatstone.

Jones' System of controlling. Mr. R. L. Jones, a former station-master at Chester, recognizing the difficulty of driving clocks by electricity, proposed to control the vibrations of the pendulum by attaching to its lower end a magnet which passed through a coil at each vibration. A standard clock, with the same length of pendulum as those controlled, was caused to transmit currents which accelerated or retarded the motion of the controlled pendulums, according as their vibrations were a little too slow or a little too fast. This system works very well in the Greenwich Observatory, where the circuit is short and constant attention is paid to the electric apparatus; but the late Mr. C. V. Walker, after many years' trial with a clock at London Bridge, controlled from Greenwich, pronounced it to be impracticable. If the current failed long enough for the controlled pendulum to get one beat out, the controlling apparatus had no means of setting the clock right again.

Hour-setting Arrangement. A very simple way of putting the minute hand forwards or backwards, as may be required, by means of an electric current transmitted from a standard clock was to attach to the pipe that carries the minute hand a heart-shaped cam, against which a lever with a pointed end is made to press exactly at the hour. This forces the cam into its lowest position, and the minute hand to the twelve numeral.

Another method is to cause two fingers to clasp the point of the minute hand, and force it to the XII. exactly at the hour.

Pneumatic Clocks.

NEUMATIC clocks of various kinds have been devised, and some of them have met with considerable favour on the Continent.

Paris Public Clocks. In the Poppe-Rescho system, used for the public clocks of Paris, air, dried by passing over lime, is pumped into strong iron reservoirs to a pressure of about forty pounds per square inch. From these reservoirs a constant pressure of ten pounds per square inch is maintained in a closed vessel, from which the air is used for driving the clocks. Behind the dials of the public clocks is a ratchet wheel fixed to the arbor of the minute hand. A click, working into this ratchet wheel, is pivoted to a lever, whose extremity is attached to a lens-shaped bellows of thin metal. Pipes are laid to all the public clocks, and at the completion of every minute a master clock at the central station opens communication between the supply vessel and the bellows, the pressure of air expands the bellows, and the ratchet wheel is advanced one tooth.

Compressed air is probably more reliable in its action than electricity, and the mechanism needed is simpler, but the time occupied by the transmission of signals appears to preclude its use for clocks at any considerable distance from the central station.

Fan Clocks. Currents of air passing up a chimney have been utilized for drawing clocks by causing the air to impinge on the blades of a fan; but although many such contrivances have been elaborated, and declared to be perfect by their fond authors, none have come into general use.

Tell-tale Clocks.

Whitehurst's Plan.

TELL-TALE, or watchmen's, clocks are those by which a record is left of the periodical visits of a watchman or other person to a particular spot. In the earliest form,

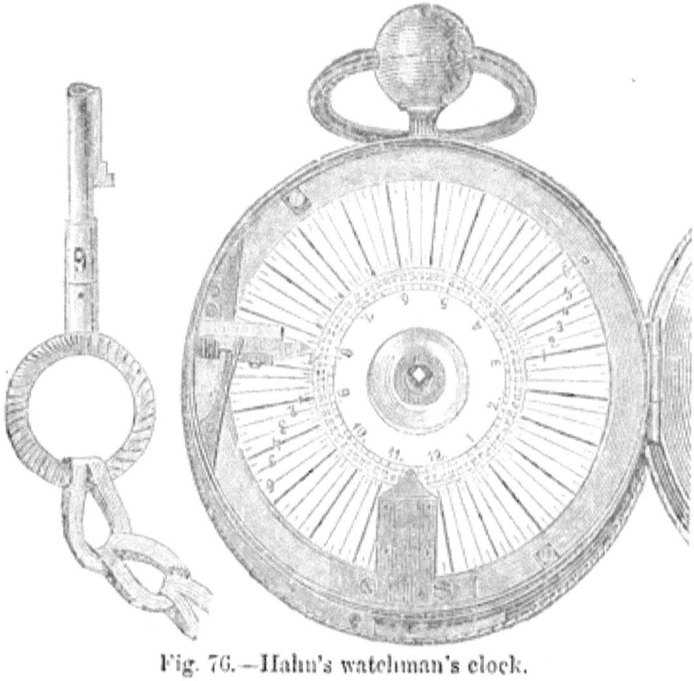

Fig. 76.—Hahn's watchman's clock.

invented by John Whitehurst, of Derby, in the last century, and still met with, a ring studded with projecting pins rotates, so that the pins successively coincide with an aperture at the desired intervals. As the watchman passes, he pushes the pin in; but should he be late,

AND OTHER TIMEKEEPERS.

it has passed the aperture, and cannot be got at. Recent improvements provide for a permanent record of the visits of the watchman. Hahn's Time Detector, one of the best examples, is shown in Fig. 76, drawn to one-half the real size. The detector is carried by the watchman, who at every station he has to visit finds a key (as shown on the left of engraving) which he inserts into a keyhole in the band of the case opposite the pendant, and gives it one turn. This lifts a steel type, and impresses a figure corresponding to the number of the key to the paper dial, so that in the morning, when the instrument is unlocked, there is recorded on the dial the time at which each station was visited. The dial is then removed, and a fresh one attached ready for the succeeding night. There is a lever by the catch on the left of the picture, which punctures the dial when the detector is unlocked, to indicate when this was done.

Hahn System.

Compensation and Adjustment of Watches and Chronometers.

Harrison's Curb.

HARRISON'S endeavours to construct a perfect portable timekeeper proved that, admirable as the balance spring is as a controller while the temperature is constant, it is far from perfect when subjected to alternations of heat and cold. He ultimately selected as a corrector, what he called a compensation curb, which was an arm composed of two thin bars riveted together. One of the bars was steel and the other brass. The coefficient of expansion of brass being superior to that of steel, the brass would struggle to lengthen more with a rise of temperature and shorten more with a fall of temperature, than the steel would. And the effect of this rigid and unnatural connection of the two metals would be a curvature of the arm, the brass side of it assuming a convex form with a rise and concave form with a fall of temperature. Then if the arm were fixed at one end, the free end of it would move to and fro in answer to changes of temperature. Harrison placed two small fingers on the free extremity to lightly clasp the balance spring near its outer end; so that as a rise of temperature weakened the force of the spring the fingers moved round and lessened its effective length, making the spring practically shorter and therefore stiffer.

Berthoud's Experiment. After Harrison's success English and French horologists turned their attention to the subject of compensating portable timekeepers. Berthoud, in 1773, tabulated the effect of temperature on one of his marine timekeepers, which he found in passing from 32° to 92° (Fahr.) lost 62 seconds through the expansion of the balance and 331 seconds from the loss of the spring's elastic force. Curiously enough he divided the loss from the spring into elastic force, and loss from elongation, but there would clearly be no loss from elongation, because with elongation from expansion of the metal there would be a proportionate increase in its breadth and thickness, and the spring would really be stronger for a rise in temperature if the alteration in its dimensions alone were considered. However, Berthoud's observation was doubtless correct as far as the totals go.

Le Roy and Berthoud in France, and Arnold and Earnshaw in England, appear to have arrived at very similar conclusions, and though French horologists consider Le Roy to be the inventor of the compensation balance, Englishmen divide the credit between their own countrymen. Though slightly altered in appearance and construction, the two modern forms of compensation balance, one being for fine watches, and the other for marine chronometers are in principle identical with the balance of Arnold and Earnshaw.

Compensation Balances. It will be observed that the unequal expansion of different metals, and their behaviour when united, which Harrison adopted as the medium of compensation, are retained. The halves of the balance rim are free at one end and fixed at the other to the central arm, which is of steel. The inner part of the rim is of steel and the outer part, which is of brass twice the thickness of the inner, is melted on the steel. The effect of an increase of temperature is that the brass bends

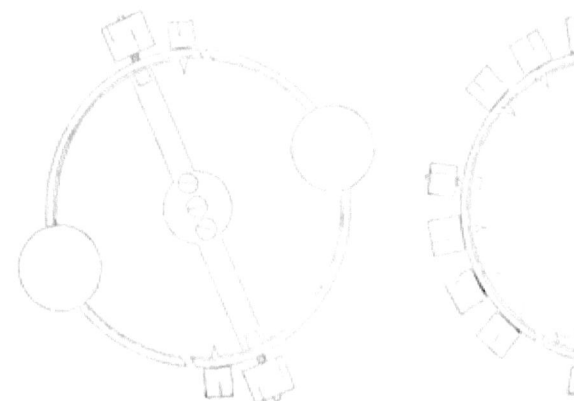
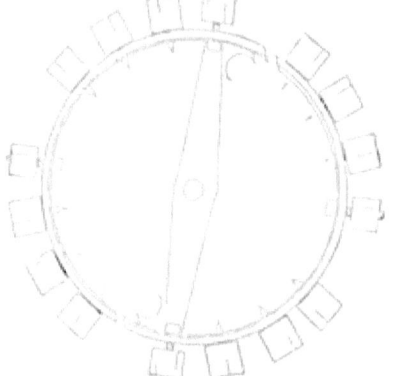

Fig. 77.—Marine chronometer balance.   Fig. 78.—Compensation balance for watches.

the rims inwards, thus practically reducing the size of the balance. With a decrease of temperature the action is reversed. The action, which is very small at the fixed ends of the rim, increases towards the free ends, where it is greatest. In a marine chronometer there is one large weight at about the middle of each half-rim, which is shifted to or from the fixed end, according as the compensation is varied by shifting screws with large heads from one hole to another, or by substituting a heavier or a lighter screw. In the marine balance there are two screws with heavy nuts on opposite sides of the rim close to the central arm for bringing the chronometer to time. In watch balances there are four such screws placed at equal distances round the rim. These of course are not touched for temperature adjustment. Figs. 77 and 78 illustrate the two descriptions of compensation balances.

Adjustment for Temperature. It must not be supposed that the difference in price of an ordinary watch, and a fine one adjusted for temperature would be merely the extra cost of the compensation balance. The adjustment for temperature is a most tedious one, and is completed only after observations and alterations extending over some weeks. The watches are tried in an oven or safe heated to the maximum temperature decided on, which is generally 90° Fahr.; tried while exposed to an average temperature, and also in a low temperature. For the last named, unless the trial is being conducted during winter, an ice box is required.

Costliness of Adjusted Watches. Watches adjusted for temperature are generally fitted with an overcoil or Breguet balance spring, and sometimes they have no index, so that any subsequent regulation that may be needed must be done by an expert. They are also adjusted for positions—that is, tried when lying flat, when hanging with the pendants upwards; then on edge, first with the pendant to the right, and then with the pendant to the left. After the various errors are noted, any necessary correction is made by the adjuster. It may be said, Surely a good watch would be right in all positions. It is true that a soundly planned, well-made watch would not have any considerable variation owing to change of position; some departure from correctness is sure to be found, and the greater part of such error can be generally eliminated by the adjuster, without much trouble, by very slightly altering the balance of the curves of the balance spring. But it is what Sir Frederick Bramwell called the " next to nothing," that gives all the trouble. It is easy to go so far towards perfection with mechanism, but after that the steps must be very short, and are very difficult, so that the man who wants a watch more perfect than the majority of his fellow-creatures are content with, will find his exactness has to be paid for.

Balance insensible to Change of Latitude. A pendulum vibrates quicker at the poles than at the equator, because gravity, which is the impelling force, has greater influence when a body approaches nearer to the centre of the earth, and many people, I find, fancy that watches are similarly affected by change of latitude. This is not so, for the *mass* of the balance remains the same, and the force of the balance spring, which really controls the vibration of the balance, is also unchanged whether the watch is far from or near to the centre of the earth.

The Going Barrel. Swiss watchmakers, as stated on page 60, abandoned the fusee for watches and formed teeth on the edge of the mainspring barrel to drive the train of wheels. This kind of barrel is called a "going barrel," because it drives the watch during the operation of winding, which the old fusee did not do until the maintaining spring which Harrison invented was applied to it, for the fusee had to be turned backwards to wind. But to wind the spring in the going barrel, the barrel arbor only, to which the inner end of the spring is fixed, is rotated, and during the going of the watch the arbor is stationary.

Reluctance of English Watchmakers to adopt it. English watchmakers fought against the change for a long time; their springers declared that with the alterations in the extent of the vibration of the balance consequent on the variations in the force of the mainspring, good performance with the going barrel was out of the question, quite oblivious of Hooke's maxim, *Ut tensio sic vis*, showing that to keep the vibrations of the balance isochronous under variations of motive force was just the province of the balance spring; and I think even now many old-fashioned workmen would stand by the assertion, notwithstanding that official trials at Kew Observatory and elsewhere have demonstrated that the going barrel is practically not inferior. What forced the hands of English watchmakers more than anything was the demand for keyless watches, and the application of keyless work to the fusee being both difficult and costly, they were obliged to find salvation against their will. Of the small number of fusee watches now made, nine out of ten are key-winding.

Fusee retained for Marine Chronometer. The fusee is still very properly retained in marine chronometers, where such extreme exactness is required that a vibration as constant as possible is desirable, and where, moreover, there is plenty of room to allow of a chain of ample strength.

Watch Movements.

Movements of Brass. 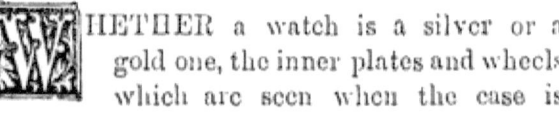 WHETHER a watch is a silver or a gold one, the inner plates and wheels which are seen when the case is opened are usually made of brass, though the brilliant matted gilding induces many to fancy that the works are of gold throughout. Occasionally there is found such a stickler for genuineness that he insists upon his watch being made all sterling, like the sailor, who, when he came into some property, refused to accept the waistcoat which Snip sent home because the back was of lining, whereas he desired it to be of blue cloth like the front, or, as he termed it, to be "stem and starn alike, and blow all

Gold Movement. sham." When the Princess of Wales was married, the enthusiastic people of Coventry presented her with a watch, every part of which was made expressly of 22-carat gold.

Such examples as these are but eccentricities which may be disregarded, for, as a matter of fact, the precious metal is too heavy and too soft to be so suitable and lasting for watch plates and wheels as the more humble brass.

Nickel. Nickel is sometimes substituted for brass, and is, if not preferable, at least not inferior for the purpose.

Arrangement of the Wheels. In an ordinary watch the centre pinion, which rotates once in an hour, occupies the centre of the pillar plate which is under the dial. Around the mainspring barrel are teeth which engage with and drive the centre pinion, and the size of the barrel is limited only by the size of the plate, to the edge of which the barrel extends. On the centre pinion is mounted the centre wheel which drives the third wheel pinion; on the third wheel pinion is mounted the third wheel which drives the fourth wheel pinion; and on the fourth wheel pinion is mounted the fourth wheel, which drives the escape pinion; and on the escape pinion is mounted the escape wheel. While the centre wheel is making one rotation, the fourth pinion, which carries the seconds hand, if there is one, makes sixty rotations, and the escape wheel goes round six hundred times; the wheels and pinions are therefore made smaller and lighter as they approach the escapement. The action of the escapement will be understood by reference to the drawings already given. The balance, like the barrel, is usually as large as the movement will allow, that is, it extends nearly from the centre pinion to the edge of the plate.

Full Plate. English verge watch movements of old were of the full plate description, that is, the pivots of the various wheels and pinions were run into two circular plates which were kept a certain distance apart by pillars. Some English lever watches are still made with full-plate movements, but the greater number are of the three-quarter plate construction, in which a portion of the top plate, or the one which is visible on opening the watch, is cut away, so that the upper escapement pivots are carried by brackets, technically called cocks. Full-plate watches of the better kind have the movement covered with a

Fig. 79.—English lever full-plate movement.

cap, affording an immunity from dirt which is not secured with an open movement. Full-plate watches are therefore to be recommended for wearers engaged in dusty avocations. The full-plate movement and cap are shown in Fig. 79.

Three-quarter Plate.
There are two advantages of the three-quarter plate—illustrated in Fig. 80—over its predecessor: firstly, the escapement can be

more readily removed and replaced, and secondly, the balance being sunk below the level of the plate, a thinner watch is possible. Occasionally the fourth wheel pivot is also carried in a cock in order to get in a slightly larger balance than could otherwise be admitted. This necessitates cutting away the plate still further, and the watch is then spoken of as a half-plate; but very few are made in this way. A bar movement has no top plate, the upper ends of all the pivots being carried either in bars or cocks. As to whether a bar

Half Plate.

Fig. 80.—English lever three-quarter-plate movement.

movement or a three-quarter plate is the better, each has its advantages, and as there is no great superiority attaching to either, the selection is really a matter of individual preference.

Last Epoch of Watches. Except for the development of the chronograph and some few other complications quite apart from the perfection of timekeeping, the general adoption of the lever escapement and the going barrel may be called the last epoch in the history of the watch. The progress of the last fifty years has been marked, but has consisted rather in the perfecting of proportions than in the introductions of new principles. Even the addition of mechanism for winding from the pendant, which is gradually but surely relegating the watch key to the limbo of obsolete accessories, is but a tardy appreciation of a contrivance patented more than half a century ago.

Watch Cases.

OLD and silver watch cases, with few exceptions, are assayed at offices under government control, and bear impressions which certify their quality. The English, Swiss, and French marks are equally reliable as guarantees, though the last-named mark is but rarely seen here.

Hall Marks. The marks of the London Hall are—for silver, a lion passant and the leopard's head; for gold, a crown, the leopard's head, and the figures 18, or such other figures as represent the quality of the gold; e.g.—

       For 15 carat gold   ..   ..   ..   15 and ·625
         „ 12   „   „   ..   ..   ..   12 „ ·500
         „ 9   „   „   ..   ..   ..   9 „ ·375

Pure gold being 24 carats, these decimals represent the proportion of gold in the article so marked.

Formerly 22 and 20 carat gold were occasionally used for watch cases, but these qualities were found to be too soft to withstand the wear, and 18 carat is now considered to be preferable.

The Swiss marks for silver are a bear and the words sterling silver or the figures 0·935, and a pheasant with the figures 0·800; for gold the head of Minerva and 18 c, (or 0·755), and a squirrel and 14 c. (or 0·583).

Gold and Silver Assays. The process of assaying to determine the quality of gold and silver is a most interesting one. A little of the metal to be tested is either cut or scraped off and very carefully weighed. After the weight is noted the metal is placed in a cupel, that is, a small bowl made from compressed bone-ash. If it is gold that is under assay a proportion of silver and lead is added, and the cupel is subjected to heat in a muffle furnace. The baser metals oxidize and pass into the pores of the cupel, leaving a button of gold and silver. This button is rolled into a thin ribbon, which is heated to redness, to anneal it, and then coiled up and boiled in nitric acid to extract the silver. The pure gold remaining is then washed, again annealed and carefully weighed; the difference between it and the original weight represents the amount of alloy. The weighing, and indeed the whole operation, requires to be conducted with exceeding exactness. The amount of silver and lead added before cupelling varies, according to the judgment of the assayer after examination of the metal to be tested; twice or three times as much silver, and five or six times as much lead as there is gold, being an average proportion.

If silver is to be assayed it is wrapped in lead and cupelled in the same way as in the gold assay just described, the second operation of boiling in nitric acid being omitted.

For assaying very small quantities of gold and silver a blow-pipe may be used in place of the muffle furnace, and in experienced hands a very close approximation may be obtained.

Assay by Touch. Formerly, precious metals were assayed by the "touch," a method still in vogue in India, and occasionally practised here when it is desired to estimate the quality of finished goods. The metal to be tested is rubbed on a piece of fine-grained dark stone, called the touchstone, and beside it is rubbed a "touch needle." The touch needles are small bars of gold, one each of all the different standards of gold likely to be tested, the one used in any particular instance being the one which, in the judgment of the operator, most closely resembles the metal under trial. The two streaks are subjected to the action of nitric acid, and the operator judges the quality by the difference in colour of the two streaks.

Single-bottomed cases have but one cover at the back.

Double-bottomed Cases. Double-bottomed cases are the kind formerly in vogue with the full-plate watch, but are not so often used now. The outer cover, when opened, disclosed another thickness of the case which was pierced with a hole for winding the watch; for setting the hands of the watch, the glazed bezel over the dial had to be opened.

Domed Cases. Domed cases are most frequently used now. In these both of the covers over the back of the watch are hinged. If the watch is to be wound with a key, the inner cover or dome has two holes, one for winding, and one for setting hands; but with a keyless watch the inner cover would be intact.

Glasses. The thin and but slightly curved watch glasses introduced in the early part of the century in place of the old highly rounded and thick "bulls-eyes," are called "lunettes" in the trade. With **Hunter.** their introduction came the "hunting" case, with a cover over the glass which has to be "sprung" open to observe the time. A "half **Half Hunter.** hunter," known also as a "cut hunter," "sight hunter," and "demi-hunter," has an aperture in the centre of the hunting cover through which the position of the hands can be approximately seen, and an hour band with figures round the aperture on the outside surface of the cover. In ladies' watches opal and other enamelled bands are favoured.

Crystal Case. Crystal cases have a thick flat glass, which allows the figures on the dial to be clearly seen, and is not nearly so liable to be broken as a "lunette." The introduction of crystal glasses obviates to a great extent the necessity of hunting covers, which are accordingly becoming less in demand except for ladies, who in many instances admire the symmetrical locket-like appearance of the hunter, and rarely exact more precision than is to be obtained by an inspection of the outer band in half hunters.

Engine Turning. Thirty years ago the backs of most watch cases were engine-turned, a form of decoration which seems to have been of French origin. It consists of a series of wavy concentric shallow groves, cut in a special lathe, and though a very elegant finish which has the advantage of not readily showing scratches, it is not so popular as it was formally. Now the public taste leans more to engraving in various styles, and polished backs, which are sometimes plain, sometimes embellished with arms, crests, or monograms either cut or enamelled.

Danger of Watches becoming Magnetized. The increasing use of electricity for lighting and other purposes has introduced a new danger for watch-wearers, who should be careful to avoid close proximity to machines for generating and distributing electro-magnetic currents, for should the quick-moving parts of a watch become magnetized, its timekeeping is sure to be deranged, and to demagnetize it is a troublesome process.

Some few non-magnetic watches are now made with the quick-moving parts of some metal other than steel. For the ordinary watch balance gold or brass may be used, and there is no great difficulty in forming the lever and pallets of some of the alloys of aluminium. Balance springs of gold were tried some years ago; latterly considerable success has been attained with springs of palladium, and palladium alloyed with other metals; but so far as the ordinary run of watches is concerned no material has yet, in my judgment, been found to answer every requirement of the balance spring so well as steel.

Alloys tried for Non-magnetic Compensation Balances. Many attempts have been made to devise a compensation balance in which the use of steel is dispensed with. Arnold and Dent used some balances of platinum and silver, which compensated fairly well, but were lacking in rigidity. Mons. Paillard has achieved considerable success with palladium, alloyed with silver, copper, and other metals. In some instances he appears to have used a palladium alloy for the inner part, and brass for the outer part of the rim, and in others to have formed both laminæ of different alloys of palladium. Still, as a matter of fact, no one system of compensation for watch and chronometer balances has come into general use, and I would advise the owners of fine watches to, if possible, keep them from becoming magnetized, rather than to rely on having them made non-magnetic by the elimination of so certain and suitable a metal as steel.

Touch Watches. Watches in which the time is indicated by the exercise of the sense of feeling have been made in a variety of forms, chiefly for the service of the blind, though for ascertaining the time during the night, travelling, or other periods of darkness, touch watches have a more extended field of usefulness. As I have already mentioned, the great Duke of Wellington always wore one.

In most of the early types there were knobs around the band of the case, to indicate the hours, and when it was desired to ascertain the time, a revolving arm was pushed round till arrested by a stop which travelled with the hour wheel. The position of the arm with relation to the knobs would then be estimated. In place of this primitive and clumsy arrangement, Messrs. Kendal and Dent provide a watch in an ordinary hunting case. On springing open the cover of the case, there is revealed a dial of oxydized silver, with extra large numerals for the hours and dots for the minutes, all in high relief. The hands are of extra strength, and, apart from its superior length, there is a tit on the end of the minute hand to distinguish it. There is no glass over the dial, so that any person can, by feeling, tell with certainty both the hour and the minute.

Diminutive Watches. As soon as watches were introduced minute specimens were attached to pins, finger-rings, and other articles of jewellery. Charles V. of Germany, and James I. of England, both had watches

set in rings. Arnold made for George III. a repeater less than a silver twopenny bit in diameter.

But, however diminutive the movement may be, a watch in a finger-ring cannot be worn in comfort. Bracelets and brooches seem to be the most fitting articles of jewellery and personal adornment for the reception of timekeepers. Representations of some of the most elegant and artistic are appended.

Two of the floral brooches are really superb. One of them is in the form of a convolvulus, the other the counterfeit of a daisy. In each case the movement is hidden in the centre of the flower, which affords excellent scope for the jeweller's art, and is tastefully enamelled

and set with diamonds. The third example is to gratify an undoubted taste which exists for jewellery in insect form, and is of a gorgeous character. Every advantage has been taken in each particular design to spread out the movement in width as far as possible beyond the liliputian dial, and to obtain adequate depth. All the movements are keyless, being generally wound by turning the bezel, the method of setting hands has to be arranged as found most convenient in each case.

Keyless Mechanism for Watches.

THE first keyless watch of which record can be found is that of Caron, in which, as already stated, the mainspring was wound by pushing round a projection on the edge of the case, very much as the spring for the repeating work is now wound in a repeating watch. In 1820, Thomas Prest patented a form of keyless work actuated by turning a button on the pendant. It did not include any provision for setting the hands, and is said to have been intended for the use of the blind. But though the convenience of dispensing with a key was so obvious, keyless watches did not come into use for some time after. The Swiss, about 1851, began to place keyless watches in the market, but English manufacturers, who still retained the fusee construction of movement, held back for a long time, till the increasing

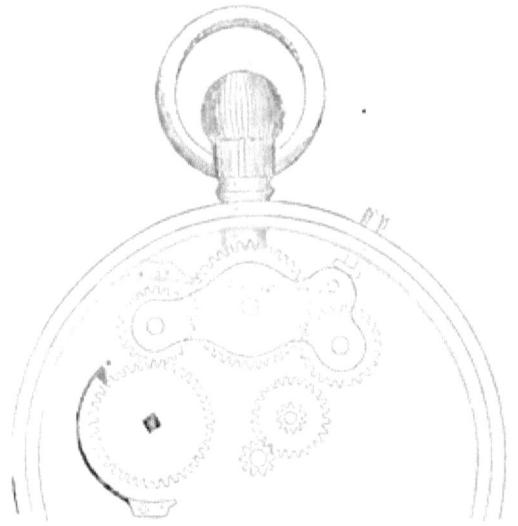

Fig. 81.—Rocking-bar keyless mechanism.

popularity of keyless work forced their hands, and compelled them to supply what the public demanded, even though it involved the abandonment of the venerable and much-loved equalizer.

"Rocking-Bar" Keyless Work. There are two kinds of going barrel keyless mechanism now in general use, the rocking bar and the shifting sleeve. The former variety is shown in Fig. 81. For winding the watch, connection has to be made between the serrated button projection above the pendant and the wheel to the left hand of the figure, which is attached to the barrel arbor For setting the hands the winding connection must be broken, and connection made with the minute wheel on the right hand of the figure, so that it may be actuated in either direction by turning the button. Three wheels, gearing together, are planted on the rocking bar. The middle one rides freely on a stud which projects from the rocking bar, which is free to move up or down, so as to engage with either the barrel wheel or the minute wheel. In its normal position the connection is with the barrel wheel. A spring, fixed at one end to the pillar plate, presses against a small stud on the rocking bar just sufficiently to keep the winding wheels in gear; a bevelled pinion or contrate wheel squared on to the stem of the winding button gears with the middle wheel on the rocking bar. As the button is turned for winding the resistance of the barrel wheel ensures the safety of its depth with the wheel on the rocking bar. When the knob is turned the reverse way the teeth of this latter wheel slip over the teeth of the barrel wheel. There is a spring click to prevent the barrel wheel running back. When any strain is thrown on the click the end of it butts against a pin screwed into the plate, but during winding there is a space between this pin and the end of the click, so that if the mainspring is wound tightly, the wheel is allowed to recoil a little till the end of the click touches the pin. Undue strain is thus taken off the mainspring, and there is no fear of overbanking, which is often observed after careless winding where no such provision is made. For setting hands, a push piece, projecting through the band of the case, is pressed with the thumbnail, so as to depress the right-hand side of the rocking bar till the wheel on that side engages with the minute wheel. The thumb-nail presses on the push piece till the operation of setting the hands is completed, and directly the push piece is released the winding wheels engage again.

"Shifting-Sleeve" Key-less Work. The shifting-sleeve form of keyless mechanism is shown in Fig. 84. A bevelled pinion, with clutch teeth underneath, rides loose on the stem of the winding button, and gears with bevelled teeth on the face of the large wheel which is just below the pendant. The part of the winding stem below the bevelled pinion is square, and upon this part is fitted a sleeve with clutch teeth corresponding with those of the bevelled pinion at its upper extremity, and a contrate pinion at its lower extremity. A groove is formed around the sleeve in which is a spring pressing the sleeve upwards, so as to keep the clutch teeth engaged. While the clutch teeth are so engaged the winding may be proceeded with. To set hands a push piece projecting through the band of the case acts on a knuckle of the spring just mentioned, so that, as the push piece is pressed in, the spring draws the sleeve away from the clutch teeth of the bevelled pinion, and brings the contrate pinion into gear with a small wheel, which latter gears with the minute wheel.

Neither of the simple keyless arrangements used for going barrels is suitable if the fusee is insisted on, because in the latter construction the mainspring is wound by turning the fusee, and accidental pressure on the winding button would most likely stop the watch if the winding wheels were left in action after winding.

Perpetual Calendar Work.

IT will be remembered that the simple calendar work attached to the old long-case clocks required the day-of-the-month dial to be adjusted by hand to suit the varying lengths of the months. A perpetual calendar to register the days of all the months as well as to provide for the extra day of leap year is a very different affair, and is now applied to both clocks and watches.

"How it is done" will be understood from an examination of the enlarged view of the calendar mechanism in a watch which is given in Fig. 82. There are several different ways of attaining the same end; this arrange-

Fig. 82.—Perpetual calendar mechanism.

ment, which is the invention of Mr. C. H. Audemars, is as good as any.

The wheel *H*, driven by the minute wheel, makes one

turn in twenty-four hours, and carries a movable finger, a, which, by contact with a pin, moves the armed lever D by its extremity p. This lever, which has its centre of motion at i, acts through its different arms. Firstly, at c it moves the day of the week star wheel (7 teeth). Secondly, at b, the star wheel for the day of the month (31 teeth). The finger a makes engagement and passes one tooth each day of the star wheel E (59 teeth), for showing the phases of the moon.

The part of the mechanism which renders the calendar perpetual is composed of a wheel of 31 teeth, F, engaging with the star wheel C. This wheel, which makes one turn per month, passes at each turn, by means of a movable finger, n, one tooth of the star wheel G (48 teeth), which latter by this means makes a revolution in four years. The circumference of account disc fixed to this star wheel corresponds to the months of thirty-one days, the shallowest notches to those of thirty days, and the four quarter notches to the month of February. At e, which is for February in leap year, the notch is hardly so deep as the other three quarter notches.

Each day, after moving the day of the week and the day of the month, the lever D, solicited by the spring h, returns its arm, r, to rest on the circumference of the count disc or in one of its notches, according to the position of the disc.

The point of the piece u, pressed by its spring, rests on the snail k. Before the last day of the month it falls on to the small part of the snail, and then its action is substituted for that of the arm b; the point of the piece u presses against the notch of the snail, and advances the star wheel the number of teeth necessary for the hand to indicate the first of the following month. It will be understood that the distance the point of the piece u falls is regulated by the position of the arm r on the disc or in one of its notches.

In the engraving the mechanism is set to the first of

December of the last year before leap year. The two pieces *m* and *t* are at the disposition of the watch wearer; the first for adjusting the day, and the second for the age of the moon. The figure *a* is movable to permit of moving the hands back without deranging the mechanism. When the wheel *H* is turned back the finger is arrested by the arm *p*, and, as it is sloped at the back, the pin carried by the wheel is able to pass easily, because the flexibility of the piece *s* permits it to give a little.

Repeating Mechanism.

A VIEW of the repeating mechanism of a watch is given in Fig. 83. It is actuated by a mainspring which is wound by pushing round a band in the edge of the case. The number of hours that will then be struck, and whether quarters or minutes will follow, depends upon the position of certain "snails," which revolve with the centre arbor. The principle is really an elaboration of Barlow's striking work, which had better be referred to first by any one who has the curiosity to trace the function of the various pieces. The gongs on which the blows are struck are not shown, but they are pieces of wire fixed at one end and curled round just on the outside of the movement.

Centre Seconds Watches.

FOR the use of doctors, scientists, and sportsmen, watches with some kind of centre-seconds hand have been made for many years. At first they were constructed, like Harrison's prize chronometer, without provision for stopping the centre seconds.

Centre Seconds Stop Watch. The centre seconds stop watch was so arranged that by moving round a slide in the band of the case a brake was brought into contact with the roller of the lever escapement. This was rather a poor device, for the whole mechanism of the

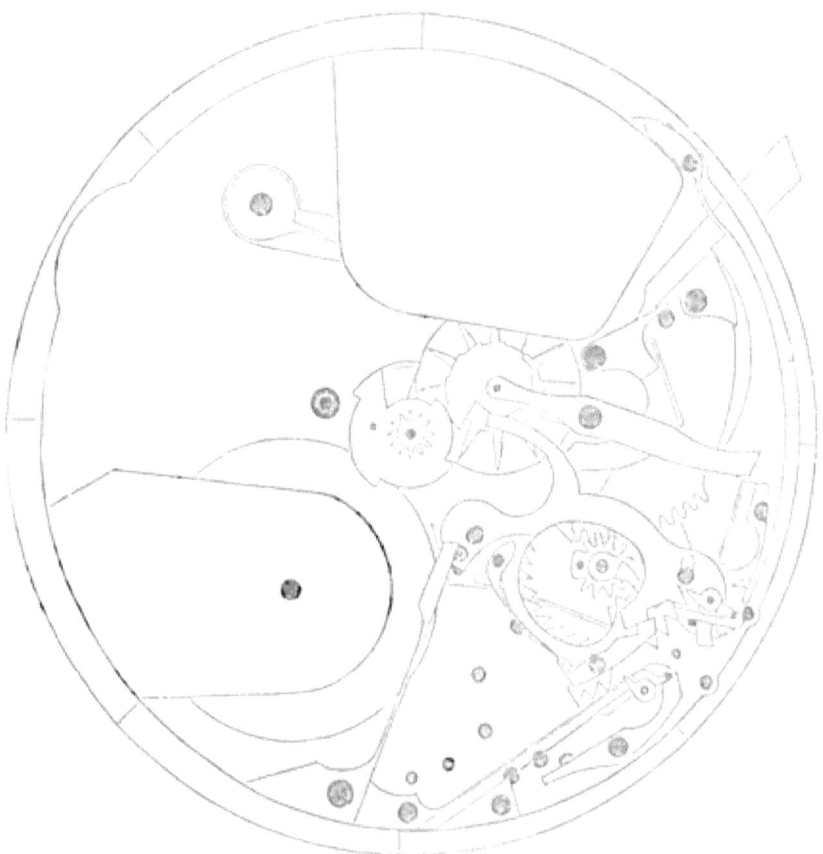

Fig. 83.—Repeating mechanism of a watch.

watch was thereby arrested. If the escapement was at all inclined to set, the watch did not readily start again when the brake was removed, and even if it did resume its course at once the watch would of course be slow by the interval during which the brake was on, and therefore cease to record the correct time.

Independent Centre Seconds. Then the independent centre seconds was introduced, in which there was a separate mainspring and train to drive the centre-seconds hand, whose course was regulated by an arm or flirt projecting from the arbor of the last pinion of the independent train, and at every revolution engaging with either the escape pinion or a special pinion on the arbor of the escape pinion. By means of a slide in the case the flirt could be stopped, and the centre-seconds hand arrested in that way at pleasure; so that the prime function of the watch was not interfered with. The independent centre seconds is a sound and durable arrangement suitable for many observations, but it fails to satisfy every requirement for race-timing.

Chronographs. The extremity of the hand of some centre-seconds timekeepers was formed into a small funnel containing ink, into which a spring pointer dipped; the pointer could at pleasure be pressed on to the dial where it would leave a dot of ink to record when the pressure was made. These were very appropriately called chronographs, a title which has been, curiously enough, retained for the sporting centre-seconds watches now in use, and which do *not* write the time.

Heart-cam. In 1862 the late Mr. A. Nicole patented the heart-cam action, by which the centre-seconds hand can by successive depressions of a button on the watch case be started, stopped, and returned to rest at zero, and this is the construction now adopted for the watches known as chronographs. It is a clever device, and will be understood by reference to the annexed drawing, Fig. 84.

Modern Chronographs.
The chronograph hand is fixed to a wheel which runs freely on the centre arbor under the canon pinion. This wheel has a finely serrated edge, and is driven by another wheel of such a proportion that the chronograph hand travels round the dial once in a minute. The serrated wheel which drives the centre one and a pinion to which it is attached are mounted on a pivoted carriage with a projecting tail. On the left of the engraving is a castle ratchet having

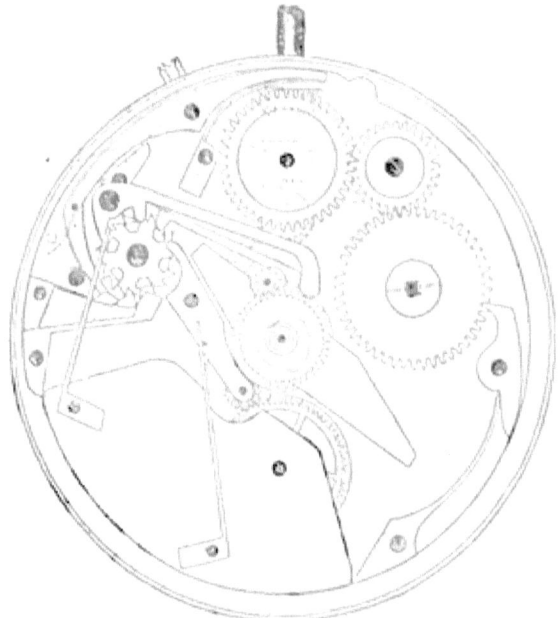

Fig. 84.—Centre seconds chronograph.

eighteen ratchet-shaped teeth around its edge and six projections or castle teeth rising from its upper face. In the figure the two serrated wheels are in contact, and the chronograph hand is consequently travelling. If now the button of the case pendant be pressed, the shorter end of the bent lever, which is lying around the movement just within the case, is depressed, and the hooked end of the lever draws the ratchet round so that the tail of the carriage, on which the driving serrated wheel is mounted, is moved far enough to take it from contact with the wheel on which the chronograph hand is fixed, and the hand consequently stops. At the same time a castle tooth which has been keeping a circular break off the chronograph hand wheel is moved out of the way so that the brake drops, thus keeping the chronograph hand from being shifted by accidental motion of the watch. When the button is again depressed, the castle ratchet is shifted still further round, and the returning lever with the pointed end is allowed to drop on the heart-shaped cam, which is fixed to the chronograph-hand wheel. As the returning lever drops, its tail lifts the brake off the wheels, and the lever, impelled by a spring, turns the cam from whatever position it may happen to be in till the lever rests on that part of the edge which is nearest to the centre of motion. The chronograph hand is then at zero.

Each time that the bent lever is pressed it draws the ratchet round one tooth, and as there are three ratchet teeth to one castle tooth, it is evident that all the pieces in contact with the castle return to their original position after three movements of the lever.

The balance of a chronograph watch makes five vibrations per second, so that the chronograph hand registers fifths of a second.

Minute Chronograph. So far the mechanism described would record the motion of the centre-seconds hand only. If the minutes are also to be registered a subsidiary minute dial is provided, the hand of which is moved forward one minute for every completed revolution of the centre-seconds hand, and returned to zero at the same time as the centre-seconds hand by means of a heart-shaped cam.

Split Seconds. To enable two intervals of varying duration from a common starting-point to be recorded, such as the time occupied by two competitors in a race, the centre-seconds hand of some chronographs is made double or "split." Then when the first interval has elapsed a subsidiary push piece in the edge of the case is depressed and one half of the seconds hand is stopped, the other continuing its course till the push piece at the pendant is pressed, when two centre-seconds hands appear stationary on the dial.

This ingenious "splitting" of the seconds is also accomplished by castle ratchet and heart-shaped cam action. There are really two distinct centre-seconds hands, and the depression of the subsidiary push piece causes a brake to clip and stop one of them, the next depression removing the brake and allowing a returning lever to fall on the cam.

Pistol Report misleading. When the starting and winning posts of a race are in sight, or where the timer can obtain a visible signal, such as the flash of a pistol from each end, one watch may be used for checking the start and the finish. But the *report* of a pistol will not do if an accurate record is desired, on account of the comparatively slow rate at which sound travels, as mentioned on page 187. For long-distance contests where the beginning and the ending are wide apart, the duration is generally checked by two chronographs of known excellence and compared just prior to the race, one of these is stopped at the start and the other at the finish. In other cases an electric signal of the start is sent from the starting-point to a watch holder at the winning-post, or *vice versâ*. For timing races in America advantage has occasionally been taken of the chronograph used by astronomers.

Rotating Chronograph and Electric Pricker. In this a large roller covered with paper is rotated by a clock, and at the moment of starting an electric current causes a pricker to mark the paper. Another mark is made when the race is finished, or at the getting home of the first and any succeeding competitors whose time it is desired to ascertain. In this way an exact and enduring record is obtained.

Appointment Reminder.

MANY of us, like Lord Dundreary, are occasionally exercised to "wecollect to wemember" the precise time of some important engagement, such as the starting of a particular train. Messrs. Kendal and Dent have devised and patented a useful "reminder." It consists of subsidiary hour and minute hands attached to a watch, or other timekeeper, and set by the wearer to the time he desires to remember. The "reminder" occupies the position of the usual seconds dial, as illustrated in Fig. 85. The reminder hands are mounted on independent motion work, and are actuated by a small shaft with a knob similar to the head of a drawing pin at one end, which is sunk in nearly level with the case. At the other end of the shaft is a pinion which takes into the minute wheel of the motion work. When it is desired to set the "reminder,"

Fig. 85.—Appointment reminder.

the knob rotates by simply pressing the thumb upon it and turning it round.

Some such addition really seems to be the natural supplement to every watch, and the wonder is that it was never introduced before. How many of us after referring to a time table in the morning and mentally repeating the exact time a train starts which we have to catch later in the day, have had a worried feeling of uncertainty as the hour approached as to whether it was—say five minutes to six or five minutes past six! But possessed of this "reminder," we can now calmly set it to the time of departure, and there it remains for reference. As often as the watch is drawn from the pocket it acts as a reminder, and as the hour for departure approaches, the difference between the hands of the watch and the "reminder" shows at a glance the minutes at disposal. As a train-catcher it may often prove to be more valuable than the timekeeper itself, for, as the intending traveller speeds along to the railway station, there are probably clocks in abundance pointing to the time of day, and no doubt nearly every person he meets can give him the same information, while neither clocks nor wayfarers supply just what he wants to know, that is, the time his train starts. Again, to record the duration of a speech, or of a race, the "reminder" is invaluable. Many other uses to which this adjunct to a watch can be put will occur to every one.

Catching a Train.

Care of Watches.

A GOOD watch deserves more care and attention than it obtains from many wearers. The pieces in a complicated watch will often number over a thousand; and a watch of the ordinary kind is composed of about 112 pieces, each one accurately designed

and finished for a particular function. The slowest wheel of the train, which is attached to the barrel containing the mainspring, completes but four rotations in twenty-four hours; while during the same period the vibrating balance, which is really the timekeeper, makes 432,000 excursions, and a variation of but two or three on either side of this number would call for further adjustment from the hands of the skilful springer. In a year the barrel has turned 1460 times, and the balance has gone to and fro the enormous number of 157,590,000 times. Seeing that every pivot in the watch requires lubrication, and that even the finest of oil rapidly dries up, a periodical cleaning and lubricating are absolutely necessary.

Advice to Watch-wearers. The works of a watch should never be exposed, except for the purpose of necessary regulation; and this operation should never be performed in the street or other place where dust is flying, nor should one attempt to regulate his watch while he is smoking, lest tobacco-ash should enter the movements. Care should also be taken that the instrument used for moving the regulator is free from dust. A fruitful cause of watches stopping is the pernicious practice of opening the inner case for curiosity, whereby grit, hair, or other foreign matter is allowed to enter, and it frequently happens that close examination by inexpert people results in damp from the breath settling on the steel work, and causing rust. I would say to all watch-wearers, do not be too hasty in regulating your watch. Owners of a new watch are especially prone to alter the regulator when there is no need of it. Give the watch plenty of time to settle down to its rate after regulation; and remember all watches, except the very finest, gain in winter and lose in summer.

When to Wind. A watch should be wound regularly once a day, whether night or morning is immaterial.

Some watchmakers recommend winding in the morning, if the watch is laid on its back during the night, because the vibration of the balance is increased when the watch is in that position, and, as the vibration is greatest when the mainspring is fully wound, there may be from winding at night danger of damage through what is called "banking," which arises from too extensive a vibration of the balance. But injury from banking may also be caused by sudden movements and jerks on the part of the watch-wearer, which is a reason in favour of winding at night, when the watch is removed from the person, and therefore not liable to be jerked or jolted; so that each person may safely study his or her convenience as to the time of winding, provided it is done regularly once a day. Whether winding with a key or by means of a button in the pendant, the winder only should be rotated, and the watch itself held perfectly still during the operation; for imparting a circular motion to the watch, as many people have a habit of doing, is very likely to increase the vibration of the balance, and cause the injurious banking just spoken of.

Warning against Meddling with the Works. If a watch is stopped, first ascertain if it is wound, for numberless instances have occurred in which the watchmaker finds the only fault is that the wearer has forgotten this very necessary routine. If the watch *is* wound, and still lifeless, take it at once to your watchmaker. No shaking, no tinkering; you can do no good, and will most likely cause further damage. I am sorry to say a word against the ladies, but many of them are most unreasonable in their treatment of watches (not you, I hope, madam, who are honouring me by reading these lines). They (some of them, that is) wind their watches at uncertain intervals, hastily, turning both watch and winder, and, if anything is wrong, they cannot rest till they have the watch open; and it has been asserted (though this *cannot* be true) that they probe the works with a pin; and occasionally go so far as to fish out the fine balance spring altogether, under the idea that it is a hair which has trespassed. But though these things are most likely to be mere malevolent and scandalous inventions, still the fact remains, and I am bound to confess it, that ladies' watches when sent for repair often do bear marks of ill-usage.

Watch Pockets. The watch-pocket should be turned inside out and brushed occasionally, to prevent an accumulation of dirt working its way through the joints of the watch-case into the movement. A piece of soft chamois leather is the best material for a watch-pocket.

Marine Chronometers.

ONE of the most important uses to which time-keepers are devoted is that of enabling the navigator to ascertain what longitude he may happen to be in as he travels over the sea.

Insufficiency of Dead Reckoning. During the sixteenth century it became evident that, if ocean navigation was to be carried on with anything like safety, there must be some more certain means of finding the longitude than depending on the dead reckoning, and, in 1598, Philip III. of Spain offered a reward of one hundred thousand crowns to any one who would solve the problem.

The Government of Holland also encouraged investigations with the same object; but no one seemed to see a way out of the difficulty; and Morin, conversing with Cardinal Richelieu as to the possibility of finding a means, remarked, "I know not what such an undertaking would be to the devil himself, but to man it would undoubtedly be the height of folly."

English Government offer £20,000. But the need was pressing, and affected maritime nations particularly, so that, in 1714, the English Government offered a reward of £10,000 to any person who invented a method of determining the longitude to within a degree, or sixty geographical miles; £15,000 if to within forty miles; and £20,000 if to within thirty miles.

Lunar Observations. Two methods of procedure were regarded as promising, one by lunar and the other by solar observations. In the first of these, which was thought to be favoured by Dr. Maskelyne, the Astronomer Royal, it was proposed to ascertain, by observation with a sextant, the distance of the moon from certain fixed stars, and then by reference to a book find the Greenwich time corresponding to that distance.

Solar Observations. As to the second method, which was eventually successful. The captain of a ship can readily ascertain the instant of noon at any place by observation of the sun, and therefore it is clear that if he had an instrument that could be depended upon to show him Greenwich time, the calculation of the longitude would, by comparison, be an easy one indeed.

Dr. Hooke gives particulars of Lord Kingcardine's Experiment. The idea of constructing such an instrument was not a new one. In the course of a paper he read before the Royal Society in 1662, Dr. Hooke said, "The Lord Kingcardine did resolve to make some trial what might be done by carrying a pendulum clock to sea, for which end he contrived to make the watch part to be moved by a spring instead of a weight, and then, making the case of the clock very heavy with lead, he suspended it underneath the deck of the ship by a ball and socket of brass, making the pendulum but short, namely, to vibrate half-seconds; and that he might be the better enabled to judge of the effect of it, he caused two of the same kind of pendulum clocks to be made, and suspended them both pretty near the middle of the vessel, underneath the deck. Thus done, having first adjusted them to go equal to one another, and pretty near to the true time, he caused them first to move parallel to one another, that is, in the plane of the length of the ship; and afterwards he turned one to move in a plane at right angles with the former; and in both these cases it was found by trials made at sea (at which I was present) that they would vary from one another, though not very much." Dr. Hooke concludes by saying that "they might be of very good use at sea if some farther contrivances about them were thought upon and put into practice."

Huygens. About the same time Huygens constructed a timekeeper, but after trial, he confessed himself baffled by the irregularities consequent on alternations of heat and cold.

In 1664, one Abraham Hill patented "a new way of makeing of watches and clocks to be vsed at sea for exact measuring of tyme, towardes the finding the longitude and knowing the true course and place of a shipp, differenced from all other sorte of watches by having instead of a ballance, a rodd of wyer, or a thynn narrow plate, with a weight at the lower end thereof, called a pendulum, and at the vpper end an arme with twoe catches or holes to move it, and certaine crooked places or cheekes for regulating the motion thereof, which motion is pduced by one or more springs or weights, the said watches being fitted with balls and socketts to hand by for goeing steadily at sea."

AND OTHER TIMEKEEPERS.

Major Holmes. Another experiment was made with a timekeeper by Major Holmes, in 1665, during a voyage from the coast of Guinea.

John Harrison to the fore. However, stimulated by the prospect of obtaining the premium of £20,000, John Harrison, a carpenter, of Faulby, in Yorkshire, who had already obtained some little local celebrity by cleaning and repairing clocks, devoted himself to the task of constructing a timekeeper for the purpose. His first efforts were in the form of clocks, and with **His First Essays.** one of those, through the generous representation of Graham and Dr. Halley, the astronomer, he was permitted to proceed in a king's ship to Lisbon, where he was able to determine the longitude to within about one degree thirty minutes. On this result the Board of Longitude, which had been created by Parliament, gave him £500 to enable him to proceed with his improvements.

After thirty years of unremitting labour, he succeeded in producing the foundation of the present marine chronometer. Harrison's timekeeper, which is still preserved at the Royal Observatory, Greenwich, is about five inches in diameter, is cased like a large watch, and has a long seconds hand moving from the centre of the dial. It contains a maintaining power to drive the fusee while the watch is being wound, and there is a laminated arm of brass and steel to lengthen and shorten the balance spring in answer to changes of temperature. Har- **His Success.** rison's son William embarked at Portsmouth on a voyage to Jamaica with the precious instrument in 1761. On arrival at Port Royal the timekeeper was found to be in error only 5·1 seconds, and on the return to Portsmouth the total variation during the whole voyage was ascertained to be but 1 minute 54·5 seconds. This was sufficiently accurate to enable the longitude to be determined within eighteen miles, a much narrower limit than the Admiralty stipulated for.

His vain Applications for the Reward. But Harrison did not get the reward yet. Another voyage was made to Barbadoes, and then in 1765 an Act of Parliament was passed awarding him the £20,000, one half to be paid on his explaining the principles on which his timekeeper was constructed, and the other half as soon as it could be ascertained that similar instruments could be made by others. Further delays occurred even after the duplicate chronometers had been made, and it was not till 1767 that John Harrison obtained the last portion of the £20,000 he had so thoroughly earned.

Lareum Kendal. Lareum Kendal, Harrison's apprentice and successor, made a chronometer closely resembling Harrison's, though somewhat slightly different in construction. The sum paid for this instrument was £400. It accompanied Captain Cook on his memorable voyages in the *Resolution*, until that intrepid officer was treacherously slain in 1779, and is now in the possession of the Royal United Service Institution. In 1774 Captain Cook wrote, "Our longitude can never be erroneous while we have so good a guide as Mr. Kendall's watch." Lareum Kendal afterwards made watches with the *remontoire* escapement and compensation curb; one of these, in excellent preservation, is in the museum of the Clockmakers' Company at the Guildhall.

Mudge adheres to the Verge. Mudge and other horologists set themselves to improve on Harrison's chronometer, which had a kind of verge escapement, driven by a *remontoire*, or auxiliary spring, wound up every few seconds. It remained for Earnshaw and Arnold to solve the problem, which they did by devising the spring detent escapement and compensation balance, the two distinguishing features of our present chronometers.

AND OTHER TIMEKEEPERS.

Harrison's Maintaining Spring alone survives.
All that has survived of Harrison's inventions is his maintaining spring. His laminated arm, or compensation curb, as he termed it, has given place to the compensation balance, and the verge escapement, however modified, was defective in principle, though Mudge, who had previously invented a far superior one in the lever, still clung to it, and allowed younger men to pass him.

Modern Chronometers.
Our modern chronometers have silvered dials $4\frac{1}{2}$ inches in diameter, the seconds hand being between the centre and the VI. The movements are $3\frac{1}{2}$ inches in diameter; they are fitted into brass boxes, which are suspended on gimbals to ensure their retaining a horizontal position, notwithstanding the motion of the ship, and enclosed in a square wooden box having an inner glazed lid. The escapement and balance have already been described.

Arnold appears to have been the first to apply the expressive term "chronometer" to portable timekeepers of precision, although in 1734 Dr. Desaguliers, Rector of St. James's, Piccadilly, wrote of "a little clock or chronometer which Mr. George Graham made for me some four years ago." In the seventeenth century the word was used as a title for a kind of metronome invented by one Loulie, of Amsterdam. As a variation of clock, watch, and timekeeper, Derham coined the expression time-engine, which was clearly too clumsy a combination for adoption by horologists generally. In France "chronometer" has not the restrictive meaning we attach to it; but is generally accepted as indicative of a timekeeper of any sort.

Keyless Mechanism for Marine Chronometers.
Ship's captains and others who have the care of chronometers often declare that the clumsy practice of turning the instrument upside down, in order to wind it, exerts more or less of

R

an injurious influence on its steady going. Whether there is any warrant for such an assertion or no it is evident that the present method is open to improvement, and various suggestions have been made for winding from the top, though hitherto no one has come into general use. It may be taken for granted that any arrangement, to be perfect, must fulfil the following conditions. There must be no extra drag on the fusee during the going of the chronometer, nor any interference with the fusee except during the time of winding; and no action of the operator must be needed to sever connection between the winder and the fusee when the winding is accomplished, otherwise the operator may omit to take such action, and then accidental pressure or other obstruction to the winder may derange or stop the chronometer. Though the convenience of a winder attached to the chronometer is obvious, manufacturers do not seem to have entered into the matter very warmly; for while the instruments are in their care and out of the gymbals, not only does the ordinary key answer well, but it is positively handier than any adjunct would be. But that the requirements of the users of chronometers must eventually prevail, and that a rational means of winding will be applied sooner or later to all marine chronometers, scarcely admits of doubt. Arnold, who was one of the pioneers of keyless watches, and some other of the early chronometer makers, did occasionally adopt what were termed turret windings to obviate overturning the chronometer. In these a movable key fitted the top of a spindle at the side of the box, and on the bottom of the spindle was a pinion which geared with a wheel on the fusee arbor. But apart from the objection to a pair of wheels and winding spindle being continually driven by the fusee, the danger of the key being left on rendered this arrangement extremely unsatisfactory, and for some years fixed winders attached to the fusee square were put forward by chronometer makers as the best

Early Windings.

solution of the problem. Some of these were winged like an ordinary key, and some in the form of a large button with serrated edge. But, at the best, they could only be accepted as an indication of the desire to improve on the primitive barbarism.

Kendal and Dent's Winding Work. Kendal and Dent's attached winder appears really to solve the various difficulties satisfactorily, and in it the following advantages are apparent:—(1) The winding is accomplished by turning a handle at the side of and above the dial, with-

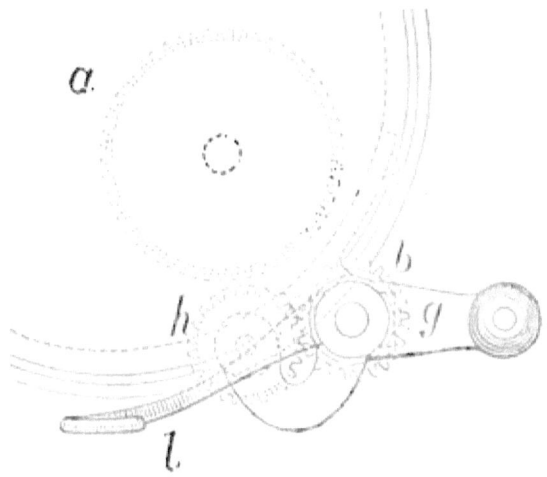

Fig. 87.

out tilting or in any way interfering with the position of the chronometer. (2) When the winding is completed, all connection with the fusee is broken automatically, and no pressure on, or turning of the winding handle will then affect the going of the chronometer. (3) It is inexpensive. (4) It can be readily applied to existing chronometers. Figs. 87 and 88 give two illustrations of this patent.

On the squared extremity of the fusee arbor is mounted a toothed wheel, a. A toothed wheel of similar pitch, b, is fixed to the lower end of a spindle, *c*, which is attached to the brass of the chronometer *d* by means of two brackets, *e* and *f*. On the upper end of the spindle *c* is the winding handle *g*. The wheels *a* and *b* are of such a size that their teeth do not engage with each other, but are just free. A third wheel, *h*, engages with *b*, and may be made to engage with the wheel *a* also, thus establishing

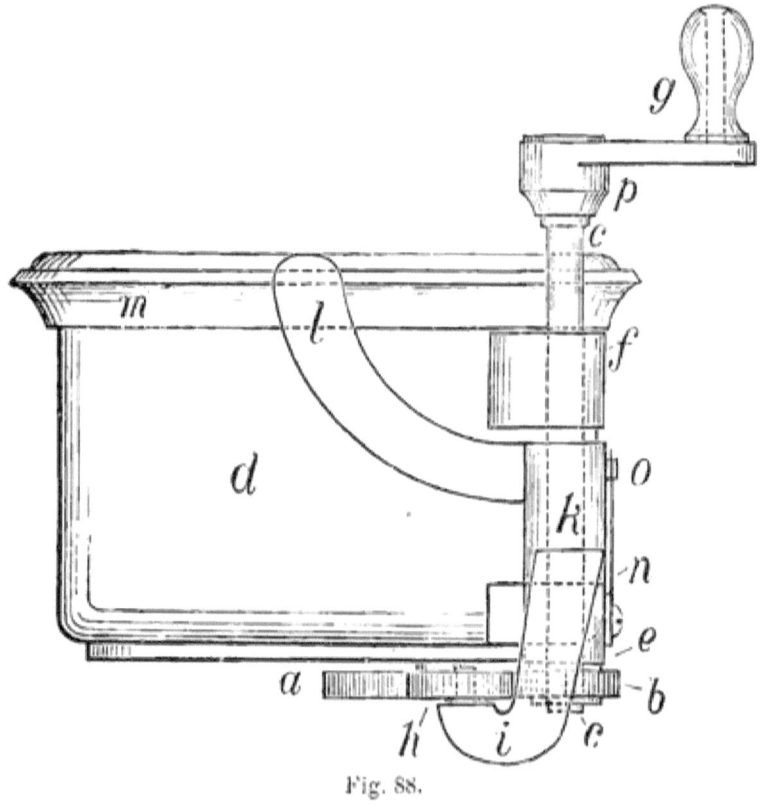

Fig. 88.

connection between *a* and *b*. The wheel *h* runs loose on a stud carried on one end of a swinging arm, *i*. The other end of this arm is in the form of a boss, *k*, which encircles and runs loosely on the spindle *c*. Rising from the top of the boss *k* is a lever *l*, curved somewhat to the shape of the bezel of the chronometer, *m*. A spring, *n*, fixed at one end to the bracket *e* bears against a pin, *o*, in the boss *k*, so that the wheel *h* is normally kept from engaging with the wheel *a*. When it is desired to wind the chronometer, the bezel of the chronometer, *m*, is steadied by the left hand of the operator, who at the same time clasps the free end of the lever *l* with his thumb. The resistance of the spring *n* is overcome, the wheel *h* engages with the wheel *a*, and the operator turns the winding handle *g* with his right hand. Directly the operator removes his thumb from the lever *l*, the wheel *h* is by the force of the spring disengaged from the wheel *a*. If desired, the boss *p* of the winding handle may contain a ratchet and click, to prevent the operator damaging the chronometer by winding it the wrong way. The winding handle may be either cranked as shown, or winged like an ordinary chronometer key.

Chronometers for the Royal Navy. It was not till about 1825 that chronometers were regularly supplied to the ships of the Royal Navy, and then the rule was that the Admiralty furnished one instrument to each ship; if the captain of the ship chose to provide a second, the Admiralty would then give him a third, and this system prevailed to within the last few years, but now the Admiralty find all necessary chronometers.

Chronometer Trials at Greenwich Observatory. The following is the mode of selection adopted by the Admiralty in purchasing chronometers. Every year there is a chronometer trial held at Greenwich Observatory. Makers have first to get permission to send chronometers for trial, and as a rule two instruments only are accepted from each maker. From 1822 till 1835 prizes were given to the makers whose instruments performed best; but now all the recompense a maker gets for his trouble and patience in adjusting his chronometers is the chance that they will be purchased. The trial at present begins in

July, and extends over about twenty-eight weeks; every morning the official in charge of the chronometers at the observatory winds each one, and notes its difference from mean time. For two periods of four weeks each during the trial all the chronometers are placed in an "oven," that is, a closed chamber heated by exterior gas-jets to a certain prearranged temperature, an automatic governor being attached to the gas supply to ensure uniformity. Before the trial is over the instruments are also subjected to the cold of winter; the total range of temperatures throughout the trial being usually from about 95° to 32° Fahr.

When the trial is over the instruments are arranged in order of excellence, according to the view of the Astronomer Royal. His formula for estimating their merit is to add to the difference between the greatest and least variation (in seconds) twice the difference between one week and the next. These factors produce what is called a trial number, and the instrument with the lowest trial number is placed at the top of the list. Then the Admiralty decide to offer a certain price for so many of the instruments from the top of the list as may satisfy their requirements, the price in each case being just what they consider the instrument to be worth from its trial number, and it is rarely that their offer is refused, although occasionally higher prices are to be obtained from foreign governments or private owners for instruments that have performed well at Greenwich. For marine chronometers, English artists have always been supreme, and the records of the Greenwich trial, extending over the last three decades, show that, although in some years the average going is not quite so good as in previous ones, we have been creeping nearer and nearer to absolute perfection. So small is the error now, that considering the imperfection inherent to all human productions, the alteration in the character of metal under different temperatures and hygrometric changes, and, above all, the unreliable behaviour of the necessary unguent applied to the working surfaces, it is hardly possible that further improvement can be made. To maintain even the present standard requires almost incredible patience and skill on the part of the adjuster.

In the Royal Navy the chronometers are never allowed out of the cabin, deck or assistant watches previously compared with the chronometer being used for noting the time of the observations. Every precaution is taken to prevent the chronometers running down. There is a board outside the captain's cabin having printed on one side "Chronometers wound." This is turned over every night revealing the other side, on which is "Chronometers not wound," and the guard is not relieved in the morning till the chronometers are wound, and the board reversed.

From the foregoing remarks it will be seen that Englishmen may justly claim the credit of inventing a very large proportion of the devices which constitute modern timekeepers. It would, however, be folly for us to arrogate to ourselves exclusive ability in the production of watches and clocks. Competition is so keen that the manufacturer of to-day, who desires to keep in the front rank, is compelled to avail himself of the skilled labour of artists in all parts of the world, and the quality and style of his goods are in great measure dependent on the judgment displayed in this respect.

INDEX.

A
Act of Parliament clocks, 157
Adjusting for positions, 208
—— —— temperature, 208
Airy, G. B., 177
Alarum, 75
American time, 45
Anchor escapement, 135
Appointment recorders, 232
Arnold, J., 149
Astronomical clock, 166

B
Balance chronometer, 207
—— watch, 207
—— spring, 122
Ball of Venice, 110
Barlow, E., 131
Bar movement, 243
Barometric error, 185
Barrel, 60
Beauvais clock, 86
Bells, St. Paul's, 173
——, Westminster, 186
Berosus, 25
Berthond, 206
Big Ben, 186
Blind man's watches, 218
Boleyn, 57
Box chronometer, 236
Bracelet watches, 249
Bradley, L., 171
Brass, movements of, 210
Breguet, 148
Brooch, watch, 219
Buonaparte, Jerome, 161
Buonaparte, Napoleon, 163
Byron, 2

C
Calendar, simple, 155
——, perpetual, 224
——, watch, 225
Cam, heart-shaped, 228
Cambridge chimes, 188
Candle clocks, 47
Cannon pinions, 119
Caron, 148
Cases, clock, 194
——, watch, 244
Centre of oscillation, 79
Centre seconds, 227
Charlemagne, 42
Charles I., 76
—— II., 76
—— V., of France, 54
—— V., of Germany, 120
Charlotte, Princess, 160
Chimes, Cambridge, 188
——, Westminster, 188
Chronograph, 229
Chronometer escapement, 150
——, marine, 236
Circular error, 80
Clepsydra, 38
Click and ratchet, 54
Clock, derivation of, 63
—— cases, 194
Clockmakers' Company, 96
Closed clock cases, 89
Compensated pendulum, 185
Compensation balance, 207
Concentric minute hand, 119
Cowper, 31
Cox, 109
Cromwell, O., 101
Crystal case, 247

Crutch, 153
Ctesibus, 40
Cumming, 142
Cunge, 111
Cut hunter, 216
Cycloidal cheeks, 129
Cylinder escapement, 123

D

Denison, 177
Derham, 58, 137
Detached escapement, 150
De Vick, 51
Dials, St. Paul's, 172
——, Westminster, 177
Dickens, C., 165
Dog watch, 22
Dome, 216
Duplex escapement, 137

E

Earnshaw, T., 149
Egyptian clepsydra, 39
Electric clocks, 201
Elizabeth, Queen, 63, 160
Ellicott, 139
Enamelling, 101
Engine turning, 217
Epact, 23
Equation of time, 12
Equational clock, 13,
Escapement, anchor, 135
——, chronometer, 150
——, cylinder, 123
——, dead beat, 125
——, double three-legged gravity, 179
——, duplex, 138
——, lever, 140
——, pin pallet, 199
——, pin wheel, 143
——, verge, 54
Expansion of fluids, 96

F

Facio, 118
Falconet, 112
Ferguson, 145
Floral watches, 219
Fob watches, 101
Foreign clockmakers, 100
Fourteenth century clocks, 52

Frodsham, 152
Fromantel, 77
Full plate, 211
Fusee, 59

G

Gathering pallet, 132
Gems for the month, 6
George III., 160
Glass dial, 113
Glastonbury clock, 50
Gnomon, 34
Going barrel, 209
Gold watch cases, hall mark for, 214
Golden number, 22
Gongs, 227
Graces, three, timekeeper, 112
Graham, 124
Grandfathers' clocks, 152
Gravity, 79
—— escapement, 179
Great Paul, 174
Gregorian rectification, 9
Grimthorpe, 177, 193
Grollier, 105
Gymbals, 241

H

Hall marks, 214
Hampton Court clock, 58
Hands, 24-hour, 192
——, Westminster, 177
Hans von Jena, 95
Harbrecht, 87
Harrison, 136
Heart-shaped cam, 228
Hele, 59
Henry de Vick, 51
—— VIII., 57, 62
Horizontal escapement, 123
Hooke, 133
Hotel de Ville clock, 116
Hour rack, 132
Huggeford, 118
Hunter, 216
Huygens, 127

I

Ice box, 208
Inclined plane clock, 107
Indian clepsydra, 44
Isochronous, 133

INDEX. 251

J

Japanese clock, 93
Jena, Hans von, 95
Jewelling, 118
Jewellery, watches in, 219
Jewel holes, 118
Jones, 202
Julian period, 24

K

Kendal, Larcum, 240
—— and Dent, 12, 192, 232, 244
Keyless mechanism, 220, 241
Kidney piece, 13

L

Legislative enactments, 156
Leopold, Prince, 160
Lepaute, 143
Leroy, 143, 144
Lever escapement, 110
Lightfoot, 50
Lippius, 88
Litherland, 142
Longitude, 236
Lunation, 3, 117
Lunetto, 216
Lyons clock, 88

M

Magniac, 108
Magnetized watches, 217
Mainspring, 60
Maintaining power, 136
Marble clock-cases, 197
Marie Antoinette, 112
Marine chronometers, 236
Martineau, Miss, sun-dial, 34
Mary Queen of Scots, 69
Mean time, 11
Merchandise Marks Act, 158
Mercurial pendulum, 81, 125
Meridian dial, 36
Milton, 2
Minute chronograph, 230
Minute spaces, 178
Mock dial, 33
—— watches, 65
Moltke, 16
Moment of inertia, 125
Months, 3

Motion work, 119
Mudge, 139
Mysterious clocks, 105

N

Napoleon Buonaparte, 163
Nautical day, 24
Nelson, 163
Nelthropp, 134
Newton, Sir Isaac, 162
Non-magnetizable watches, 217

O

Oliver Cromwell, 101
Oven, 208

P

Palais de Justice clock, 145
Pair-cased watches, 103
Paley, 163
Palladium balance-springs, 218
Pallets, 141
Paris, clocks of, 115
Pedometer watch, 164
Pendulum, 77
——, compensated, 81, 185
—— bobs should be heavy, 81
——, circular error of, 80
——, length of, 79
——, length of, sidereal, 79
——, mercurial, 81, 125
Pendulum, wood rod, 81
——, zinc tube, 81
Pinchbeck, 142
Pin pallet escapement, 199
Pin wheel escapement, 113
Plantus, 26
Pneumatic clocks, 203
Pyrenean dial, 35

Q

Quare, 129
Quarter clocks, 181, 191
—— bells, 187
Queen Elizabeth's watches, 63
Queen of Scots' watch, 69

R

Rack striking work, 131
Ramsay, 72
Recoiling escapement, 124
Remontoire, 179

INDEX.

Repeaters, 119, 131, 227
Ring dial, 34
Rocking-bar keyless work, 221

S

Safety-pin, 141
St. Dunstan's clock, 91
St. Paul's clock, 170
Sand-glass, 47
Savage, 142
Self-winding watches, 164
Seventeenth century, 117
Shagreen, 103
Shakespeare, 2
Ship's chronometer, 236
Skull watch, 69
Silvered dials, 241
Schwilgue, 83
Solar time, 11
Sound, velocity of, 187
Split seconds, 230
Spring, balance, 122
———, gold, 150
———, main, 60
Standards of time, 11
Stogdon, 149
Strasburg clocks, 82
Striking work, 131
——— count-wheel, 55, 181
——— locking plate, 131
——— rack, 132
Sully, 137
Sun, cycle of, 22
Sun dials, 25
Suspension of pendulums, 81, 121
Sussex, Duke of, 161

T

Tamborine and bee, 114
Tax on timekeepers, 157
Tell-tale clocks, 204
Thiout, l'Aine, 144
Three graces, 113
Transparent dial, 113
Three-quarter plate, 212
Time, 1
——— chart, 12
Ting-tang quarters, 194

Tompion, 120
Touch watches, 218
Toutiu, 102
Train, 52
Transit instrument, 18
Trial number, 246
Twenty-four hour timekeepers, 17, 192

U

Urn timekeepers, 112

V

Velocity of sound, 187
Venice, ball of, 110
———, clock in piazza at, 94
Vertical escapement, 54
Vitruvius, 39
Voltaire, 162
Vulliamy, 152

W

Watch balance, 207
Watches, care of, 233
Watch jewelling, 118
——— movements, 210
Watchman's clocks, 204
Weeks, 8
Wellington, 165
Wells clock, 50
Westminster Abbey, 169
Westminster clock, 177
Wheatstone, 202
Whitehurst, 204
Wimborne clock, 56
Windsor Castle clocks, 57
Wolsey, Cardinal, 57
Wood, E. J., 65
Worcester, Marquess of, 161

Y

Year, duration of, 8
Young, 1

Z

Zech, 59

KENDAL & DENT,

𝕎atchmakers to the Admiralty,

THE SHAH AND COURT OF PERSIA, Etc.,

106, CHEAPSIDE, LONDON, E.C.

GENTS' STERLING
SILVER ENGLISH LEVER WATCHES.

Capped and Jewelled Movement. Heavy Double-Bottom Cases.
Best Finish Throughout.

A Written Warranty with each Watch for Five Years.

Prices: 75s., 84s.; £4 15s., £5 5s., £5 15s., £6 6s., £7 7s., etc.

DITTO, in 18-Carat Hall-marked Gold Cases,
From 14 Guineas Upwards.

KENDAL & DENT'S ENGLISH LEVERS
GAINED THE
Gold Medal, Paris International Exhibition.

GENTS' AND LADIES'
Sterling Silver Patent Lever Watches.

Crystal Glass. Three-quarter Plate. Fully Jewelled Movement.
Compensation Balance.

Warranted for Three Years. 42/-, 50/-, 55/-, 63/-, etc.

GENTS' AND LADIES'
STERLING SILVER HORIZONTAL WATCHES.

Three-quarter Plate Movement. Crystal Glass. Warranted for Three Years. Price 30s.

KENDAL & DENT,
106, CHEAPSIDE, LONDON, E.C.

AGENTS WANTED TO FORM CLUBS.

WATCHES

AS SUPPLIED TO

THE ROYAL NAVY.

KENDAL & DENT,

CHRONOMETER MAKERS

TO THE

ADMIRALTY,

106, CHEAPSIDE, LONDON,

HAVE always in stock a choice selection of WATCHES, same as supplied to the **Board of Admiralty**, specially examined and rated, fitted with palladium balance-spring, and adjusted for all climates.

Also a stock of well-seasoned **2-Day** and **8-Day** Marine Chronometers in rosewood and mahogany cases.

PRICES FROM 18 GUINEAS UPWARDS.

www.ingramcontent.com/pod-product-compliance
Lightning Source LLC
Chambersburg PA
CBHW021356230426
43666CB00006B/541